Forschungs-/ Entwicklungs-/ Innovations-Management

Edited by
H. D. Bürgel (em.), Stuttgart, Germany
D. Grosse, Freiberg, Germany
C. Herstatt, Hamburg, Germany
H. Koller, Hamburg, Germany
C. Lüthje, Hamburg, Germany
M. G. Möhrle, Bremen, Germany

Die Reihe stellt aus integrierter Sicht von Betriebswirtschaft und Technik Arbeitsergebnisse auf den Gebieten Forschung, Entwicklung und Innovation vor. Die einzelnen Beiträge sollen dem wissenschaftlichen Fortschritt dienen und die Forderungen der Praxis auf Umsetzbarkeit erfüllen.

Edited by

Professor Dr. Hans Dietmar Bürgel (em.),
Universität Stuttgart

Professorin Dr. Diana Grosse vorm. de Pay,
Technische Universität Bergakademie Freiberg

Professor Dr. Cornelius Herstatt
Technische Universität
Hamburg-Harburg

Professor Dr. Hans Koller
Universität der Bundeswehr Hamburg

Professor Dr. Christian Lüthje
Technische Universität Hamburg-Harburg

Professor Dr. Martin G. Möhrle
Universität Bremen

Weitere Bände in der Reihe http://www.springer.com/series/12195

Florian Denker

The Crucial Role of Domain Knowledge in Evaluating Early-Stage New Product Ideas

With a foreword by Univ. Prof. Dr. Cornelius Herstatt

Florian Denker
Hamburg, Germany

Dissertation Technische Universität Hamburg, 2017

Forschungs-/ Entwicklungs-/ Innovations-Management
ISBN 978-3-658-19783-4   ISBN 978-3-658-19784-1   (eBook)
https://doi.org/10.1007/978-3-658-19784-1

Library of Congress Control Number: 2017954982

Springer Gabler

Printed on acid-free paper

This Springer Gabler imprint is published by Springer Nature
The registered company is Springer Fachmedien Wiesbaden GmbH
The registered company address is: Abraham-Lincoln-Str. 46, 65189 Wiesbaden, Germany

Foreword

Successfully developing and launching new products is one of, if not the most important driver of a company's growth and profitability. Two equally important activities are fundamental for successful new product development (NPD): (i) developing new product ideas, and (ii) selecting the most promising ideas for further development. However, early-stage new product ideas entail high uncertainties regarding their market potential and feasibility that make their first evaluations extremely challenging. Thus, the successful evaluation and subsequent selection of the most promising new product ideas poses a major challenge for research and practice alike, since there are currently no tested methods or procedures which help with overcoming these uncertainties.

Research has already recognized this problem for a long time. However, the literature presents contradictory opinions on the question whether the evaluation of new product ideas can only be carried out by experts with a very distinct domain knowledge or whether laypersons or persons with expertise in other areas can also evaluate early-stage new product ideas. The latter actors play an increasingly important role particularly concerning recent developments, such as innovation platforms, crowdsourcing, or crowdfunding. Especially with the most recent trend leaving the initial evaluation of new product ideas to consumers, or the "crowd," it becomes necessary to develop a deeper understanding of the influence that domain knowledge has on evaluation decisions, and thus the quality of the evaluation.

Mr. Denker addresses this topic in his dissertation by raising the following research questions as the focus of his work: 1) What is the role of individuals' domain knowledge for the proficient evaluation of early-stage new product ideas in the front-end of innovation? 2) Should firms give more, or less, consideration to domain knowledge as an important factor in selecting appropriate judges – both internal and external to the firm – for the evaluation of early-stage new product ideas?

To investigate these research questions, Mr. Denker conducted an empirical study in which 333 evaluators with different levels of domain knowledge evaluated various early-stage new product ideas. The innovation degree of these product ideas was manipulated so that the evaluators had to evaluate both incremental and radical product ideas. In summary: The results of the study show that evaluators with little domain knowledge overestimate the originality and the user value of incremental ideas and underestimate the user value and the feasibility of radical ideas, while evaluators with a distinct domain knowledge are more reliable with recognizing the potential of radical ideas, especially with regard to higher user value.

With his dissertation, Mr. Denker makes an important contribution to innovation management research and to the management practice. Based on the results, a clear recommendation can be made: in order to ensure an effective evaluation, evaluators of early-stage new product ideas should have comprehensive knowledge of consumers' needs and wants, as well as distinct knowledge about the opportunities and limits of available technologies in the respective domain. In this context, the results also show that not only company-internal experts can have this knowledge. The results indicate that also external users, particularly lead users (i.e. users who are ahead of the majority on major market trends and innovations), could be suitable for effectively evaluating early-stage new product ideas.

Mr. Denker contributes to theory by extending the research field which aims at increasing the effective evaluation of new product ideas by focusing on the evaluator's individual characteristics beyond the process design aspect. The results also conclude that the selection of suitable evaluators depends strongly on the evaluation object's degree of innovativeness. However, most importantly, the results of the study indicate that domain knowledge is one of the key factors in deciding whether or not a company should employ external users to evaluate new product ideas.

I regard Mr. Denker's dissertation as a very successful, insightful, and independent scientific contribution that is relevant to both researchers and innovation managers.

Hamburg, June 2017

Univ. Prof. Dr. oec. publ. Cornelius Herstatt

Acknowledgements

I would like to express my gratitude to my supervisors Professor Herstatt and Dr. Eling who, in a genuinely caring manner, always provided research guidance, practical support, and continuously inspired me to push forward. I highly appreciate all their contributions of time, ideas, and experience that helped me tremendously in developing this thesis.

I also want to thank my colleagues and friends from the Institute of Technology and Innovation Management for the feedback, stimulating discussions, practical help, and moral support.

In particular, I am grateful for my wonderful, ever-supportive girlfriend Verena and my amazing friends, who helped me to overcome the more difficult times throughout this project and, thus made the completion of this work possible. Life would not be same without you!

Last but not the least, I would like to thank my family for raising me and for supporting me throughout this project and in my life in general.

Thanks for all your support!

Content overview

Table of content

Index of figures

Index of tables

List of abbreviations

AT	Ahead of trend
AVE	Average variance extracted
b	Unstandardized regression coefficient
CDK	Consumer domain knowledge
CFA	Confirmatory factor analysis
CITC	Corrected item-total correlation
DK	Domain knowledge
DV	Dependent variable
EFA	Exploratory factor analysis
e.g.	Exempli gratia (English: for example)
et al.	Et alii (English: and others)
etc.	Et cetera (English: and so forth)
F	F-statistic value
FEI	Front-end of innovation
i.e.	Id est (English: that is)
IP	Intellectual property
H	Hypothesis
HC	Heteroscedasticity-consistent standard error estimators
HEB	High expected benefits
ICC	Intraclass correlation coefficient
IRR	Interrater reliability
IV	Independent variable
KMO	Kaiser-Meyer-Olkin (criterion)
LLCI	Lower level confidence interval
LU	Lead userness
M&S	Marketing and Sales
MSA	Measure of sampling adequacy
N	Sample size
n.d.	Not dated
n.s.	Not significant
n/a	Not applicable
NPD	New product development
OLS	Ordinary least squares
p	Probability (p-value)
R&D	Research and Development
R^2	Coefficient of determination/explained variance
RQ	Research question
SD	Standard deviation
SEM	Structural equation model
Sig.	Significance
TE	Technical expertise
ULCI	Upper-level confidence interval
VIF	Variance inflation factor
#	Number
ρ	Dillon-Goldstein's rho (composite reliability)
λ	Standardized outer item loadings

"Why [...] do we have such a high rate of new product failures? Is it possible, as some of the research studies suggest, that the problem is one of people, not technology?"

(Crawford, 1977: 54)

1 Introduction

1.1 Research problem

Launching a "differentiated product with unique customer benefits and superior value for the user" (Cooper, 1999: 117) is one of the foremost drivers of firms' profitability (Cooper, 2011). Two central activities need to be undertaken, with equal proficiency, at the very beginning of the new product development (NPD) process to lay the foundation for successfully developing and launching such innovative new products (Evanschitzky et al., 2012): (i) generating high quality new product ideas, and (ii) selecting the most promising ideas for inclusion in a firm's innovation funnel (Girotra, Terwiesch, and Ulrich, 2010). Thus, generating a large number of ideas is in itself not sufficient; firms must also select their early-stage ideas very carefully, as choosing the right idea sets the basis for future commercial success (Kornish and Ulrich, 2014).

Successful idea screening decisions will avoid both "false positives," i.e., selecting bad ideas based on overestimating their potential, and "false negatives," i.e., rejecting good ideas based on underestimating their potential. False negatives may lead firms to neglect opportunities that might have produced successful products, which could have significantly increased the firm's future NPD success (Girotra, Terwiesch, and Ulrich, 2010). False positives, on the other hand, may result in wasting resources on ideas that could eventually fail in the marketplace and/or are likely to be terminated during the development process due to their low possibility of being successful (Martinsuo and Poskela, 2011).

Additionally, idea screening at the front-end of innovation requires a portfolio approach (Eling, Griffin, and Langerak, 2016). Firms should select a balanced portfolio of incremental and radical new product ideas to enter their innovation funnels, thereby maximizing their probability of achieving innovation success (Chao and Kavadias, 2008). Nevertheless, many firms continue to develop increasingly incremental innovations, potentially leading to unbalanced innovation portfolios (Barczak, Griffin, and Kahn, 2009). Thus, it is not surprising that the question of how to proficiently screen for radical innovation ideas has been proposed as a priority for innovation management research (Barczak, 2014).

Based on the importance of selecting the right ideas for further development, the "screening of new product ideas is perhaps the most critical new product development (NPD) activity" (Calantone, DiBenedetto, and Schmidt, 1999: 65). Unfortunately, selecting the most promising ideas for further development still poses a major challenge for many organizations (Pisano and Verganti, 2008).

The challenges inherent in decision making at the front-end of innovation might explain many firms' severe problems with discerning good ideas from bad ones. Before selecting ideas at this early stage, they are usually evaluated on a number of criteria for ease of comparison, and to ensure that the decision making is objective (Hart et al., 2003; Martinsuo and Poskela, 2011). Although a gatekeeping committee usually performs the actual idea selection, individuals within the front-end team generally perform the first evaluation of early-stage new product ideas. They either do so informally to decide which ideas to elaborate on further (Eling, Langerak, and Griffin, 2015; Kim and Wilemon, 2002), or more formally to prepare for the gatekeeping committee's go/no-go decisions (Eling, Griffin, and Langerak, 2016). With the recent proliferation of open innovation strategies (Chesbrough, Vanhaverbeke, and West, 2006; Chesbrough, 2006b), individuals external to the firm are also increasingly undertaking this evaluation. Including industry experts, users or laymen (Magnusson, Wästlund, and Netz, 2016; Velamuri et al., 2015) adds evaluation capacity to the firm in an effort to cope with the massive numbers of ideas (Piezunka and Dahlander, 2015; Ocasio, 2011) that can result from utilizing innovation tournaments/contests (Girotra, Terwiesch, and Ulrich, 2010), online communities (Dahlander and Wallin, 2006), innovation tournaments/contests (Terwiesch and Ulrich, 2009; Terwiesch and Xu, 2008), innovation toolkits (Piller and Walcher, 2006), and crowdsourcing (Jeppesen and Lakani, 2010; Ebner, Leimeister, and Krcmar, 2009).

Despite firms' attempts to rationalize and control this evaluation process, they are heavily dependent on these individuals' correct first assessments to ascertain which ideas are high potential ones and which are not. Especially when evaluating early-stage new product ideas, these individual idea evaluators are frequently confronted with highly uncertain and ambiguous information (Kim and Wilemon, 2002). In addition, per definition, ideas for radical new products involve new technologies not currently found in existing products and provide users with completely new benefits (Garcia and Calantone, 2002). These attributes of early-stage new product ideas pose formidable challenges in understanding the benefits and shortcomings, and evaluating these ideas proficiently.

Studies on the evaluation of creative outcome (Amabile, 1982; Amabile, 1996), innovation management research (Ozer, 2005), and practice, have acknowledged that proficient evaluation might be largely dependent on selecting appropriate evaluators for the task, while also presuming that an appropriate evaluator has to be an expert in the particular domain (Salas, Rosen, and DiazGranados, 2010; Shanteau and James, 1992). It is therefore likely that the individual evaluators' specific abilities or characteristics, and especially their domain knowledge, could have an impact on their evaluation performance (Ozer, 2005). In this context, domain knowledge is defined as knowledge about users' needs and wants (Lüthje, 2004; Homburg, Wieseke, and Bornemann, 2009), and about the opportunities and limitations of applied technologies in a domain (Magnusson, 2009). Unfortunately, existing research has not yet ascertained whether only evaluators with high-level domain knowledge are appropriate judges of early-stage new product ideas at the front-end of innovation.

Existing studies that investigated new product idea evaluation in respect of whether, or not, "non-experts" – represented by users, employees outside the R&D department, and even laymen – could match experts' evaluation decisions, yield inconclusive results. On the one hand, innovation management studies concluded that non-expert evaluators can be leveraged as a valuable source to evaluate new product ideas (Magnusson, Wästlund, and Netz, 2016), indicating that high domain knowledge is not a necessary prerequisite to ensure a sound evaluation outcome. Some researchers have even argued that "online consumer panels are a better way to determine a 'good' idea than are evaluations by experts" (Kornish and Ulrich, 2014). On the other hand, creativity research studies stated a need for caution when using evaluators with low domain knowledge, because their judgments tend to be inconsistent and do not match those of evaluators with high level domain knowledge (Kaufman et al., 2008; Kaufman, Baer, and Cole, 2009).

Furthermore, domain knowledge may play an even more significant role in evaluating new product ideas that are more radical by nature (Peracchio and Tybout, 1996). The uncertainty inherent in radical new product ideas has been shown to greatly influence individuals' behavior in evaluation tasks (Veryzer, 1998b). Psychology research studies allow the conclusion that individuals attempt to avoid uncertainty, thus demonstrating a strong tendency to prefer feasible and desirable ideas that provide short-term benefits at the cost of originality (Licuanan, Dailey, and Mumford, 2007; Blair and Mumford, 2007). Consequently, in an NPD setting, evaluators might be biased against radical new product ideas in favor of highly producible incremental ideas. Previous research determined that comprehensive domain knowledge might either alleviate (Graeff and Olson, 1994), or reinforce (Moreau, Lehmann, and Markman, 2001), such uncertainty-related evaluation problems.

To summarize, although there seems to be widespread agreement that proficient idea evaluation is of crucial importance for innovation success (Calantone, DiBenedetto, and Schmidt, 1999), research and practice have paid limited attention to the human factor in new product idea evaluation. They thus largely follow the longstanding belief that experts are the most appropriate evaluators of early-stage new product ideas. However, a detailed review of the existing literature on new product idea evaluation and screening reveals that the level of domain knowledge required to effectively evaluate early-stage new product ideas at the very beginning of the front-end has not yet been clarified. Furthermore, research has largely neglected that the selection of appropriate evaluators may even be more important in the evaluation of highly innovative new product ideas. Accordingly, it is the objective of this thesis to develop a deeper understanding of the role of an individual evaluator's domain knowledge in evaluating early-stage new product ideas in order to determine whether or not more, or less, consideration should be given to domain knowledge as the central factor in selecting appropriate judges – both internal and external to the firm.

1.2 Research objectives and contribution

Inspired by the belief that both research and management practice would benefit significantly from developing a deeper understanding of the central characteristics that could identify individuals as appropriate judges of early-stage new product ideas, I dedicate this dissertation to uncovering the role of domain knowledge in the proficient evaluation of early-stage new product ideas. To the best of my knowledge, there are no studies in the field of innovation management that have explicitly explored the influence of domain knowledge in terms of how, why, when, or, under which conditions, domain knowledge influences evaluation behavior and outcomes at the individual level. Thus, my thesis attempts to clarify this important topic by addressing the following two research questions:[1]

RQ1: What is the role of individuals' domain knowledge in the proficient evaluation of early-stage new product ideas in the front-end of innovation?

RQ2: Should firms give more, or less, consideration to domain knowledge as an important factor in selecting appropriate judges – both internal and external to the firm – for the evaluation of early-stage new product ideas?

Having developed a deeper understanding of the topic throughout this thesis, my research contributes to innovation management research in a number of ways. First, it augments available research on proficient idea evaluation, which largely had process design aspects as their foci (Eling, Griffin, and Langerak, 2016; Riedl et al., 2013; Dean et al., 2006), to also address individual evaluators' characteristics, and to argue for the importance of domain knowledge in selecting appropriate evaluators for the evaluation of early-stage new product ideas. Second, my research attempts to answer the question whether the selection of evaluators should vary depending on whether the innovation is incremental or radical (Barczak, 2014) when investigating the role of domain knowledge in the evaluation of early-stage new product ideas. Finally, my research delivers new insights into the question of who should be involved in early-stage idea evaluations. Therefore, this thesis informs prior ambiguous findings regarding the role of experts, users, and laymen in respect of idea evaluation.

1.3 Outline of the thesis

In approaching these research objectives, this thesis is structured into six chapters (see Figure 1). Following the introductory remarks in relation to the research problem, as well as to the research objective and contribution, a frame of reference is provided in chapter 2. The purpose of this second chapter is to briefly introduce the reader to the basic concepts

---

[1] The first research questions encompasses a set of sub questions, including;
RQ1a: How does domain knowledge influence criteria-based evaluation outcomes by affecting the assessment of the three dimensions that constitute a new product idea's quality (originality, user value, and feasibility)?
RQ1b: How does domain knowledge influence holistic evaluations of new product ideas?
RQ1c: Does the idea's degree of innovativeness moderate the influence of domain knowledge on new product idea evaluation outcomes?

of innovation, the front-end of innovation, and the open innovation paradigm, thus providing the context for the research problem and objectives.

Chapter 3 provides the theoretical foundation for this thesis. This chapter explores relevant prior research, and details the idea evaluation activity in the front-end of innovation. Based on an analysis of currently available literature, the role of individuals' domain knowledge in the proficient evaluation of early-stage new product ideas is identified as a research gap, and research questions are formulated to address this important research opportunity. Furthermore, this chapter introduces relevant theories from psychology, creativity, and consumer behavior research that form the foundation of the thesis's research framework. Chapter 3 concludes with the introduction of the research framework and the reasoning behind the underlying hypotheses.

Chapter 4 is dedicated to the research design chosen for the purpose of testing the hypotheses. This chapter describes the quantitative online survey, including the sequence of the survey, the reasoning behind the chosen sample, and the operationalizing of the constructs used to reflect the variables in the research framework. At the end of the chapter, the data cleansing methods, the constructs' reliability and validity checks, and the common method bias test are described in preparation for the empirical analysis.

Chapter 5 focuses on the empirical analysis of the survey data. The chapter begins with a descriptive analysis of the sample and of the evaluation outcomes. The purpose of this descriptive analysis is to provide an easier understanding of the subsequent, more complex multiple regression analyses. These multiple regression analyses are developed to test all the formulated hypotheses, including all the proposed direct effects, interaction effects, mediation effects, and moderated mediation effects.

In chapter 6, the empirical findings are discussed in the light of the hypotheses on the reasoning behind the research framework and in respect of the preceding research findings. Based on this detailed discussion of the results, chapter 6 highlights the implications for theory and managerial practice. Finally, the limitations of this study are discussed, and suggestions for future research opportunities are provided.

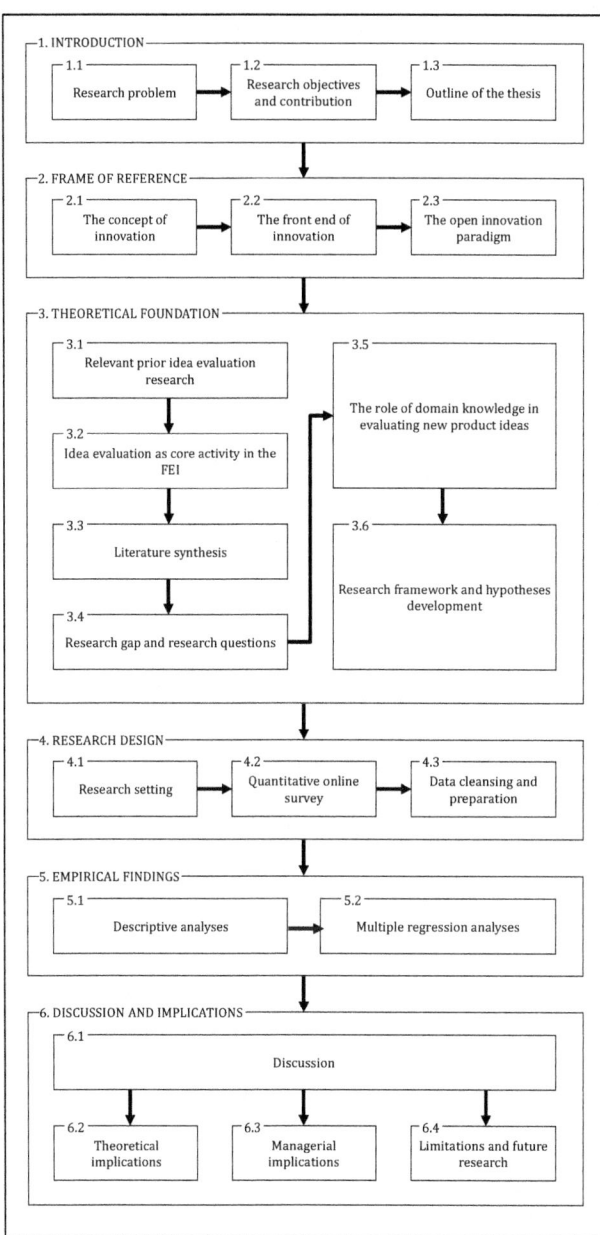

Figure 1: Outline of the thesis

2 Frame of reference

The objective of this chapter is to provide a frame of reference for the study's research questions. I will therefore introduce the innovation concept (section 2.1) by distinguishing between innovation as an outcome (section 2.1.1) and innovation as a process (section 2.1.2). Subsequently, I will highlight the front-end of innovation as the innovation process phase that is most relevant in the context of this study (section 2.2). The chapter closes with a short introduction to the open innovation paradigm, and the major idea evaluation challenges that firms need to face when obtaining large numbers of new product ideas from external sources (section 2.3).

2.1 The concept of innovation

What is innovation? In research, as well as practice, innovation is a broadly defined term used in a variety of contexts (Gaubinger et al., 2015). Theory and practice have failed to agree on a generally accepted definition of the term "innovation." Over the years, the innovation concept has been expanded and modified, resulting in various definitions of innovation (Hauschildt and Salomo, 2007). These various definitions of innovation might also be a reason why the term is often confused with the term "invention." An "invention comes either from combining technological components in a novel manner, or through reconfiguring existing combinations" (Fleming and Sorenson, 2004: 910). However, an invention does not qualify as an innovation. Only by introducing an invention to the market and, thus, diffusing the invention to other parties beyond the inventor, do inventions become innovations (Hauschildt and Salomo, 2007). Despite these various definitions, the literature seems to agree that innovation can be categorized into two groups: (i) innovation as an outcome (what is created), and (ii) innovation as a process (how it is created) (Crossan and Apaydin, 2010). Both interpretations will be discussed in the following sections.

2.1.1 Innovation as an outcome

Following the belief that the successful development and commercialization of different types of innovations may require different processes, skills, and techniques (Reid and Brentani, 2004; Veryzer, 1998a; Song and Montoya-Weiss, 1998), research scholars have for decades been discussing classification schemes for defining innovations (Garcia and Calantone, 2002). The classification scheme that has received most attention in research and practice refers to the degree of innovativeness that captures the change when compared to the given status quo, i.e., "highly innovative products are seen as having a high degree of newness" (Garcia and Calantone, 2002: 112).

However, determining the newness of an innovation is not a trivial task, as it depends on (i) the perspective from which the newness is assessed, as well as (ii) the dimensions against which the newness is measured (Garcia and Calantone, 2002; Schultz, Salomo, and Talke, 2013). Innovation management literature has developed an abundance of different constructs in an effort to accurately measure an innovation's degree of newness. Consequently, conceptualizing innovativeness varies across different studies (Szymanski, Kroff, and Troy, 2007). Nonetheless, researchers seem to have reached agreement that it is beneficial to define innovativeness as a continuous, multi-dimensional construct (Gatignon et al., 2002; Green, Gavin M. B., and Aiman-Smith, 1995). With this multi-dimensional approach having become the state-of-the-art approach to measure innovativeness (Gemünden, Salomo, and Hölzle, 2007), two dimensions have emerged as the predominant measurements of innovativeness: (i) the market-related dimension and (ii) the technology-related dimension (Garcia and Calantone, 2002).[2]

The *market-related dimension* reflects that highly innovative products deliver a substantially higher user value compared to preceding or competitive products by either fulfilling unsatisfied needs, and/or creating completely new consumer benefits (Chandy and Tellis, 1998; Veryzer, 1998a). In some cases, this might ultimately lead to the creation of an entirely new market (Song and Montoya-Weiss, 1998).

The *technology-related dimension* reflects the belief that highly innovative products are based on the introduction of new technological principles, or the use of completely new components that call for a new knowledge base in the firm (Schultz, Salomo, and Talke, 2013). Developing highly innovative new products thus usually involve expanding

---

[2] Research scholars have added further dimensions to measure innovativeness. One example is the scale of innovativeness developed by Schultz, Salomo, and Talke (2013). This scale measures innovativeness as a multi-dimensional construct along market-related, technology-related, firm-related, and environment-related dimensions. However, this dissertation adopts the more widely used approach of Garcia and Calantone (2002), and only defines innovativeness along market-related, and technology-related dimensions.

technological capabilities beyond the existing boundaries (Veryzer, 1998a). Consequently, existing knowledge may become obsolete to some degree (Gemünden, Salomo, and Hölzle, 2007).

Acknowledging these two dimensions, the degree of innovativeness can therefore either be assessed separately for each dimension, or by combining both dimensions into an overall degree of innovativeness (Schultz, Salomo, and Talke, 2013; Green, Gavin M. B., and Aiman-Smith, 1995; Garcia and Calantone, 2002). Following common language in the innovation management literature, the two extremes of these two-dimensional construct are described as incremental innovations and radical innovations (see Figure 2).

Incremental innovations (also referred to as "sustaining," "continuous," "minor," or "evolutionary innovations" (Garcia and Calantone, 2002)) are defined as refinements, modifications, or improvements to an existing product or product line that help firms maintain, or strengthen, their positions in extant markets through product enhancements and increases in production efficiencies (Hartmann, 2014). Consequently, incremental innovations build on firms' existing knowledge and are characterized by minor technological changes (Green, Gavin M. B., and Aiman-Smith, 1995). Thus, lower risk and high predictability characterize incremental innovations (Garcia, 2010).

Radical innovations (also referred to as "breakthrough," "discontinuous," or "disruptive" innovations (Garcia and Calantone, 2002)) are defined by changes in technology components embodied in a new product, enabling it to fulfill currently unsatisfied consumer needs, or even create completely new ones (Chandy and Tellis, 1998; Veryzer, 1998a). Based on these characteristics, radical innovations offer a significant product advantage providing firms with the means to gain competitive advantages, but also come at the cost of lower consumer familiarity and difficulties with successfully developing and marketing the products (Calantone, Chan, and Cui, 2006). Thus, radical innovations require significant changes in consumer usage patterns, as well as consumer thinking (Veryzer, 1998b), and bear sizable financial risks for firms (Green, Gavin M. B., and Aiman-Smith, 1995).

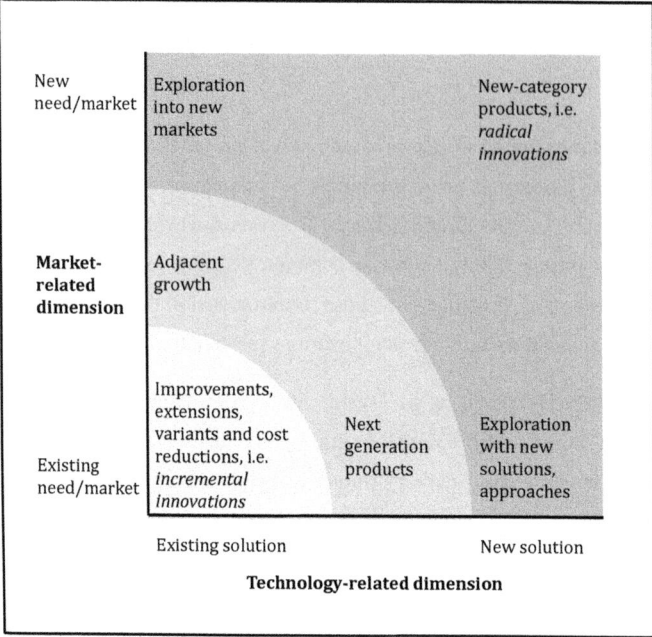

Figure 2: Types of innovation[3]

To summarize, the outcome of an innovation process can be classified by its degree of innovativeness. This innovativeness can be defined as a multi-dimensional construct believed to have a market-related, as well as a technology-related, dimension. Depending on the magnitude of innovativeness in both dimensions, innovations can thus be classified on a continuous construct with incremental innovations forming the lowest level of innovativeness and radical innovations forming the highest.

2.1.2 Innovation as a process

The second interpretation of the term innovation does not refer to a static outcome, but to the dynamic element of innovation. In this sense, innovation refers to the process that

---

[3] Author's illustration, adapted from Terwiesch and Ulrich (2009).

starts with the identification of an opportunity, and ends with the commercialization of the outcome of the process (Song and Montoya-Weiss, 1998; Cooper, 2011; Koen et al., 2001).

Over the years, the innovation management literature has developed many process models to structure the innovation process in order to provide firms with a structure to move product development projects proficiently from idea to launch and beyond (Cooper, 2011). However, despite the differences between these models, innovation management research scholars seem to agree that the innovation process comprises three major phases: (i) the front-end of innovation, (ii) new product development, and (iii) commercialization (Song and Montoya-Weiss, 1998; Cooper, 2011; Koen et al., 2001).

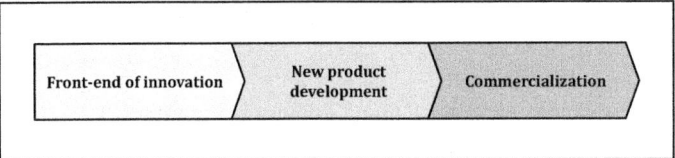

Figure 3: Simplified innovation process[4]

The front-end of innovation (FEI) includes all activities with regard to the generation, evaluation, and selection of new product ideas, the formulation of potential concepts, and the initial planning of the potential development project (the FEI is discussed in more detail in section 2.2). In the new product development phase, the selected concepts are developed, tested, and validated. The last phase constitutes the commercialization of the product. This includes commencing with full operations or production, as well as marketing and selling the product (for details on these two phases see Cooper and Kleinschmidt, 1986; Cooper, 2011; Song and Montoya-Weiss, 1998).

Among the many different innovation process models, the Stage-Gate® system, developed by Cooper (1983), has probably garnered the researcher and practitioner most attention. A large number of major NPD firms have implemented more, or less, modified versions of

---

4   Author's illustration, based on Koen et al. (2001: 51).

the Stage-Gate system (Barczak, Griffin, and Kahn, 2009; Griffin, 1997). That is why I will refer to a stage-gate system throughout this thesis when I use the term innovation process.

The Stage-Gate system breaks the innovation process down into a set of information-gathering stages, each followed by a go/no-go decision gate (Cooper, 2008). This system of stages and gates aims to provide a clear structure for moving an idea to the launch stage, and is therefore referred to as "idea-to-launch system" (Cooper, 2008: 213). According to Cooper (2011), each stage consists of a set of activities to gather the information needed to advance the project to the next gate. The information gathered helps reduce the decision makers' uncertainty at the gates and supports the decision making process on whether, or not, to proceed with the project. A typical Stage-Gate system consists of the following stages (Cooper, 2011: 100):

- *"Discovery*: pre-work designed to discover and uncover opportunities and generate ideas.
- *Scoping*: a quick, preliminary investigation and scoping of the project [...].
- *Build the Business Case*: a much more detailed investigation involving primary research – both market and technical – leading to a Business Case, including product and project definition, project justification, and project plan.
- *Development*: the actual detailed design and development of the new product, and the design of the operations or production processes.
- *Testing and validation*: tests or trials in the marketplace, lab, and plant to verify and validate the proposed new product, and its marketing and production/operations.
- *Launch*: commercialization–beginning of full operations or production, marketing and selling."

Each stage is followed by a gate that serves as Go/Kill decision point where projects are prioritized, are allocated resources, or are rejected. Thus, the gates in the Stage-Gate system are checkpoints in the development process to determine whether, or not, the firm is (i) selecting the projects correctly, and (ii) is selecting the right projects (Cooper, 2011). Each gate follows a similar structure comprising the following (Cooper, 2008: 215):

- "Deliverables: [define][5] what the project leader and team bring to the decision point (e.g. the results of a set of completed activities). These deliverables are

---

[5]   Added by the author.

visible, are based on a standard menu for each gate, and are decided at the output of the previous gate.

- *Criteria* against which the project is judged: These include *must-meet criteria* or knock-out questions (a checklist) designed to weed out misfit projects quickly; and should-meet criteria that are scored and added (a point count system), which are used to prioritize projects.

- Outputs: a decision (*Go/Kill/Hold/Recycle*), along with an approved action plan for the next stage (an agreed-to timeline and resources committed), and a list of deliverables and date for the next gate."

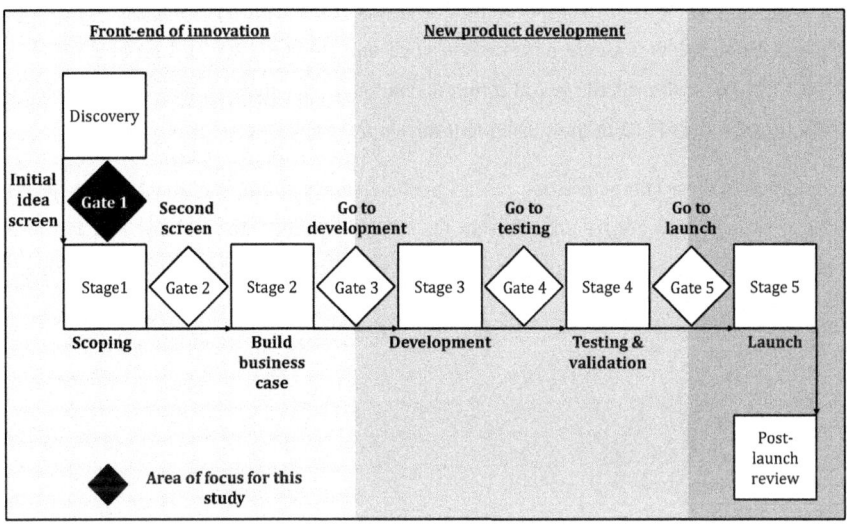

Figure 4: Five-stage, five-gate Stage-Gate system[6]

As depicted in Figure 4, the evaluation of early-stage new product ideas is an activity carried out to reduce the decision makers' uncertainty at the first gate of the innovation process. Thus, new product idea evaluation is an activity in the front-end of innovation. This first phase of the innovation process is described in more detail in the following section.

---

6   Author's illustration, based on Cooper (2008: 215).

2.2 The front-end of innovation

The front-end of innovation (FEI)[7] is the first phase of the innovation process, comprising the generation, evaluation, and selection of new product or service ideas, the formulation of potential concepts, and the initial planning of the potential development project (Koen et al., 2001). The FEI ends when the company decides to start the formal, and well-structured, new product development phase (Murphy and Kumar, 1996; Koen et al., 2001; Herstatt and Verworn, 2007).

The literature on the FEI has shown that the characteristics of this phase differ fundamentally from those of the subsequent development phase (Kim and Wilemon, 2002). Although the characteristics of the FEI may be specific to the firm and its context, and might therefore not follow a single pattern (Verworn and Herstatt, 2007), Kim and Wilemon (2002: 270) have identified several common characteristics that can be used as a baseline to distinguish the FEI from the subsequent development phase (see Table 1).

In addition to these characteristics, research scholars have pointed out that the high degree of uncertainty with regard to strategic fit, customer needs, technology, and required resources is the FEI's most important characteristic (Gaubinger et al., 2015; Verworn and Herstatt, 2007).

---

[7]   Also referred to as fuzzy front end of innovation, e.g. Koen et al. (2001); Khurana and Rosenthal (1997).

Table 1: Comparison of characteristics between the FEI phase and the development phase

Factors	General characteristics of the FEI phase	General characteristics of the development phase
State of an idea	Probable, fuzzy, easy to change	Determined to develop, clear, specific, difficult to change
Features of information for decision-making	Qualitative, informal, approximate	Quantitative, formal, precise
Outcome (/action)	A blueprint (/diminishing ambiguity to decide whether to make it happen)	A product (/making it happen)
Width and depth of focus	Broad but thin	Narrow but detailed
Ease of rejecting an idea	Easy	More difficult
Degree of formalization	Low	High
Personnel involvement	Individual or small project team	A full development team
Management methods	Unstructured, experimental, creativity needed	Structured, systematic
(Visible) damage if abandoned	Usually small	Substantial
Commitment of the CEO	None or small	Usually high

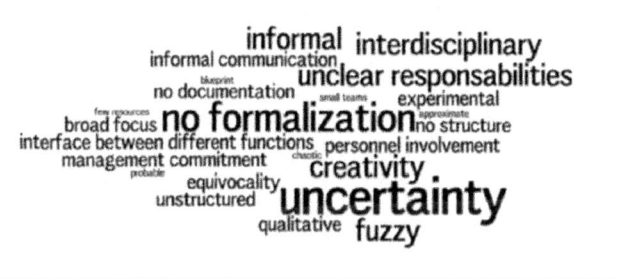

Figure 5: Characteristics of the front-end of innovation[8]

---

[8]   Source: Gaubinger et al. (2015: 46).

Therefore, the innovation management literature has repeatedly underlined the need to reduce uncertainty in the FEI in order to ensure successful product development (Herstatt and Verworn, 2007; Moenart et al., 1995; Kim and Wilemon, 2002; Zhang and Doll, 2001). Thus, it is not surprising that the majority of authors agree that the most important purpose of the activities carried out throughout the FEI is to reduce uncertainty in the dimensions related to consumer uncertainty, competitive uncertainty, resource uncertainty, and technological uncertainty (Moenart and Souder, 1990; Zhang and Doll, 2001).

This reduction in uncertainty has such specific relevance in the FEI, because, in this phase, decision makers still have the greatest possibility to influence the overall outcome of the innovation process (Wheelwright and Clark, 1995; Herstatt and Verworn, 2001). They can do so, because the activities and decisions during the FEI affect all downstream decisions in the innovation process, including the development time and cost (Cooper, 2011; Verworn and Herstatt, 2007; Herstatt and Verworn, 2007; Zhang and Doll, 2001).

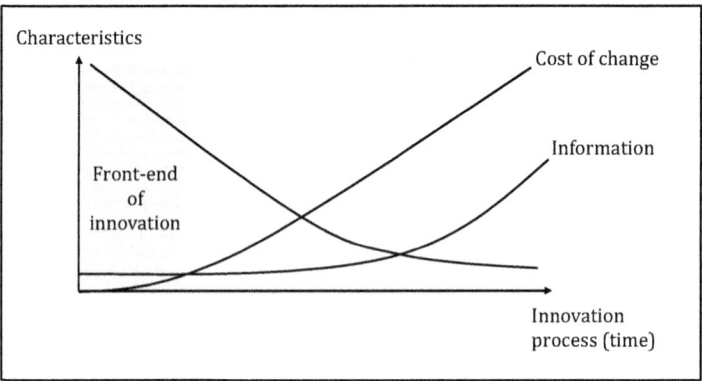

Figure 6: Influence, cost of changes, and information during the innovation process[9]

Given the FEI activities' high impact on the development outcome, it is not surprising that a number of empirical research studies have found that proficiency in carrying out FEI activities is a key success factor in new product development (Evanschitzky et al., 2012;

---

[9]   Author's illustration, based on Herstatt and Verworn (2001: 5).

Langerak, Hultink, and Robben, 2004; Markham, 2013). Based on several empirical studies comparing the best practices of the best, and the worst, performing NPD firms, leading innovation management researchers have even concluded that the biggest differences between successful and unsuccessful NPD firms lie in the execution quality of pre-development activities in the FEI (e.g. Cooper and Kleinschmidt, 1995).

In an effort to improve proficiency in the FEI, innovation management researchers have developed a number of theoretical process models. Some well-known process models include the *Stage-Gate® Process* of Cooper (2011) – as explained in section 2.1.2 – the *Three Phase Front End Model* of Khurana and Rosenthal (1997) and the *New Concept Development Model* of Koen et al. (2001). Gaubinger and Rabl (2014: 16) summarized the pros, and cons, of these different models:

However, despite the existence of these process models, neither academics nor practitioners seem to fully understand how to execute the FEI proficiently (Eling, 2014). Therefore, it is not surprising that many firms still strive to improve the outcomes of this critical phase (Markham, 2013).

Table 2: Pros and cons of front-end process models

Model	Pros	Cons
Stage-gate process (Cooper)	Very famous and frequently cited model	Product concepts can be stopped too early
	Flexible to both radical and incremental innovations	Gatekeepers low level of knowledge can lead to wrong decisions
	Integrates both the market and technological perspective	Lack of flexibility due to sequential approach, except third generation
	Activities are performed in parallel model fashion	
Three phase front end model (Khurana and Rosenthal)	Additional consideration of elements of the organizational environment (foundation elements)	No feedback loops
	Useful tool to visualize and structure front-end activities, reduce the fuzziness and ease communication	No description of the preliminary opportunity identification and idea generation in detail
		Tool lacks flexibility
		Decision making could be enhanced by a more structured process (especially in the pre-phase zero and phase one phases)
New concept development model (Koen et al.)	Includes all company related factors	Abstract model that is hardly transferable to a business situation
	Stimulates innovation due to its non-sequential order of phases	Practitioners criticize the lack of application of these methodologies
	Flexible with regards to both radical and incremental innovations	Model mainly focuses on product development
		Influencing factors are not controllable

2.3 The open innovation paradigm

At the beginning of this millennium, Chesbrough (2006b)[10] postulated a paradigm shift in the way firms innovate, moving from a closed innovation model to an open innovation model. This paradigm shift has received extensive attention in the literature,[11] and – more than 10 years later – is still proposed as a research priority for innovation management research (Barczak, 2014).

The open innovation paradigm proposes that the abilities and assets for creating innovation do not necessarily have to be collocated with those of commercialization. In other words, "Open Innovation is a paradigm that assumes that firms can and should use external ideas as well as internal ideas [...] as they look to advance their technology" (Chesbrough, 2006a: 1). The underlying logic of the open innovation paradigm is summarized as follows (Chesbrough, 2006b: xxvi):

- A firm does not need to employ only smart people, but should instead work with them inside and outside the firm.
- Internal innovation activities are needed to gain some significant value, which external innovation efforts can create.
- In order to beat the competition, it is more important to have a better business model than to get to the market first.
- Beating the competition does not require producing the best and most ideas, but making the best use of internal and external ideas.
- Proactive IP management allows other firms to use the firm's IP. It also considers buying other firms' IP whenever advancing the own business model.

Following this logic, firms should supplement their traditional R&D practices with the sourcing of external knowledge throughout the entire innovation process (Chesbrough, Vanhaverbeke, and West, 2006; Chesbrough, 2006b). Thus, open innovation applies to all major phases of the innovation process, and is not limited to the FEI. Based on an extensive

---

[10] The first edition of "Open innovation - The new imperative for creating and profiting from technology" published in 2003.

[11] A comprehensive review of research on open innovation can be found in West and Bogers (2014), and West et al. (2014).

literature review, open innovation research scholars have depicted the major steps that constitute the open innovation approach in a four-phase, integrated model (Figure 7).

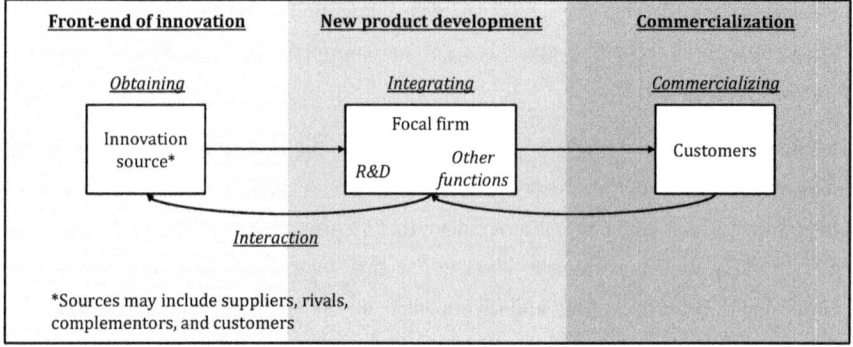

Figure 7: A four-phase process model for leveraging external sources of innovation[12]

According to this model, firms have to follow three major steps in order to successfully engage in open innovation: (i) obtaining innovations from external sources, (ii) integrating innovations, and (iii) commercializing innovations[13] (West and Bogers (2014) provide a comprehensive review of the published literature on each of these steps).

Obtaining new knowledge and ideas from external sources during the front-end of innovation is of special importance in the context of this study. In recent years, firms have increasingly started exploring new ways of obtaining innovations from external sources in an effort to source market knowledge, technical knowledge, components, or even actual new product ideas/inventions (Bogers and West, 2012) by facilitating online communities (Dahlander and Wallin, 2006), innovation tournaments/contests (Terwiesch and Ulrich, 2009; Terwiesch and Xu, 2008), innovation toolkits (Piller and Walcher, 2006), crowdsourcing, and broadcast searches (Jeppesen and Lakani, 2010; Ebner, Leimeister, and Krcmar, 2009).

---

[12] Author's illustration, based on West and Bogers (2014: 816).
[13] To account for innovation not following a unidirectional linear path, West and Bogers (2014) extend the phases with a fourth phase – interaction mechanisms.

However, leveraging external sources to obtain new product ideas results in a major follow-up challenge – how to effectively identify the most valuable new product ideas from hundreds, or even thousands, of submissions (West and Bogers, 2014). Once a firm has elicited ideas from external sources, these ideas need to be evaluated. The challenge then arises that the massive number of new product ideas resulting from these initiatives can be overwhelming for many firms (Piezunka and Dahlander, 2015; Blohm, Leimeister, and Krcmar, 2013). This is due to the traditional method of employing experts internal to firms (see chapter 3.2.3.1) being useless (Terwiesch and Ulrich, 2009) due to limited in-house expert resources. Research scholars have suggested outsourcing the idea evaluation process beyond the firms' internal experts (see chapter 3.2.2.3), thus leveraging external knowledge in an effort to accelerate and improve new product idea evaluation, as a strategy to face this challenge. Strongly related to the open innovation model, this approach has also been referred to as open evaluation (Haller, 2013; Velamuri et al., 2015).

To summarize, by leveraging external sources to obtain new product ideas, firms might face a major challenge in the initial evaluation of early-stage new product ideas as they will have to evaluate a massive number of ideas. Thus, proficient idea evaluation in the front-end of innovation becomes increasingly important if firms want to truly benefit from obtaining knowledge and ideas from external sources.

2.4 Interim summary

The term innovation refers to innovation as an outcome and as a process. The outcomes of an innovation process can be classified as more incremental and more radical innovations, depending on their degree of innovativeness. In the context of this dissertation, innovativeness includes a market-related dimension and a technology-related dimension.

Another interpretation of the term innovation describes the process to move new product development projects from idea to launch, and beyond. This process can be divided into three major phases: (i) the front-end of innovation, (ii) new product development, and (iii) commercialization. Research has shown that proficient execution of the front-end phase is a key success factor in new product development (Evanschitzky et al., 2012; Langerak, Hultink, and Robben, 2004). Nonetheless, neither academics, nor practitioners, seem to fully understand how to execute the FEI proficiently (Eling, 2014).

With the emergence of the open innovation paradigm, NPD firms face a new challenge compelling them to confer even more importance to the proficient execution of front-end activities. In an effort to obtain new product ideas from external sources, firms have increasingly started facilitating these, for example, innovation tournaments/contests (Terwiesch and Ulrich, 2009; Terwiesch and Xu, 2008), crowdsourcing, and broadcast searches (Jeppesen and Lakani, 2010; Ebner, Leimeister, and Krcmar, 2009). Such initiatives can easily generate hundreds, or thousands, of ideas (Piezunka and Dahlander, 2015; Blohm, Leimeister, and Krcmar, 2013) that subsequently need to be evaluated proficiently for firms to ultimately benefit from open innovation.

Therefore, in order to advance the existing knowledge of how to proficiently execute the FEI, this dissertation focuses on developing a deeper understanding of increasing the proficiency of one key activity during the FEI – the evaluation of early-stage new product ideas.

3 Theoretical foundation

This chapter starts with a short introduction to the different streams of research that have provided the theoretical foundation for this thesis (section 3.1). This is followed by portraying idea evaluation as a core activity in the front-end of innovation (section 3.2). As part of this portrayal, the discussion will focus on: (i) why proficient idea evaluation is important for NPD success, (ii) how new product ideas are evaluated, and (iii) who should evaluate early-stage new product ideas. Based on this discussion, the relevant research gap for this study is identified (section 3.3), and the central research questions for the thesis are formulated (section 3.4). Subsequently, a theory is developed to explain how domain knowledge influences the perception, judgment, and thus the evaluation of early-stage new product ideas (section 3.5). Following the introduction to this theory, the study's theoretical research framework and the underlying hypotheses are presented (section 3.6).

3.1 Relevant prior idea evaluation research

Idea evaluation is one of the central activities at the front-end of innovation. However, focusing the thesis's research objectives regarding the role of an individual's domain knowledge and, thus, the human factor in idea evaluation requires extending the view beyond the existing innovation management literature to adjacent fields of research. Endeavoring to identify pertinent research questions and develop a thorough theory on the influence of domain knowledge on the perception and judgment of new product ideas, research from innovation management, psychology, creativity, marketing, and consumer behavior scholars was integrated into the research efforts underlying this thesis (see Figure 8). A summary of the most relevant research studies for this thesis is provided in appendix A.

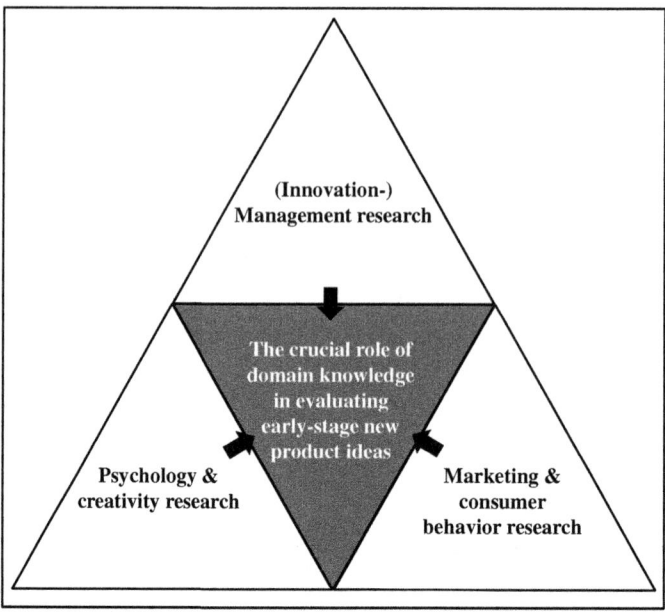

Figure 8: Academic schools of thought forming the theoretical foundation of the thesis[14]

3.2 Idea evaluation as core activity in the FEI

According to Cooper (2011), there are two fundamental ways of winning at product innovation: (i) doing projects right and (ii) doing the right projects. New product idea evaluation in the FEI is concerned with the latter by supporting the goal to select the *right* projects for further development. This means identifying those new product ideas with: (i) the highest potential for return-on-investment, and (ii) those that best fit the firm's strategy with regard to the overall NPD portfolio. This is important, because scarce organizational resources may otherwise be wasted on the development of ideas that will eventually fail in the market place and/or are likely to be terminated somewhere in the development process due to their low chances of development success, or are a strategic mismatch with the firm's innovation portfolio (Martinsuo and Poskela, 2011; Calantone, DiBenedetto, and

---

[14] Author's illustration.

Schmidt, 1999; Griffin, 1997). It is thus not surprising that a number of renowned studies have linked proficient idea evaluation to NPD success.

Identifying and selecting the most promising ideas require accurate evaluation with regard to the ideas' potential success in the market place. In this context, research and practice face the challenge that the evaluation of early-stage new product ideas is particularly difficult, as the assessment of their quality relies on the subjective judgment of appropriate evaluators, because the idea's "true" quality cannot be known until the finished innovation is commercialized in the market place (Onarheim and Christensen, 2012).

That is why appropriate evaluators need to assess early-stage new product ideas for their overall quality in terms of their uniqueness, potential value for future customers, and the possibility to develop, produce, and successfully commercialize them within a "reasonable time" and under "reasonable investments." Making such assessments can be very challenging, as the best choice is frequently very difficult to determine, especially when ideas show similar potential (Calantone, DiBenedetto, and Schmidt, 1999; Kim and Wilemon, 2002), or when an evaluator has to compare ideas with strengths and weaknesses on different dimensions. In this context, proficiency in idea evaluation increases if evaluators can correctly evaluate the differences in potential in terms of the important dimensions of an idea's quality (Eling, Langerak, and Griffin, 2015). The most commonly used approaches to carry out this evaluation is to either employ a rational evaluation process using specific evaluation criteria and/or to evaluate ideas holistically on the basis of intuition.

The evaluation of early-stage new product ideas has traditionally been undertaken inside the firm – both informally and formally. On the one hand, individuals or (small) front-end teams informally evaluate new product ideas to decide which ideas to drop and which to elaborate on further (Eling, Langerak, and Griffin, 2015; Kim and Wilemon, 2002). On the other hand, screening and/or gate committees perform more, or less, formal idea evaluation activities in preparation for go/no-go decisions (Eling, Griffin, and Langerak, 2016). Firms increasingly engage in obtaining new product ideas from external sources (Chesbrough, 2006b; Chesbrough, Vanhaverbeke, and West, 2006) by facilitating new idea generation methods, such as innovation tournaments (Terwiesch and Ulrich, 2009) or crowdsourcing (Bayus, 2013; Piezunka and Dahlander, 2015). Research and practice have thus recently explored the possibility of outsourcing idea evaluations to users (Magnusson,

Wästlund, and Netz, 2016; Toubia and Florès, 2007) or online communities (Velamuri et al., 2015) in an effort to cope with the massive number of ideas that can result from such activities. This has raised the question of who is best suited to evaluate new product ideas: firm-internal experts or external sources, such as users.

After this brief introduction to new product idea evaluation as a core activity in the FEI, selected topics of special importance in the context of this thesis are discussed in more detail in the following sub sections.

3.2.1 Why is proficient idea evaluation important?

Proficient idea evaluation can be defined as the effective and efficient evaluation of new product ideas. The effectiveness of idea evaluation refers to the ability to identify those ideas with the highest potential to become successful (Kim and Wilemon, 2002; Girotra, Terwiesch, and Ulrich, 2010). In this context, effective idea evaluation can help decision makers avoid "false positives," i.e., selecting bad ideas based on overestimating their potential and "false negatives," i.e., rejecting good ideas based on underestimating their potential (Berg, 2016). False negatives may lead firms to neglect opportunities that might have produced successful products, which could have significantly increased the firm's future NPD success (Girotra, Terwiesch, and Ulrich, 2010). False positives, on the other hand, may waste resources on ideas that could eventually fail in the marketplace and/or are likely to be terminated during the development process due to their low probability of success (Martinsuo and Poskela, 2011).

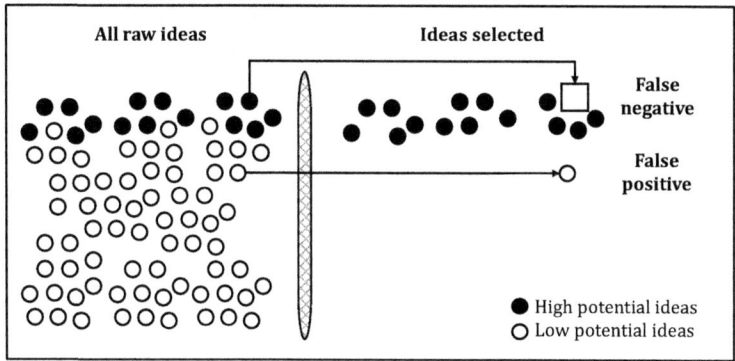

Figure 9: False negatives and false positives in idea evaluation[15]

The efficiency of new product idea evaluation refers to the ability to evaluate even vast numbers of ideas within a reasonable time frame (Velamuri et al., 2015). Efficiency can also be interpreted as the speed of the evaluation and thus refers to the ability to take less time to make idea evaluation decisions. Efficient idea evaluation has been shown to matter from an individual project perspective, as well as from an organizational perspective (Eling, Langerak, and Griffin, 2015). From a project perspective, efficient idea evaluation might contribute to a faster completion of the front-end phase, which might enable a firm to reduce its cycle time throughout all phases of the NPD process and, thus, to increase its new product performance (Eling, Langerak, and Griffin, 2013). From an organizational perspective, efficient idea evaluation means spending less time evaluating ideas, which in turn has been suggested to increase the overall efficiency of a firm's NPD workforce (Eling et al., 2015).

Overall, the importance of proficient idea evaluation in the front-end of innovation can be linked to two important antecedents of a firm's NPD success: (i) the need to successfully identify exceptional new product ideas (see section 3.2.1.1), and (ii) the need to develop a balanced innovation portfolio, including a fair balance between more incremental vs. more radical ideas (see section 3.2.1.2). Consequently, research scholars have argued that the "screening of new product ideas is perhaps the most critical new product development (NPD) activity" (Calantone, DiBenedetto, and Schmidt, 1999: 65). It is thus not surprising

---

[15] Author's illustration.

that a number of renowned studies have been able to link proficient idea evaluation to new product success (Cooper, 1979, 1988; Cooper and Kleinschmidt, 1986; Dwyer and Mellor, 1991; Parry and Song, 1994; Sanchez and Elola, 1991; Evanschitzky et al., 2012; Langerak, Hultink, and Robben, 2004).

3.2.1.1   The need to identify exceptional new product ideas

Launching a unique, superior product with a compelling value proposition is one of the foremost keys to profitability (Cooper, 2011). Consequently, in the context of new product development (NPD), innovation should focus on high-quality ideas with the potential to be developed into a "differentiated product with unique customer benefits and superior value for the user" (Cooper, 1999: 117), instead of developing "one more me-too, ho-hum, tired and vanilla product, much the same as competitors'" (Cooper, 2011: 27).

In line with this argument, it has been suggested that the quality of the best new product idea generated, identified, and selected for further development, determines the success of the front-end of innovation. This is because the extreme values in innovation are what matter – i.e., a firm is likely to prefer 99 bad ideas and one out-standing idea to 100 average ideas (Dahan and Mendelson, 2001; Terwiesch and Ulrich, 2009). This argument not only supports the importance of generating exceptional ideas, but also the critical importance of the ability to distinguish exceptional ideas from average or bad ones through idea evaluation (Girotra, Terwiesch, and Ulrich, 2010). Proficiency in the initial evaluation of early-stage new product ideas is therefore of the utmost importance. Generating a large number of ideas of average quality is in itself not sufficient; firms must also be able to discern and select the best ideas very carefully, as choosing the right idea sets the basis for future commercial success (Kornish and Ulrich, 2014). This logic is illustrated in Figure 10. Although generating a large number of new product ideas is likely to increase the probability of exceptional ideas being generated, these exceptional ideas need to be accurately identified to avoid false negatives and false positives in the final selection of the ideas.

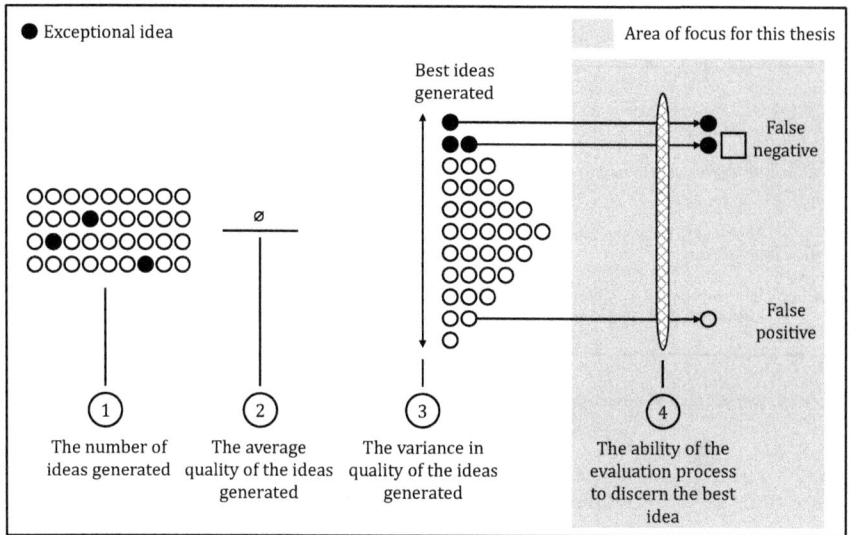

Figure 10: Four factors underlying the performance of the idea generation process[16]

3.2.1.2   The need to balance the innovation portfolio

Firms should develop, and successfully launch, a balance of more incremental and more radical new product ideas in order to maximize their innovation success (Cooper, Edgett, and Kleinschmidt, 2002; Loch and Kavadies, 2002). Unfortunately, today's firms encounter an increasingly dynamic and complex environment, forcing them to develop new products in increasingly shorter time intervals (Gaubinger et al., 2015). According to Cooper (2011), drivers of this development are: (i) the exponential rate with which the world's technology base and know-how increase, (ii) rapidly changing customer needs, (iii) radically shortened product life cycles (on average by 75 per cent in the past 50 years), and (iv) increased globalization. Consequently, many firms have reacted to that pressure by shifting the focus of their development offerings to more incremental products. Empirical studies have shown that, in development portfolios, the share of "new-to-the-world, new-to-market innovations" decreased from 20.4 per cent in the 1990s to 11.5 per cent in the 2000s, whereas the share of "improvements & modifications to existing firm products" increased from 20.4 per cent to 36.7 per cent (see Figure 11).

---

[16]   Author's illustration, adapted from Girotra, Terwiesch, and Ulrich (2010: 594).

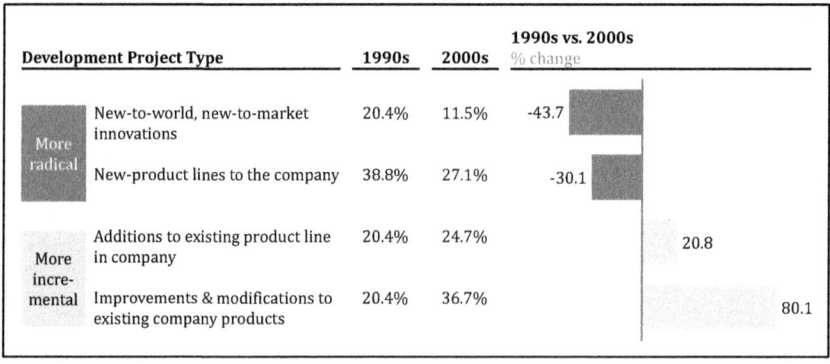

Development Project Type	1990s	2000s	1990s vs. 2000s % change	
More radical New-to-world, new-to-market innovations	20.4%	11.5%	-43.7	
New-product lines to the company	38.8%	27.1%	-30.1	
More incre-mental Additions to existing product line in company	20.4%	24.7%		20.8
Improvements & modifications to existing company products	20.4%	36.7%		80.1

Figure 11: Breakdown of development portfolios by project type[17]

In fact, firms seem to continue along this path by becoming more conservative in their innovation portfolios with lower percentages of their total number of projects in the new-to-the-world and new-to-the-firm categories. Such an imbalance in a firm's innovation portfolio can have critical consequences for long-term success. Despite success rates and NPD efficiencies having remained largely stable in recent years, the emphasis on incremental innovation seems to have negatively impacted the revenue and profits of the new products that have been commercialized (Barczak, Griffin, and Kahn, 2009).

Therefore, innovation management research scholars have argued that in an effort to establish a balanced portfolio and, thus, ensure an overall NPD performance in the long run (Lerch and Spieth, 2013), it is important to take a portfolio perspective at the very beginning of the FEI (Kock, Heising, and Gemünden, 2015; Eling, Griffin, and Langerak, 2016). In other words, an important aspect of proficient idea evaluation in the front-end of innovation lies in accurately evaluating and, thus, identifying promising radical new product ideas. These actions allow such ideas to be funneled into the firm's development pipeline, which will ensure that a balanced innovation portfolio is regained.

3.2.2 How to measure the quality of new product ideas?

All generated early-stage new product ideas need to be accurately measured for their quality in order to identify exceptional new product ideas. This quality measure is a

---

[17] Author's illustration, source: Cooper (2011: 3).

prediction of how successful an innovation might be (Berg, 2016). In this context, research and practice face the challenge that the evaluation of new product ideas is particularly difficult, as their "true" quality cannot be known for certain until they are fully developed, tested, and commercialized in the market (Onarheim and Christensen, 2012).

The literature has solved this dilemma by taking the point of view that a new product idea is the outcome of a creative process (Csikszentmihalyi, 1996; Amabile, 1996; Mumford and Gustafson, 1988). Logically, the creativity of a new product idea is considered a reliable measure of its quality, just as the creativity of a painting or poem is believed to reflect its quality (Im, Montoya, and Workman, 2013). However, to be useful in the context of new product idea evaluation, this point of view requires an appropriate method to actually measure creativity.

Building on extant creativity research, a number of innovation management research scholars have established the consensual assessment technique (CAT) as a widely used and well validated instrument to assess new product ideas (see Table 3 and Table 4)[18]. As such, the CAT provides the theoretical foundation for individuals' subjective judgments of new product ideas being regarded as reliable measures of idea quality. Therefore, the CAT will be explained in more detail in the following section.

---

[18] Rbesearch has identified, developed, and discussed a large number of methods and tools that can be used for the evaluation of new product ideas (examples include the Analytic Hierarchy Processes by Calantone, DiBenedetto, and Schmidt (1999), the Benefit Measurement Models by Baker, Kenneth, G. and Albaum (1986), Idea Markets (see e.g. Dahan, Soukhoroukova, and Spann (2010); Soukhoroukova, Spann, and Skiera (2012)), the Adaptive Concept Screening (see e.g. Toubia and Florès (2007); Cui, Peng, and Florès (2015)); for an overview of other relevant evaluation methods see Ozer (1999)). However, these methods will not be discussed in this dissertation and the remainder of the thesis will focus on simple criteria-based and holistic evaluation mechanisms, because these two are the most commonly applied idea evaluation methods (see e.g. Hart et al. (2003)). As it is the goal of this thesis to investigate idea evaluation in the front-end from an individual's behavioral point of view, we expect the investigated behavior to also be generally exhibited when we use other idea evaluation tools and processes.

Table 3: Selected (innovation-) management research studies employing the CAT for idea evaluation (part I)

Source	Idea domain	Expert definition	Evaluation criteria
Franke et al., 2014	Carpentry, roofing, inline skating	Carpentry experts (n=3), roofing experts (n=2), inline skating experts (n=3)	Novelty, usefulness
Somech and Drach-Zahavy, 2013	Health care (services)	Senior people employed in a health maintenance organization (n=2); researchers in the area of organizational behavior in health care organizations (n=2)	Magnitude, radicalness, useful
Schuhmacher and Kuester, 2012	Online services for soccer clubs	Experts in the domain, i.e., a frequent user of soccer club homepages, and a manager of a soccer club running a homepage for soccer fans (n=2)	Novelty, relevance, feasibility
Poetz and Schreier, 2012	Feeding of babies	CEO and head of R&D (n=2)	Novelty, customer benefit, feasibility
Bretschneider et al., 2012	SAP software	Employee at the SAP University Competence Center (n=4) and SAP employees (n=4)	Novelty, originality, paradigm relatedness, technical feasibility, economic feasibility, acceptability, effectiveness
Witell et al., 2011	Microwave ovens	Employees of a microwave manufacturer with a tenure > 5 years (n=4)	Originality, value
Piller and Walcher, 2006	Sport shoes	Experienced managers (innovation, product management, communication) from different hierarchies in the organization (n=5)	Originality, customer benefit, number of beneficiaries, level of elaboration
Magnusson et al., 2016 & Magnusson et al., 2014	Mobile telephony services	Developer for wireless services with a tenure > 5 years (n=4)	Originality, user value, producibility

Table 4: Selected (innovation-) management research studies employing the CAT for idea evaluation (part II)

Source	Idea domain	Expert definition	Evaluation criteria
Kristensson and Magnusson, 2010	Mobile telephony services	Panel A: Technical experts working at a university (=2) Panel B: CEO, CTO and former marketing manager of a telecommunications service firm (n=2)	Originality, value, producibility Holistic judgment
Magnusson, 2009	Mobile telephony services	Engineers, employed in the firm's R&D department with a tenure > 5 years (n=3); judges with "a mix of technical and marketing experience," employed outside the firm (n=3)	Originality, user value, producibility
Kristensson et al., 2004	Mobile telephony services	Panel A: Telecom operators who held a master's degree in engineering, employed inside the firm (n=6) Panel B: Consultants in the telecom field, employed outside the firm (n=6) Panel C: Students with orientation in computer science (n=3) or business administration (n=3) Panel D: Employees inside the firm without further specification (n=6)	Originality, value, realization
Magnusson, 2003	Mobile telephony services	Experts, experienced in evaluating mobile communications service ideas (n=6)	Originality, user value, producibility

3.2.2.1   The consensual assessment technique (CAT)

Amabile (1982) initially developed and validated the CAT as a tool to assess creativity in the 1980s, but since then she and other researchers have developed it further (Baer, Kaufman, and Gentile, 2004; Amabile, 1983, 1996; Baer, 1993; Kaufman et al., 2007). The CAT has its theoretical roots in the product-based view of creativity[19], which defines creativity according to the impression that a creative outcome (such as a new product idea) evokes in an appropriate observer:

"A product or response is creative to the extent that appropriate observers independently agree it is creative. Appropriate observers are those familiar with the domain in which the product was created or the response articulated. Thus, creativity can be regarded as the quality of products or responses judged to be creative by appropriate observers, and it can also be regarded as the process by which something so judged is produced." (Amabile, 1996: 33)

Furthermore, the following assumptions are made about how evaluators judge creativity:

"A product or response will be judged as creative to the extent that (a) it is both novel and appropriate, useful, correct or valuable response to the task at hand, and (b) the task is heuristic rather than algorithmic" (Amabile, 1996: 35).

Several important facets of this definition should be highlighted in the context of new product idea evaluation. First and foremost, Amabile's definition abandons "the hope of finding objective criteria for creativity and, instead, [...] relies on clearly subjective criteria" (Amabile, 1996: 34). Second, it is assumed that, although creativity might be difficult to characterize in terms of specific features, it is something that individuals can recognize and agree upon. Third, this definition assumes that there is a basic form of creativity to which observers respond when they refer to something as being "creative." Fourth, it is assumed that creativity judgments are based on an idea's novelty and appropriateness, as these two characteristics constitute the major hallmarks of creativity. Finally, Amabile's definition assumes that there are degrees of creativity, so that observers can state that some

---

[19]   Modern creativity research encompasses a complex body of knowledge with various views on "creativity" (Amabile, 1996). According to Rhode's (1987) meta-analysis research study, creativity definitions can be categorized into four groups: (1) person, (2) process, (3) press, and (4) product.

outcomes are more creative, or less creative, than others rather than assuming that creativity is a dichotomous quality (outcomes are either creative or not creative) (Amabile, 1996).

The CAT has been well validated in creativity research and has been called the "gold standard" of creativity assessment (Carson (2006), cited in Kaufman, Baer, and Cole (2009)). The CAT was originally created and validated to measure the creativity of parallel works – artifacts created under the same firmly controlled settings (e.g. collages created by students given the same assignment and in the same class room) (Amabile, 1982), but Baer, Kaufman, and Gentile (2004) have shown that the CAT can also be used to validly evaluate nonparallel creative work – artifacts created under different and uncontrolled conditions. Baer et al.'s findings have set an important prerequisite for the CAT's broad field of applications, because most creative outcomes are rarely created under the exact same conditions. These findings are thus largely attributed to the recognition that the CAT can be used on almost any type of creative product.

In fact, research scholars have shown that the CAT can be used in virtually any domain, whether it is evaluating artistic creative outcomes, such as poems, collages, short stories, photographs, designs, music compositions, and dramatic performances, or non-artistic outcomes, such as mathematical equations and problems, responses to science-based questions, solutions to everyday problems, business solutions, and ideas for high-tech products (Amabile, 1996).

Amabile (1996: 41) identified several requirements with regard to the CAT's evaluation procedure in order to evaluate creative outcomes:

1. Evaluators need to be experienced in/familiar with the domain in question. However, the evaluators' level of experience/familiarity does not need to be identical.
2. Evaluators need to make their evaluations independently. The CAT principle relies on agreement being reached without the evaluators (or the researcher) attempting to influence the outcome. Consequently, evaluators should not be trained to agree with another, nor be able to confer while making their assessments.
3. Evaluators should evaluate an idea's creativity and, thus, the overall quality on the basis of (i) a holistic judgment and (ii) a criteria-based judgment. With regard to the

latter, these criteria should at least include the novelty and appropriateness dimensions. Applying both approaches allows for determining whether the creativity judgment is related to, or independent of, those dimensions.

4. Evaluators should rate the ideas relative to one another, rather than rating them against some subjective absolute.[20]

5. The ideas should be presented to each evaluator in varying random order and each evaluator should assess the various criteria in a different random order.

Once these conditions have been met and all evaluations have been collected, the ratings in respect of each criterion need to be analyzed for interrater reliability, because in the CAT, "reliability [...] is equivalent to construct validity. If appropriate judges independently agree that a given product is highly creative, then it can and must be accepted as such" (Amabile, 1996: 43). Therefore, it has been largely accepted that evaluations of idea creativity have to be considered valid indicators of the idea's quality as long as appropriate judges independently agree on their evaluations. Furthermore, in the context of new product idea evaluation, the assumptions of the CAT imply that (i) it is the evaluator's perception, rather than the objective reality, that explains the evaluations of new product ideas (Christiaans, 2002), (ii) evaluators familiar with the domain intuitively adhere to the aspects of novelty and appropriateness when judging creativity, and that (iii) creativity is something that can be measured on the basis of criteria that reflect the latter two aspects on a continuous scale.

3.2.2.2 Criteria-based evaluations

Research and practice have been confronted with the challenge of defining a reliable set of criteria that best reflects the quality of each individual idea, in order to carry out meaningful idea evaluations. There have not been uniformly accepted criteria for the evaluation of new product ideas for a long time (Balachandra and Friar, 1997). Acknowledging that the key objective of the front-end of innovation is the generation of a creative product concept (Im, Montoya, and Workman, 2013), innovation management research has started building on extant knowledge in the creativity research field to develop a meaningful set of evaluation criteria with which to measure an early-stage idea's

---

[20] However, Amabile (1996: 75) acknowledged that this might be impossible in some settings and evaluators are thus not necessarily required to evaluate all creative outcomes relative to one another.

quality. Voices in the literature have convincingly argued that the creativity of new product ideas can be used as a meaningful indicator of a new product idea's future success in the marketplace, and can thus also be used to measure an idea's quality in a new product development setting (see section 3.2.2.1). Consequently, exploring the dimensions that constitute creativity has been considered a good starting point to determine the criteria that are appropriate for the evaluation of new product ideas (Haller, 2013).

Creativity research scholars have suggested deconstructing creativity into several sub dimensions to enable its measurement. In this context, it has often been suggested that creativity should be divided into the two dimensions: novelty and usefulness (Amabile, 1996; O'Quin and Besemer S., 1999). A comprehensive literature review, including more than 50 conceptualizations of creativity, reveals that, although there seem to be many different dimensions to measuring creativity, most of the dimensions have similar meanings. The meanings can be summarized as *novelty, relevance, workability,* and *specificity* (Dean et al., 2006).

Recognizing the overlap between the creativity concept and the characteristics that determine the quality of new product ideas, innovation management scholars have adapted the dimensions that primarily determine an idea's creativity. These scholars have also established three predominant criteria against which to evaluate the quality of early-stage new product ideas: *originality, user value,* and *feasibility*[21] (Kristensson, Gustafsson, and Archer, 2004; Magnusson, 2009; Poetz and Schreier, 2012; Riedl et al., 2013; Magnusson, Wästlund, and Netz, 2016; Magnusson, Netz, and Wästlund, 2014; Kudrowitz and Wallace, 2013, Kristensson and Magnusson, 2010). In the following paragraphs, the meaning of these three criteria and their relevance for new product idea evaluation are described in more detail.

Originality is most often referred to as the most obvious attribute of creativity in new product ideas, because it reflects an idea's novelty (Kristensson, Gustafsson, and Archer, 2004). More specifically, originality reflects how unusual or unexpected an idea is compared to other ideas or products already available in the domain (Shah, Smith, and Vargas-Hernandez, 2003). Furthermore, originality determines the extent to which an idea

---

[21] Other studies have used different terms with a similar meaning (Dean et al., 2006), e.g., originality is also called novelty, user value is called customer benefit, and feasibility is called producibility.

or concept is transformational and breaks with existing paradigms in the sense that it might force a shift in the market. As such, originality also determines whether or not new elements and relationships between elements are included in an idea (Dean et al., 2006). Consequently, originality does not only capture the newness of an idea, but also the uniqueness of its characteristics, which can be considered an important indicator of such an idea's "innovativeness"[22] (Haller, 2013).

The *user value* criterion is used to assess whether or not an idea is (i) useful in respect of the extent to which it responds to, or solves, a certain target users' needs, and (ii) whether or not solving this need is considered valuable (Besemer S. P. and O'Quinn, 1987). Thus, from a customer's point of view, user value refers to the idea's benefits for future users (Piller and Walcher, 2006). From a firm's perspective, an idea's user value indicates the extent to which an idea solves a relevant need that potential customers may have and are willing to pay for, which can therefore be seen as an indicator of market demand (Haller, 2013). That is why the user value criterion has also been referred to as the demand side of an idea's quality equation (Magnusson, Wästlund, and Netz, 2016).

Feasibility captures the probability of developing an idea into a final product and the ease with which this can be done under reasonable resource investments, thus allowing the product to be sold at a price that still includes a profit (Magnusson, Wästlund, and Netz, 2016). More feasible ideas can therefore be transformed more timely and cheaper, allowing firms to achieve short-term benefits (Dean et al., 2006). Although not included as a criterion in some prior studies, assessing an idea's feasibility is of particular importance in the context of innovation management. New product ideas do not automatically evolve into innovations, thus stressing the importance of considering the feasibility of the final product (Kristensson, Gustafsson, and Archer, 2004). An idea or concept considered impossible or highly difficult to realize is probably of zero to little interest to firms (Haller, 2013; Magnusson, Netz, and Wästlund, 2014). Accordingly, this criterion reflects the supply side dimension of the idea's quality equation (Magnusson, Wästlund, and Netz, 2016).

Altogether, these three criteria fulfill the theoretical requirements of Amabile's CAT, because they resonate well with her definition of creativity as "the production of novel, useful ideas or problem solutions" (Amabile et al., 2005: 368). Simultaneously, these three

---

[22] The term innovativeness is defined in chapter 2.1.1.

criteria represent the most important aspects of successful innovation (Magnusson, Wästlund, and Netz, 2016), i.e., something (i) that is unusual and unique compared to existing products (*originality*), (ii) that solves an underlying problem and thus creates value for the user (*user value*), and (iii) that is possible to realize given both its technical and economic aspects (*feasibility*) (Poetz and Schreier, 2012). Furthermore, by evaluating an idea against these three dimensions, ideas can be assessed with regard to their innovativeness and classified as more incremental or more radical ideas (Magnusson, 2009). Incremental ideas are those that provide the user with additional value and are easy to realize, but are not specifically original. A moderate user value, high feasibility, but low originality therefore characterize valuable incremental ideas. On the other hand, radical ideas can be defined by their high originality paired with high user value, but with the downside of low feasibility (Kristensson and Magnusson, 2010).

Empirical studies that have investigated the evaluation criteria used in practice to assess new product ideas throughout the new product development process support the external validity of these three criteria. These studies have shown that firms weed out impractical ideas in the initial assessment of early-stage new product by evaluating the uniqueness of the product ideas (i.e., originality) together with their market potential, perceived customer acceptance (i.e., user value), and their technical feasibility (i.e., feasibility) (Tzokas, Hultink, and Hart, 2004; Hart et al., 2003).

3.2.2.3 Holistic evaluations

A commonly used alternative to criteria-based idea evaluation is to ask evaluators to simply state their overall impression regarding an idea's quality in one holistic judgment (Hart et al., 2003; Tzokas, Hultink, and Hart, 2004). This type of judgement allows evaluators to undertake an evaluation without being given any specific guidance or criteria in respect of their decision. Consequently, evaluators must not only decide what aspects are important in order to assess an idea's quality, they must also determine the relative weight of these aspects in order to reach their judgment. The validity of such judgments is thus based on the assumption that an evaluator will automatically and intuitively take all relevant information into account (Magnusson, Netz, and Wästlund, 2014).

These holistic judgments differ from criteria-based evaluations in the sense that holistic judgments can be interpreted as an intuitive decision-making task (Haller, 2013). A comprehensive body of research points towards two important aspects of intuitive-based decision making that should be acknowledged in the context of new product idea evaluations. [23] First, intuitive decision-making carries a higher risk regarding evaluation biases (Tversky and Kahnemann, 1974). Evaluators might thus assess ideas as good or bad without considering all relevant dimensions, or by weighting the dimensions in different ways. For example, research studies have found that individuals who have been instructed to intuitively select the best ideas based on their own subjective evaluations, show a strong tendency to select feasible and effective ideas at the cost of originality (Rietzschel, Nijstad, and Stroebe, 2010). This tendency to select desirable and feasible ideas that provide short-term benefits at the cost of originality has also been found in other research studies (Licuanan, Dailey, and Mumford, 2007; Blair and Mumford, 2007). This indicates that individuals might, either (i) not take all relevant information into account, (ii) might assign different weights to certain aspects of the idea, or (iii) revert to the selection criterion that is most important to them when forming a holistic judgment.

From this perspective, research scholars have argued that user value and/or feasibility might be perceived as the predominant criteria and originality might even be regarded as irrelevant in some evaluation situations (Rietzschel, Nijstad, and Stroebe, 2010). Based on their research findings, Blair and Mumford (2007) conclude that originality might even be perceived as a negative trait, because individuals seem to have an "undeniable disdain for risky and original ideas" (Blair and Mumford, 2007: 215). Contrary to these findings, a more recent empirical research study indicates that evaluators unconsciously include originality, user value, and feasibility as criteria in their holistic judgments, but also that the weighting of these criteria depends largely on the task instruction and interpretation (Magnusson, Netz, and Wästlund, 2014). However, this study employed experts for the evaluation of ideas, which points towards the second important aspect that should be considered in the context of intuitive new product idea evaluation.

This second aspect signifies that intuition's positive contributions regarding increasing efficient and effective decision making (Dane and Pratt, 2007; Eling, Griffin, and Langerak,

---

[23] Research on intuition in decision-making has a long history, with ongoing research in several disciplines. Different schools of thought consider the benefits and shortcomings of intuitive-based decision-making well-researched (Akinci and Sadler-Smith, 2012), while innovation management research scholars have developed a framework for how intuition can be used beneficially to evaluate decisions in the FEI (Eling, Griffin, and Langerak, 2014).

2014) seem to be limited to evaluators whose intuition is based on their high domain knowledge (Sadler-Smith and Shefy, 2004; Salas, Rosen, and DiazGranados, 2010). Therefore, domain knowledge might be even more likely to influence intuitive-based judgments than criteria-based evaluations.

3.2.3 Who should evaluate early-stage new product ideas?

Regardless of the processes, methods or criteria used in new product idea evaluation, the choice of who evaluates new product ideas will always be at the center of the evaluation outcome (Ozer, 2005). Based on the relevant idea evaluation literature, the following two general possibilities can be employed in an evaluation task: (i) domain experts[24] (section 3.2.3.1.), or (ii) "quasi-experts" and "non-experts" in the form of users, customers, community members, regular firm employees, or even laymen (section 3.2.3.2). However, prior research has been unable to provide a conclusive answer on whether or not less knowledgeable individuals can replace experts in the crucial task of idea evaluation. Neither have the kinds and levels of knowledge deemed appropriate in an evaluator when assessing early-stage new product ideas been fully understood, nor whether, depending on the domain and/or innovativeness of the ideas to be evaluated, evaluators need to have less or more knowledge.

3.2.3.1   Idea evaluation by experts

The individuals comprising the front-end teams traditionally undertake idea evaluations to decide which ideas to drop, to further elaborate on, and/or which ideas need to be reported in the firm's idea management system or communicated to the management (Eling, Langerak, and Griffin, 2015; Kim and Wilemon, 2002; Boeddrich, 2004). Furthermore, these evaluations provide the informational base for go/no-go decisions (Eling, Griffin, and Langerak, 2016).

In this context, literature and practice have accepted the basic assumption that a judge who is appropriate for idea evaluation needs to be an expert in the field (Salas, Rosen, and DiazGranados, 2010; Shanteau and James, 1992; Ozer, 2009, 2005; Rochford, 1991; Cooper, 2011). The primary distinction that separates experts from non-experts is the breadth and

---

[24] In the following paragraphs, the term, domain expert is used interchangeably with the term individuals with high domain knowledge.

depth of their domain-specific knowledge (Phillips, Klein, and Sieck, 2004). Individuals are therefore assumed to qualify as appropriate evaluators on the basis of their higher level of domain knowledge in the respective industries (Velamuri et al., 2015; Salas, Rosen, and DiazGranados, 2010).

A large body of research that investigates the general benefits of expertise broadly supports only considering individuals with high domain knowledge as appropriate judges for the assessment of new product ideas (see Ericsson et al., 2006 for an overview). Research in this field has shown that experts have a large and well-organized knowledge base that allows the development of intuitive pattern recognition capacities (Klein et al., 1993) based on complex domain-specific schemas (Dane and Pratt, 2007). Thus, experts have a unique cognitive architecture (Dane, 2010, see chapter 3.5.2), which may enable them to be more efficient and effective in judgment and decision making tasks, to exhibit superior domain-relevant memory skills, and to solve problems more competently (Ericsson et al., 2006; Hoffmann, 1992). Furthermore, in respect of predictions, the literature suggests that experts should be able to make more accurate predictions in their respective domains. This suggestion is based on experts not only recognizing the relevant issues in their prediction task, but being able to simplify complex problems, generate meaningful interpretations based on the given information, and being willing to process all the required information (Alba and Hutchinson, 1987; Shanteau and James, 1992; Ozer, 2009).

However, relying on experts might also have its downside and limitations. First, finding universal experts to evaluate new product ideas in different domains is impossible, which is a general problem. Expertise is always domain-specific and its meaningful application outside the domain diminishes (Anderson, 2015). Furthermore, research suggests that expertise can lead to a phenomenon referred to as "cognitive entrenchment" (Dane, 2010: 583). Dane (2010) proposes that experts' cognitive schemas are not only becoming more complex, but also more stable and, thus, resistant to modification over time. Such cognitive entrenchment may limit experts in their problem solving, adaptation, and creative idea generation in a way that essentially restricts their flexibility to think beyond known boundaries (for detailed consequences of cognitive entrenchment see Dane (2010)). These limitations might explain why experts have been shown to often fail to recognize new and highly original ideas (Blohm et al., 2011), or might be the reason for experts displaying poor judgment in predicting the market success of ideas in the field of highly advanced technologies (Galbraith, Ehrlich, and DeNoble, 2006).

3.2.3.2 Substituting experts with non-experts

Research has recently raised the question whether or not experts are the only appropriate judges that can evaluate creative outcomes, such as new product ideas (e.g. Velamuri et al., 2015; Magnusson, Wästlund, and Netz, 2016; Toubia and Florès, 2007; Onarheim and Christensen, 2012; Haller, 2013; Kornish and Ulrich, 2014). This doubt finds support in the fact that about 20 years ago, Amabile (1996) revised the CAT's initially stated requirement that an appropriate judge of creativity needs to be an expert in the domain.

> "In the 1983 edition we asserted that appropriate judges are those familiar with the domain [...]. We [...] used the term "expert" to describe appropriate judges, but we are now convinced that for most products in most domains, judges need not to be true experts in order to be considered appropriate. [...] We suggest that the best guideline is to use judges who have at least [...] experience in the target domain, if at all possible."
> (Amabile, 1996: 72)

This change in the CAT's requirements provides theoretical justification for employing quasi-experts, or even novices, for the evaluation of new product ideas.

Practical justification for substituting experts arises from resource and absorptive capacity constraints within firms (Cohen and Levinthal, 1990). Firms currently engage in open innovation strategies (Chesbrough, Vanhaverbeke, and West, 2006; Chesbrough, 2006b), increasingly facilitating the acquisition of ideas from external sources by utilizing distant search (Piezunka and Dahlander, 2015), online communities (Dahlander and Wallin, 2006), innovation tournaments/contests (Terwiesch and Ulrich, 2009; Terwiesch and Xu, 2008), innovation toolkits (Piller and Walcher, 2006), and crowdsourcing/broadcast searches (Jeppesen and Lakani, 2010; Ebner, Leimeister, and Krcmar, 2009). They can thus easily generate hundreds, or even thousands, of new product ideas (Haller, 2013).

Despite this problem, meta-analysis research of hundreds of open innovation papers has found that most research on open innovation is only concerned with obtaining externally generated ideas and not with how to proceed with these ideas in the subsequent phases of the innovation process (West and Bogers, 2014). Utilizing experts to evaluate such large numbers of ideas has been found to be challenging, time consuming, and expensive (Pisano and Verganti, 2008; Soukhoroukova, Spann, and Skiera, 2012). Firms have therefore been advised to rethink the established expert evaluation process. Research scholars have proposed that using experts to evaluate such large amounts of ideas is neither effective nor efficient (Poetz and Schreier, 2012; Terwiesch and Ulrich, 2009). Improving the proficiency efficiency of evaluating a multitude of ideas has sparked the interest of research and practice alike, and has been declared a research priority for innovation management (Barczak, 2014).

Consequently, the potential of outsourcing idea evaluations as a means to (i) accurately identify the most promising ideas (effective evaluation), while simultaneously (ii) managing a vast number of ideas in a reasonable time frame and under reasonable resource investments (efficient evaluation), has also received increasing attention in the management literature (e.g. Velamuri et al., 2015; Magnusson, Wästlund, and Netz, 2016; Toubia and Florès, 2007; Onarheim and Christensen, 2012; Haller, 2013; Kornish and Ulrich, 2014).

Despite the potential advantages of outsourcing idea evaluation processes once left to experts, it is also problematic. For example, most innovation contests' common practice of inviting all registered participants to the idea evaluation task (Poetz and Schreier, 2012; Haller, 2013), irrespective of their domain knowledge (Velamuri et al., 2015), largely contradicts the requirements logic behind the traditional approach of expert jury evaluations, and this practice might also disregard the CAT requirement to select "appropriate" evaluators (see section 3.2.2.1). Research scholars have stressed that little is known about how non-experts and experts differ in their abilities to judge new product ideas, since "remarkably little attention has been paid to investigating the characteristics deemed appropriate in people judging new product/service ideas" (Magnusson, Wästlund, and Netz, 2016: 3).

Consequently, from a theoretical, as well as a practical perspective, research has been confronted with the question to clarify what kind of knowledge is essential to accurately evaluate ideas in a given domain and for a particular purpose (Kaufman et al., 2008). Several studies, both in the creativity and management literature, have tried to answer this question by investigating whether or not non-experts (individuals with no specific domain knowledge) or quasi-experts (individuals familiar within the domain considered to possess moderate domain knowledge) can mimic the evaluation decisions made by experts (individuals with high domain knowledge). The results of these studies are summarized in Table 5, Table 6, Table 7, and Table 8, and will be discussed in the following sections.

Table 5: Expert / non-expert comparison studies – creativity research studies (part I)

Source	Domain	Expert / quasi-expert / non-expert definitions	Criteria	Core findings
Kaufman et al., 2013	Short stories	**Experts:** professional writers with either MFAs in creative writing or PhDs in English (n=10) **Quasi-experts:** Group 1: advanced undergraduate and graduate students in creativity (n=12) Group 2: students with elementary education majors (n=10) Group 3: students with senior secondary education/English double majors (n=10) Group 4: English teachers with at least two years of experience teaching English (n=9) **Non-experts:** students from a psychology class (n=106)	Creativity	- Experts and quasi-experts show a high degree of agreement, thus quasi-experts can be used as substitutes for experts - Non-expert judgments are not similar to those of experts
Kaufman et al., 2013	Mouse trap designs	**Experts:** professional engineers with > 10 years experience (n=15) **Quasi-experts:** first year undergraduate engineering students (n=31) **Non-experts:** students from a psychology class (n=274)	Overall creativity, novelty, relevance, elegance, genesis	- The ability of non-experts and quasi-experts to substitute experts depends on the dimension being assessed - For overall creativity, elegance, and genesis: quasi-experts and non-experts are poor substitutes for experts - For novelty: quasi-experts might be suitable substitutes for experts, while non-experts are not - For relevance: quasi-experts and novices are capable of substituting experts
Kaufman et al., 2009	Short stories	**Experts:** professional writers with either MFAs in creative writing or PhDs in English (n=10) **Non-experts:** students from a psychology class (n=106)	Overall creativity	- Little difference between experts' and students' ratings

Table 6: Expert / non-expert comparison studies – creativity research studies (part II)

Source	Domain	Expert / quasi-expert / non-expert definitions	Criteria	Core findings
Kaufman et al., 2008	SciFaiku poems	Experts: published poets with multiple publications in respected publications (n=10) Non-experts: students from a psychology class (n=106)	Overall creativity	- Non-expert raters' judgments of creativity are inconsistent and do not match those of the expert raters - Experts and non-experts rate creative work in different ways with expert raters being more critical
Kaufman et al., 2005	Poems, short stories	Experts: middle school teachers teaching creative writing (n=4) published creative writers (n=4) psychologists who focus on creativity research (n=5) Quasi-experts: gifted creative writers from a renowned school of arts (n=8)	Overall creativity	- Quasi-experts' ratings have good interrater reliability and are significantly correlated with the ratings of experts
Dollinger and Shafran, 2005	Drawings	Experts: artists (n=5) Quasi-experts: psychologists (n=5)	Overall creativity, quality of drawings	- Experts and quasi-experts ratings were nearly identical for both criteria*

Table 7: Expert / non-expert comparison studies – innovation management research studies (part I)

Source	Domain	Expert / quasi-expert / non-expert definitions	Criteria	Core findings
Magnusson et al., 2016	Wireless services	Experts: experienced professionals within the field of wireless communications with > 5 years experience in evaluating wireless ideas (n=4) Quasi-experts: members of an internet based community of interest focusing on Android mobile phones (n=19) Non-experts: users of mobile phones without in-depth knowledge about wireless communication (n=11)	Originality, user value, producibility	- Firms can employ users during the initial screening process (using criteria-based assessment) as a proxy for in-house experts in order to select the best ideas for further elaboration - User panels' absolute criteria scores are not conformant with those of experts; users overestimated the ideas - User panels' relative criteria scores are conformant with those of experts - Users can rank a set of ideas, but cannot assess a very limited number of ideas reliably
Kornish and Ulrich, 2014	Consumer products (gadgets)	Experts: experts in consumer products marketing and product development with > 25 years professional experience (n=7) Non-experts: Anonymous consumer panel (recruited by a vendor)	Units sold (for experts), purchase-intent (for non-experts)	- Online consumer panels are a better way to determine a "good" idea than ratings by experts - Asking consumers to state purchase-intentions of early-stage ideas, better predicts market outcomes than asking experts to predict sales
Haller, 2013	Services in healthcare, education, and leisure	Experts: experts in innovation management/information systems from industry and academia (n=12) (each category was evaluated by 5 judges) Non-experts: students (60.5% management; 14.0% industrial engineering; 25.5% other) (n= 300) (100 randomly assigned per idea)	Originality, effectiveness, feasibility, elaboration, willingness to pay	- Users might be able to substitute experts in the assessment of originality and feasibility, but not in respect of relevance, elaboration, and financial potential

Table 8: Expert / non-expert comparison studies – innovation management research studies (part II)

Source	Domain	Expert / quasi-expert / non-expert definitions	Criteria	Core findings
Riedl *et al.*, 2013	SAP software	Experts: professors in information systems, employees of SAP's marketing and R&D department, or the German SAP University Competence Centers (n=11) Quasi-experts: undergraduate and graduate students from two information systems courses related to SAP, and research assistants in the field of information systems (n=219)	Novelty, relevance, feasibility, elaboration	- Idea selection based on user ratings lead to similar results as ratings of a jury of experts
Onarheim and Christensen, 2012	Medical equipment	Experts: senior marketers within the firm (n=7) Quasi-experts: employees from various functions within the firm with > 4 years experience in the product domain (n=35)	Intent to further pursue the idea*	- Employees' ratings cannot replace expert ratings - Employees' votes significantly correlate with the preferences of the experts - Correlation between employees and experts increases when only include the most experienced employees

* The executive team selected the 12 best ideas in the course of a full-day workshop in which all 99 ideas were assessed.

3.2.3.3   Research comparing experts and non-experts evaluations

Similar to the motivation to leverage non-experts to evaluate new product ideas, creativity research studies comparing expert and non-experts evaluations have been motivated by experts being a scarce resource, costly, and difficult to bring together. The sourcing of panels of experts can therefore be a challenge, especially when researchers need to evaluate the creativity of a vast number of creative outcomes (Kaufman et al., 2008).

Based on the argument that it is "not clear how essential it is to use expert raters when using the CAT, nor exactly what kind of expertise is essential to be an expert rater in a given domain and for a particular research purpose" (Kaufman et al., 2008: 172), research scholars conducted various studies to determine the appropriateness of using non-expert judges to evaluate creative outcomes. The theoretical justification of these studies is based on the CAT methodology and its reliance on expert judgments. Kaufman, Baer, and Cole (2009) have argued that, if non-experts' ratings can be shown to be virtually indistinguishable from experts' ratings, "then there is no reason not to allow nonexperts to stand in for experts in making creativity ratings for that particular kind of artifact" (Kaufman, Baer, and Cole, 2009: 227). Consequently, non-experts are deemed appropriate substitutes for experts if their evaluations provide (i) sufficient interrater reliability according to the CAT's assumptions and (ii) are highly correlated with expert ratings (Kaufman, Baer, and Cole, 2009).

In the past, several studies were conducted in the psychology and creativity research fields to investigate this topic. The core findings of these studies can be summarized as follows (for references see Table 5 and Table 6):

- Non-expert raters are, generally, not appropriate substitutes for expert raters, because non-expert judgments tend to be inconsistent and do not match those of experts;
- Quasi-experts might appropriately replace expert judges in some domains, as they have been shown to achieve consistent ratings very similar to those of experts;
- Some domains might require more expertise than others;
- Evaluators become more critical (i.e., give lower ratings) as their level of domain knowledge increases.

For the further interpretation of these results in the context of this thesis, two points should be considered. First, it is important to acknowledge that the majority of these findings are based on a comparison of intuitive-based, holistic judgments of creativity. As such, the studies' findings that domain knowledge seems to be a significant driver of evaluation outcomes appear to be in line with prior research in the field of expert intuition (see section 3.2.2.3). Thus, different, unconsciously internalized standards of what to consider creative, or how to internally weight different dimensions of creativity, might explain the differences between individuals with less and more domain knowledge. For example, Hekkert and Wieringen (1996) have shown that experts seem to attach more value to originality when evaluating creativity than non-experts. However, in a more recent study, Kaufman et al. (2013) investigated both holistic evaluations and criteria-based evaluations of mouse-trap designs. The results indicate that the influence of domain knowledge might depend on the dimensions against which an idea is being assessed. For example, while non-expert evaluators have been shown to be appropriate evaluators of the mouse-trap design's relevance, they fail to match experts' evaluation in terms of the overall creativity, elegance, and genesis.

Second, these studies have been conducted in various domains, including the evaluation of short stories, poems, drawings, etc. The studies reached different conclusions, perhaps arising from some domains or evaluation objects requiring more knowledge than others to evaluate creative outcomes within the domain. This might be related to the possibility that individuals possess moderate domain knowledge in some fields based on everyday experience. On considering these two points, it should be acknowledged that the appropriateness of non-expert evaluators might strongly depend on the purpose of the assessment (Runco, McCarthy, and Svenson, 1994).

To summarize, prior psychology and creativity research studies conducted in recent years support the conclusion that the evaluator's domain knowledge significantly influences idea evaluation outcomes. Furthermore, the importance of domain knowledge seems to differ depending on the domain, the object of evaluation, and the criteria being assessed. Nonetheless, there is reason to believe that evaluators do not always have to possess expert-domain knowledge, at least not when evaluating creativity in some domains (e.g. short stories) or some dimensions (e.g. relevance). However, the assignability of these results to a new product idea evaluation context might be questionable. Most of these studies were (i) carried out in the field of artwork (short stories, poems, drawings, or collages) and (ii) their designs differed in the way in which non-experts, quasi-experts, and experts were defined, making it difficult to identify the type of knowledge that is actually relevant for idea evaluation.

Contrary to the findings of the aforementioned psychology and creativity research studies, management research scholars have been far more optimistic about leveraging non-experts (usually represented by user and consumer panels) to evaluate and select early-stage new product and service ideas. The following quotes from selected studies highlight this optimism:

- "companies can employ users during the initial screening process using criteria assessment to select the best ideas for further elaboration" (Magnusson, Wästlund, and Netz, 2016: 1);
- "online consumer panels are a better way to determine a 'good' idea than are ratings by experts" (Kornish and Ulrich, 2014: 14);
- "open evaluation might be used to substitute expert juries in the assessment of originality and feasibility" (Haller, 2013: 168);
- "around 20 user ratings per idea are sufficient for creating stable idea rankings" (Riedl et al., 2013: 7);
- "employee voting significantly correlates with the preferences of the executives: overall, in the top 12 selected ideas and in the choice of idea categories" (Onarheim and Christensen, 2012: 661);
- "individuals in creator roles [i.e., the idea generators] are more likely to give promising novel ideas the support they deserve than individuals in manager roles [i.e., traditional gate committee members]"[25] (Berg, 2016: 27).

It should be acknowledged that although these research studies come to somewhat similar conclusions, the designs of these studies were vastly different in respect of all the major parameters that might possibly influence the evaluation outcomes, for example, the evaluator's degree of domain knowledge, idea domains, and evaluation criteria (see Table 5 and Table 6). For example, Kornish and Ulrich (2014) base their conclusion on the finding that a consumer panel's purchase-intent related to early-stage new product ideas

---

[25] Brackets added by the author.

(measured on a 5-point Likert-scale) is a better predictor of future sales volume than estimates by marketing and product development specialists (measured in units sold). Onarheim and Christensen (2012) asked firm employees from different departments to state whether or not ideas presented to them should be further developed and worked on. The employees' top selections were then compared to the top selections of an executive team. However, the executives did not evaluate the ideas with such a simple evaluation scheme. Their selection was developed during the course of a full-day workshop.

The studies by Haller (2013) and Magnusson, Wästlund, and Netz (2016) at best resemble a criteria-based idea evaluation approach as described in this thesis (see section 3.2.2.2). A closer look at the results of these two studies reveals an interesting pattern. First, expert judgments were shown to be more reliable (i.e., higher interrater reliability) than those of non-experts, with both experts and non-experts reaching acceptable levels of reliability (Haller, 2013; Magnusson, Wästlund, and Netz, 2016).

Second, the criteria-based evaluations of experts, quasi-experts, and non-experts were shown to be correlated. Nevertheless, the correlations hardly reached the threshold of what can be considered substantial agreement.[26] For example, in the study that Magnusson, Wästlund, and Netz (2016) conducted, the correlations between the firm-internal experts and quasi-experts (technically skilled users) might only be considered high in respect of the user value criterion,[27] whereas correlations between experts and non-experts (technically naïve users) did not display substantial agreement in all the other dimensions.[28] Similarly to Magnusson, Wästlund, and Netz's (2016) results, the study by Haller (2013) finds that non-experts (students) and experts only reach moderate agreement on originality and feasibility, and only reasonable agreement on the other dimensions.[29]

---

[26] Kaufman, Baer, and Cole (2009) refer to standard criteria for the minimum recommendation of a correlation of about .90 (Anastasi and Urbina, 1998) for comparing individual scores. However, these authors acknowledge that somewhat lower levels are acceptable for group comparisons.

[27] Correlation analysis showed the following results: originality ($r = .544$, $p < .001$), user value ($r = .803$, $p < .001$), and producibility ($r = .378$, $p < .001$).

[28] Correlation analysis showed the following results: originality ($r = .515$, $p < .001$), user value ($r = .559$, $p < .001$), and producibility ($r = .555$, $p < .001$).

[29] Correlation analysis showed the following results: originality ($r = .426$, $p < .001$), feasibility ($r = .508$, $p < .001$), effectiveness ($r = .255$, $p < .001$), elaboration ($r = .398$, $p < .001$), willingness to pay ($r = .238$, $p < .001$) Haller (2013: 166). A threshold of 0.61 reflects substantial agreement according to Landis and Koch (1977).

Third, evaluators seem to become more critical with an increase in domain knowledge, which is reflected in the lower absolute idea ratings in all the dimensions (Magnusson, Wästlund, and Netz, 2016).

These results indicate that experts, quasi-experts and non-experts evaluate the dimensions of an early-stage idea's quality in very different ways. This has also been acknowledged by Magnusson, Wästlund, and Netz (2016: 12): "none of the two user panels' [...] idea assessments [...] could be considered conformant with the professional expert panel in absolute scores [...]. In comparison with the experts, both user groups overestimated the ideas."

3.2.3.4   Interim summary

Research from various fields has explored the possibility of substituting experts in evaluation tasks. The motivation for this research is largely based on experts being expensive, difficult to source, and perhaps being overwhelmed when faced with the task of evaluating hundreds, or even thousands, of ideas. Unfortunately, these various studies yield somewhat inconclusive results regarding whether or not individuals with high domain knowledge, are the only appropriate evaluators for an idea's quality.

Overall, creativity management studies seem to suggest a need for caution when using non-expert evaluators for the evaluation of an idea's creativity, because judgments have been found to be inconsistent and do not match those of expert-evaluators. However, these research studies have also shown that quasi-experts might be leveraged as suitable substitutes for experts, in some domains.

Management studies, on the other hand, generally conclude that non-experts or quasi-experts are a valuable source to be leveraged in the evaluation of early-stage new product ideas. However, these conclusions are not based on the finding that non-expert evaluations match those of experts in absolute terms, but rather on the rankings of ideas based on non-experts' evaluations being somewhat similar to those of experts' rankings.

Furthermore, when comparing these studies, it should be acknowledged that synthesizing the findings becomes very difficult due to the extremely diverse study settings. Creativity management studies have largely investigated the evaluation of artwork (not ideas) based on holistic judgments, whereas management studies have applied an even more diverse range of evaluation settings, including estimations of the sales volumes, criteria-based evaluations, and purchase-intent statements. In addition, different research scholars have very differently interpreted the correlation threshold to determine whether experts' and non-experts' evaluations can be considered similar, which might have contributed to the different conclusions.[30]

3.3 Literature synthesis

Proficient evaluations of early-stage new product ideas are of critical importance for NPD success. Accurate idea evaluations can help decision makers identify and select exceptional new product ideas, and identify radical new product ideas to be funneled into the firm's development pipeline in order to develop a balanced innovation portfolio (see section 3.2.1).

In the search for a method to accurately evaluate early-stage new product ideas, innovation management literature has taken the view that the quality of new product ideas is largely reflected in their creativity. Consequently, innovation management literature has mostly accepted the consensual assessment technique (CAT) as a valid approach to evaluate new product ideas. According to the CAT, subjective assessments can be considered a valid indicator of an idea's quality, as long as appropriate judges' evaluations independently agree with respect to the idea's degree of creativity (see section 3.2.2.1).

Therefore, in order to determine the quality of new product ideas, a reliable set of criteria needs to be defined that best reflects the quality of each individual idea. Building on criteria used in creativity research to determine an idea's creativity, innovation management research scholars have developed three predominant criteria to evaluate early-stage new product ideas. These criteria are: originality, user value, and feasibility (see section 3.2.2.2). An established alternative to the criteria-based evaluation approach is the holistic evaluation of new product ideas. A key difference with the aforementioned approach is that evaluators are not provided with any specific guidance or criteria to reach their decisions, but instead have to rely on their intuitions (see section 3.2.2.3).

---

[30] For example, whereas Kaufman, Baer, and Cole (2009) argue that correlations of .70 can be considered, whereas Magnusson, Wästlund, and Netz (2016) consider correlations of .40 to .60 sufficient.

Literature and practice have traditionally made the assumption that an appropriate judge of new product ideas needs to be an expert in the field, i.e., needs high-level domain knowledge in the relevant field (see section 3.2.3.1). However, with firms being confronted with the challenge of evaluating hundreds, or even thousands, of new product ideas in the front-end of innovation, outsourcing the idea evaluation process to alleviate pressure on internal experts has sparked the interest of innovation management scholars and practice alike. Consequently, research has started exploring whether or not non-experts, constituting employees outside the realm of new product development, users, or even laymen, might have the ability to mimic experts' new product idea evaluations (see section 3.2.3.2). Creativity research and management research scholars have conducted several studies in this context. However, these studies yield somewhat inconclusive results on the abilities of non-experts to replace experts in new product idea evaluation (see sections 3.2.3.3 and 3.2.3.4). The research opportunity that arises from these inconclusive results is depicted in the following section.

3.4 Research gap and research questions

Given new product failure rates of up to 90 per cent in some industries, current idea evaluation outcomes still seem to lack predictive power, despite the extensive research efforts to develop more effective and efficient evaluation methodologies (Andrew and Sirkin, 2003). In this context, it has been argued that a formal system of idea evaluation with its tools, procedures, and criteria is not a value in itself (Martinsuo and Poskela, 2011). Interestingly, research scholars already hinted at this problem 40 years ago (Crawford, 1977: 54):

> "Why [...] do we have such a high rate of new product failures? Is it possible, as some of the research studies suggest, that the problem is one of people, not technology?"

Irrespectively of the evaluation methodology applied, idea evaluation outcomes are largely dependent on the choice of appropriate evaluators (Amabile, 1996; Ozer, 2005). Despite the importance of the human factor in idea evaluation, only limited attention has been paid to the characteristics deemed appropriate in individuals judging new product ideas (Magnusson, Wästlund, and Netz, 2016).

The most obvious and important characteristic that defines appropriate evaluators in the context of new product idea evaluations might be their domain knowledge. However, prior research studies comparing expert and non-expert evaluations were unable to deliver conclusive results with regard to the level of domain-relevant knowledge needed to ensure proficient idea evaluations. Nonetheless, these studies seem to indicate a shared finding that opens up an interesting avenue for research.

The individual's level of domain knowledge seems to influence idea evaluation outcomes and this influence might be more, or less, severe, depending on (i) the evaluation approach and/or dimension to be evaluated, and (ii) the object of evaluation. Consequently, I decided to dedicate this dissertation to extend the literature on this topic by investigating the following research question:

> *RQ1: What is the role of individuals' domain knowledge for the proficient evaluation of early-stage new product ideas in the front-end of innovation?*

To explore this research question to its fullest extent, I will present additional sub-research questions. The literature suggests that the influence of domain knowledge might differ between a rational decision making task – i.e., criteria-based evaluation – and an intuition-based decision making task – i.e., holistic judgments. Consequently, I raise the following sub-research questions:

> *RQ1a: How does domain knowledge influence criteria-based evaluation outcomes by affecting the assessment of the three dimensions that constitute a new product idea's quality (originality, user value, and feasibility)?*

> *RQ1b: How does domain knowledge influence holistic evaluations of new product ideas?*

Furthermore, prior research indicates that a new product idea's degree of innovativeness might moderate the influence of domain knowledge on evaluation outcomes (Moreau, Lehmann, and Markman, 2001; Gregan-Paxton et al., 2002; Peracchio and Tybout, 1996). Prior research studies comparing new product idea evaluations by experts and non-experts neglected the possible moderation effect. Acknowledging that the effective evaluation of radical ideas is of the utmost importance for NPD success, I aim to explore whether or not the influence of domain knowledge is of equal importance in the evaluation of incremental and radical new product ideas.

> *RQ1c: Does the idea's degree of innovativeness moderate the influence of domain knowledge on new product idea evaluation outcomes?*

Developing a deeper understanding of the role of individuals' domain knowledge might be important in many aspects. First, understanding the role of domain knowledge in more detail might help firms decide whether domain knowledge should play a more important role in the staffing of individual evaluators in front-end evaluation teams, or gate committees, in order to achieve more proficient evaluations. Second, the findings of this study might focus more attention on the domain knowledge of users and/or laymen in the context of open evaluations than is currently the case (Velamuri et al., 2015). Third, investigating the influence of domain knowledge on criteria-based evaluations, as well as on holistic judgments, might indicate which evaluation approach might require more or less domain knowledge. Thus, answering the first research questions might also contribute to answering the more overarching research question:

> *RQ2: Should firms give more, or less, consideration to domain knowledge as an important factor in selecting appropriate judges – both internal and external to the firm – for the evaluation of early-stage new product ideas?*

To summarize, this thesis will focus on increasing idea evaluation proficiency by contributing to the important question of who is best suited to the early-stage evaluation of new product ideas, in order to lay the foundation of subsequent decisions on idea selection in the FEI. The thesis thus explores domain knowledge as a core characteristic that might distinguish appropriate judges from inappropriate ones in the context of early-stage idea evaluations. Therefore, this thesis addresses an area of research that has received remarkably little attention before – exploring the characteristics deemed appropriate in individuals' judging new product ideas (Magnusson, Wästlund, and Netz, 2016). By answering the outlined research questions, this thesis aims to contribute to theory and practice in a number of ways, and might help increase our understanding with regard to a number of recently proposed research priorities for innovation management (Barczak, 2014: 641):

- "How do you effectively screen radical innovation ideas?
- How do you screen multitudes of ideas that come from crowdsourcing?
- Should the gatekeepers vary depending on whether the innovation is incremental or radical?"

3.5 The role of domain knowledge in evaluating new product ideas

Experts and non-experts interpret information, form judgments, and reach decisions differently. The literature on these differences has therefore developed into a dedicated field of research (Chi and Glaser, 1988; Ericsson et al., 2006; Klein, 2008). However, recognizing that the role of individuals' domain knowledge in the proficient evaluation of early-stage new product ideas is not yet fully understood, I decided to dedicate this research to developing a deeper understanding of the influence that domain knowledge might exert on individuals' perceptions and judgments of early-stage new product ideas (see previous section).

In this section, I will present the theoretical basis of the role of domain knowledge in evaluating early-stage new product ideas. First, I will narrow down the definition of domain knowledge by introducing the two most relevant types of knowledge in the context of innovation – need knowledge and solution knowledge (see section 3.5.1). Second, domain knowledge will be related to the formation of cognitive schemas (see section 3.5.2) and, third, theories from prior research in the adjacent field of consumer behavior research will be introduced to link these cognitive schemas to the evaluation of early-stage new product ideas (see section 3.5.3). On the basis of these theories, I developed the central research framework for this dissertation (see section 3.6).

3.5.1 Need knowledge and solution knowledge as constituents of domain knowledge

According to von Hippel (1994, 1998), there are two types of knowledge that can be considered important antecedents of successful innovation – need knowledge and solution knowledge. Need knowledge is the knowledge of the preferences, needs, wants, desires, satisfaction, motives, etc. of the customers and users in a specific domain (Piller, Ihl, and

Vossen, 2011). This knowledge thus provides insight into how a new product creates value for a user (Lüthje, 2004). In other words, need knowledge informs the accurate perception of a customer's hierarchy of needs (Homburg, Wieseke, and Bornemann, 2009). Furthermore, need knowledge has also been recognized as providing knowledge about the "needs [innovators] will face in current or future markets" (Alexy, George, and Salter, 2013: 270), thus allowing for the anticipation of needs that might arise in future. In an idea evaluation context, need knowledge is thus required to understand the benefits that an idea for current or future customers creates, and to analyze whether or not customers would be willing to pay for having these needs satisfied.

Solution knowledge is the knowledge of how to best apply domain-specific technologies to transform customer needs into new products (Piller, Ihl, and Vossen, 2011). In an idea evaluation context, solution knowledge provides a general and abstract understanding of possible applications of the given technology in the domain, independently of what is already known about specific products in which these technologies might have been used before (Danneels, 2007). Solution knowledge is thus needed to understand how an idea might be implemented, and can be considered as the ability to analyze technical feasibility in the light of the given domain technologies' chances and boundaries (Magnusson, 2009).

At the core of new product idea evaluation, the evaluator has to assess the technology that is presented as the solution to a specific need. Simultaneously, the evaluator also has to assess the market potential that the new product fulfilling this need, creates. It can therefore be assumed that domain knowledge, as a combination of need knowledge and solution knowledge, has major relevance for the evaluation of new product ideas. This is achieved by (i) providing a frame of reference – including facts, principles, and opinions, as well as knowledge of performance scripts and paradigms in the domain (Amabile, 1983) – and by (ii) reducing uncertainty with regard to the benefits and shortcomings of the idea (Alba and Hutchinson, 1987; Gregan-Paxton and Roedder John, 1997). The reasoning behind this assumption is presented in the following sections.

3.5.2   The structure of domain knowledge in schemas

Understanding the role of an individual's domain knowledge in the evaluation of new product ideas requires insight into how domain knowledge manifests itself in an individual, and how individuals with low domain knowledge, as opposed to high domain knowledge, differ in this respect.

The literature largely reflects agreement that domain knowledge manifests itself in an individual in the form of organized knowledge structures "about a concept or type of stimulus, including its attributes and the relations among those attributes" (Fiske and Taylor, 1991: 98). These organized knowledge structures are also referred to as schemas. Such schemas have been found to differ markedly among individuals, depending on the level of domain-specific knowledge acquired over time through experience, practice, implicit learning, and experiential learning (Dane, 2010). Individuals with high domain knowledge tend to have schemas that are more complex (Rousseau, 2001; Dane and Pratt, 2007). This means that (i) their domain schemas are relatively larger in terms of the overall quantity of attributes and components contained in a schema, and (ii) that their domain schemas involve more interrelationships than those of individuals with low domain knowledge (see Figure 12).[31]

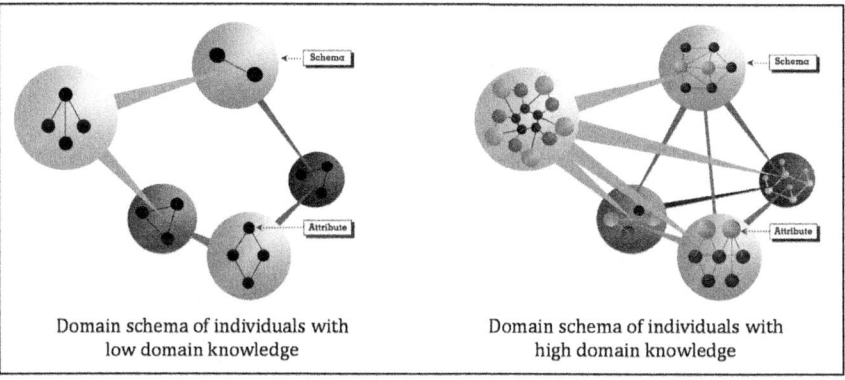

Domain schema of individuals with
low domain knowledge

Domain schema of individuals with
high domain knowledge

Figure 12: Comparison of schemas between individuals with low domain knowledge and those with high domain knowledge[32]

---

[31] In this context, "the term *attribute* refers to an independent property or component of an object [...]. The term *relation* refers to an interconnected system of properties and components. The distinguishing feature of a relation is the link (or links) that defines the relationship between attributes" Gregan-Paxton and Roedder John (1997: 268).

[32] Source: Dane (2010: 581 & 582), slightly adapted by replacing the term "novice" with individuals with low domain knowledge and the term "expert" with individuals with high domain knowledge.

Research has found that possessing a large number of complex domain schemas can provide individuals with a number of benefits, including more effective decision-making, superior recall and memory skills, and exceptional problem-solving capabilities (Ericsson and Lehmann, 1996; Klein, 1998; Chi and Glaser, 1988). However, possessing a large number of complex domain schemas might also lead to inflexible problem-solving due to functional fixedness (Duncker, 1945), problems with adjusting to novel tasks, and difficulties with radical idea generation (Dane, 2010).

Despite the numerous benefits and shortcomings that might result from possessing a large number of specific schemas, little is known about how the complexity of schemas might influence the evaluation of early-stage new product ideas. However, adjacent fields of research might be leveraged in this context. Consumer behavior research scholars have established theories and have empirically tested how domain knowledge – structured in schemas – influences the evaluation of tangible new products. Consequently, these theories and findings can be considered a solid theoretical basis for also explaining how domain knowledge might influence the evaluation of early-stage new product ideas. Selected theories that form the foundation of this thesis's research framework are therefore described in more detail in the following sections.

3.5.3 Domain knowledge and new product idea evaluations

Cognitive psychology research has shown that novices differ from experts in the content, extent, and organization of their domain knowledge (Chi, Glaser, and Rees, 1982). These differences have been found to influence fundamental information-processing activities, such as problem solving (Chi, Glaser, and Rees, 1982), the recall and recognition of presented information (Fiske, Kinder, and Larter, 1983), judgment (e.g. Bettman and Sujan, 1987), and decision-making (Klein, 1998; Lipshitz et al., 2001; Salas, Rosen, and DiazGranados, 2010). In line with these findings, a number of consumer behavior research studies have shown that domain knowledge can influence new product evaluations by affecting the comprehension, attribute interpretations, inferences, and, thus, the overall evaluations of new products (Gregan-Paxton et al., 2002; Gregan-Paxton and Roedder John, 1997; Meyers-Levy and Tybout, 1989; Moreau, Lehmann, and Markman, 2001; Peracchio and Tybout, 1996; Meyers-Levy, Louie, and Curren, 1994; Bettman and Sujan, 1987).

However, to my knowledge, these research findings have not yet been considered in the context of early-stage new product idea evaluation in the front-end of innovation.

Acknowledging the research findings from these adjacent research fields, I propose that – similarly to the evaluation of new products – the evaluation of early-stage new product ideas can be considered a problem-solving task under uncertainty. This involves the recognition and interpretation of limited, and sometimes ambiguous, information to reach a judgment, which can subsequently form the basis of decision-making. The difference between an early-stage new product idea and a new product is that ideas are often intangible, incomplete, ill-defined, unspecific, and vague, whereas finished products provide more specific information and are tangible (Hatchuel and Weil, 2009). In this thesis, I therefore assume that even more uncertainty and ambiguity surround the evaluation of new product ideas, which might in turn even amplify the influence of domain knowledge on the evaluation outcome.

Consequently, I propose that theories applied in the field of consumer behavior are a promising theoretical foundation to explain the influence of domain knowledge on the perception and evaluation of early-stage new product ideas. The following sections explain the three theories that provide the theoretical basis of the dissertation's framework: (i) schema-based evaluation, (ii) inference making, and (iii) the knowledge transfer paradigm.[33]

3.5.3.1 Schema-based evaluation

The availability and structure of relevant schemas have been found to play a central role in guiding product evaluations (Meyers-Levy and Tybout, 1989; Meyers-Levy, Louie, and Curren, 1994). Consumer behavior research studies have shown that new products are evaluated more favorably when the products' attributes are perceived as only moderately incongruent with their associated domain schemas (Meyers-Levy and Tybout, 1989).

This effect has its theoretical basis in Mandler's hypothesis (Mandler, 1982). This hypothesis posits that encountering a stimulus (e.g. a new product) that is congruent (conforms to expectations), does not arouse and simply evokes a mild positive response,

---

[33] Although all the theories are presented separately, their boundaries are sometimes blurred, which means that these theories can sometimes overlap.

because the evaluator is familiar with such a product. On the other hand, encountering a stimulus that is incongruent (disrupts expectations), prompts arousal and cognitive elaboration. When this incongruity is at a moderate level, it can be resolved by utilizing prior knowledge, which, generally, results in greater positive effects than that associated with congruity. However, if the incongruity is strong enough, it is likely to remain unresolved. The absence of a resolution and the remaining uncertainty usually result in feelings of frustration and helplessness, which, in turn, evoke negative responses to a new product. In the light of this theory, domain knowledge has thus been identified as an important factor that moderates how an activated schema affects product evaluations (Peracchio and Tybout, 1996).

Individuals with low domain knowledge possess a knowledge structure that is structured in a rudimentary fashion with few linkages between its elements (Fiske and Taylor, 1991; Alba and Hutchinson, 1987). A limited amount of information, few interconnections, and a lack of strong affective associations with specific attributes characterize this knowledge structure (Peracchio and Tybout, 1996, see section 3.5.2). As a consequence, individuals with low domain knowledge tend to interpret new information literally (Alba and Hutchinson, 1987). Owing to the characteristics of their knowledge structures, these individuals have a higher probability of experiencing schema incongruity when confronted with new products. They thus have to invest considerably more cognitive effort in reconciling incongruities (Peracchio and Tybout, 1996). Following Mandler's hypothesis, it can be assumed that, if the invested cognitive effort proves successful, new products or attributes might be perceived more positively. If the effort is unsuccessful, individuals will experience high uncertainty in their evaluations and negative effects are likely to occur (Meyers-Levy and Tybout, 1989).

Conversely, individuals with high domain knowledge have knowledge structures (schemas) that are "extensive, affords complex inferential processing, and includes extreme affect toward product features" (Peracchio and Tybout, 1996: 178). These knowledge structures can further be characterized by the many links occurring among elements, and by the formation of abstract representations (Alba and Hutchinson, 1987; Fiske and Taylor, 1991). Consequently, these individuals have a generally reduced perception of incongruity and relate new information more strongly to their domain knowledge. Thus, in their evaluations, individuals with high domain knowledge are more likely to rely on strong inferences regarding the products' features (Alba and Hutchinson, 1987). Therefore, schema congruity is less likely to influence these individuals' evaluations than evaluative inferences that their schemas activate (Peracchio and Tybout, 1996).

In an idea evaluation context, it is thus more likely that evaluations of individuals with low domain knowledge are likely to reflect congruity-based-effects, whereas evaluations of individuals with high domain knowledge are likely to reflect inference-based effects. The influence of inference-based effects is discussed in more detail in the following section.

3.5.3.2 Inference making theory

Research has shown that the inferences individuals make about a new product can have a significant impact on attitude, judgment, and choice (Alba and Hutchinson, 1987). In the context of new product evaluations, individuals draw inferences about product attributes, product benefits, as well as regarding the new product idea's appropriateness for various users and situations. This might include inferences about the product's ability to help individuals achieve their goals and values, as well as how a product works, how it is used, and its relationship with other products (Graeff and Olson, 1994).

According to Alba and Hutchinson (1987), inferences in a product evaluation context can be divided into four types: (i) evaluation-based, (ii) correlation-based, (iii) similarity-based, and (iv) schema-based. In making evaluation-based inferences, individuals retrieve a previously formed summary judgment (e.g. an overall evaluation) from memory that then serves as the basis of a specific judgment (e.g. an attribute rating). Individuals do not make any efforts to separate their judgments into constituent causes. Correlation-based inferences may occur if two attributes are perceived as being highly correlated, so that the value of one is believed to lead to the value of another, and sufficient information is only perceived to be available for one attribute, but not the other (Roedder John, Scott, and Bettman, 1986). A well-known and researched example is that many consumers infer that a very expensive product is also of high quality. In the case of similarity-based judgments, individuals form inferences about an unfamiliar product based on its similarity to a familiar product. In essence, this process is a form of reasoning by means of knowledge transfer (Gregan-Paxton and Roedder John, 1997, see section 3.5.3.3). These three kinds of inferences are defined by heuristic connections between known and inferred facts, and are also called nonanalytic inferences (Alba and Hutchinson, 1987).

Domain knowledge has been argued to play an important role in inference making, as individuals with low domain knowledge are more likely than individuals with high domain knowledge to base their judgments on nonanalytic inferences: "all things being equal, experts will be more judicious in their use of such heuristics (cf. Downing, Sternberg, and Ross 1985). Specifically, experts [...] should distinguish between relevant and irrelevant features when judging product similarity; they should question the validity of analogical reasoning [...] and they should be less prone to overinterpret noncausal covariation." (Alba and Hutchinson, 1987: 421). Furthermore, it has been argued that while domain knowledge may moderate nonanalytic inferences, schema-based inferences cannot be made unless individuals possess requisite levels of domain knowledge represented by complex schemas (Alba and Hutchinson, 1987). These schema-based inferences play a central role, because as they simplify the evaluation by allowing individuals to link the new product to prior knowledge about a list of attributes that is common to a given group or category of products (Wyer and Srull, 1994).

Acknowledging the role of domain knowledge as a prerequisite for schema-based inferences, Alba and Hutchinson (1987: 428) have hypothesized that schema-based inferences should:

- facilitate the comprehension of product-related information;
- generally increase the accuracy with which product-related information is simplified;
- facilitate the generation of simplifications for technical information;
- enable the inference of intended product benefits from technical information, and infer likely technical causes.

More recent consumer research studies have shown that inferences can also directly influence product evaluations. According to Mukherjee and Hoyer (2001), individuals tend to evaluate new products based on the weights assigned to benefit-related value inferences and the learning cost inferences that occur during the evaluation of new products. When individuals perceive a new product to be superior in terms of its benefits in relation to other products, they may form positive value inferences. If a new product is perceived to be difficult to understand and use, individuals may make negative learning cost inferences. Consequently, whether the evaluator relies more on positive inferences regarding potential benefits, or on negative inferences regarding potential risks may influence the evaluation of a new product (Mukherjee and Hoyer, 2001). In this context, research scholars have shown that the formation of such inferences depends on two important factors: (i) the individual's domain knowledge (see above), and (ii) the idea's degree of innovativeness (Mugge and Dahl, 2013; Gregan-Paxton et al., 2002).

To summarize, individuals form different kinds of inferences – positive (e.g. value inferences), as well as negative (e.g. learning-cost) inferences – when evaluating new product ideas. In this context, domain knowledge has been found to play an important moderating role. Moreover, individuals with low domain knowledge rely primarily on nonanalytic inferences, whereas individuals with high domain knowledge are more likely to base their judgments on schema-based inferences.

3.5.3.3   The knowledge transfer paradigm

Decades ago, research established that individuals attempt to understand something new by relating it to something familiar in order to facilitate comprehension (Davidson, 1976). Transferring this finding to the context of product evaluation, consumer behavior research scholars have argued that individuals' learn about a new product by transferring existing knowledge (the base) to a new product (the target). This process is known as "consumer learning by analogy" (Gregan-Paxton and Roedder John, 1997: 269).

The process of analogical learning through knowledge transfer comprises four stages: "*(a)* accessing the base domain, *(b)* mapping the elements of the target onto the base, *(c)* transferring knowledge from the base to the target, and *(d)* inducing a schema" (Gregan-Paxton and Roedder John, 1997: 267). Gregan-Paxton and Roedder John (1997) describe the function of each of the four stages as follows:

- *Access stage*: this stage is concerned with the target's ability to activate the individual's mental representation of a base domain (a schema) as a potential source of information about the target domain.
- *Mapping stage*: the goal of this stage is to compare the content and structure of the base with the target domain. The objective of the comparison is to map the elements of both domains in order to create paths through which knowledge can be transferred from the base to the target.

- *Transfer stage*: in this stage, knowledge is transferred from the base to the target. Having understood the relevance of previously acquired knowledge as a potential source of information (access stage), and having aligned the target and the base (mapping stage), individuals transfer knowledge from the base to the target in the belief that if the base and the target are known to be similar in certain aspects, they are likely to be similar in other aspects as well.

- *Schema induction*: in the course of analogical learning, a new schema may be created that then serves as a basis of future analogical learning.

What an individual can learn from the comparison of the base (i.e., the schema) and the target determines the individual's ability to comprehend a new product, which in turn determines this individual's attitude towards the new product (Moreau, Lehmann, and Markman, 2001). Perceptions of new products are thus largely dependent on the types of mappings constructed in the mapping stage of the analogical learning process. In this stage, the base and the target domains are either aligned according to their attributes (independent property or component of an object), or their relations (interconnected system of properties and components). These relational-based mappings allow individuals to create goal-relevant inferences about a new product's performance and have been found to have greater explanatory power than comparisons based on attributes (Gregan-Paxton and Roedder John, 1997).

Given the influence of individuals' domain knowledge in this process, it has been proposed that the ability to construct relational mappings is a function of the number and complexity of schemas that an individual possesses (Gregan-Paxton and Roedder John, 1997). Following the line of argumentation that the schemas of non-experts may not provide sufficient information to recognize relational similarities between a base and a target, individuals with low domain knowledge might be unable to construct relational mappings and, consequently, have to rely more on attribute-based mappings, such as explicit product attributes (Gregan-Paxton and Roedder John, 1997).

Thus, also applying the concept of knowledge transfer within the context of new product idea evaluation provides a strong informative basis for how individuals' domain knowledge may influence the perception and evaluation of early-stage new product ideas. According to the framework by Gregan-Paxton and Roedder John (1997), individuals with high domain knowledge should be able to transfer a significant amount of useful attribute-based and relation-based knowledge from their domain knowledge base, i.e., schemas, to the new product idea under evaluation. This should empower these individuals to generate useful goal-relevant inferences about the characteristics and potential of the new product idea, and may thus enable individuals to more effectively evaluate new product ideas (Moreau, Lehmann, and Markman, 2001). Furthermore, this "prior knowledge can be used to facilitate current learning even when the target entity defies classification in terms of existing product concepts" (Gregan-Paxton and Roedder John, 1997: 275). In other words, high domain knowledge may influence the evaluation of a new product idea, even if the idea does not exactly fit a schema stored in memory. Individuals with low domain knowledge, on the other hand, are unlikely to recognize relational similarities and may face difficulties with evaluating early-stage new product ideas (Moreau, Lehmann, and Markman, 2001).

3.5.3.4 Interim summary

Knowledge influences how people perceive and interpret information, as well as how they reach judgments and decisions. This may be true for any type of knowledge, but in the context of new product idea evaluation, there is reason to believe that domain knowledge, in the form of need knowledge and solution knowledge, plays an especially influential role.

Based on the presented literature it can be expected that individuals domain knowledge influences the meanings assigned and the inferences drawn from the presented idea description during new product idea evaluations (Graeff and Olson, 1994). Differences in the evaluation outcomes may thus arise between individuals with either low, or high, domain knowledge. These differences are due to individuals with high domain knowledge leveraging their complex schemas to more easily categorize external information into existing schemas. These individuals can also transfer more useful attribute-based and relation-based knowledge to the new product idea being evaluated (the process of internal knowledge transfer is conceptually depicted in Figure 13). Consequently, individuals with high rather than low domain knowledge are presumed to generate different meanings from the new product idea description. These individuals are (i) better able to discern appropriate meaning from the external information provided and (ii) can build goal-relevant inferences about the benefits and shortcomings of the idea. Domain knowledge should therefore play a major role in how individuals perceive new product ideas and in how they evaluate these ideas. This general proposition forms the foundation of this study's research framework, which will be introduced in the following section.

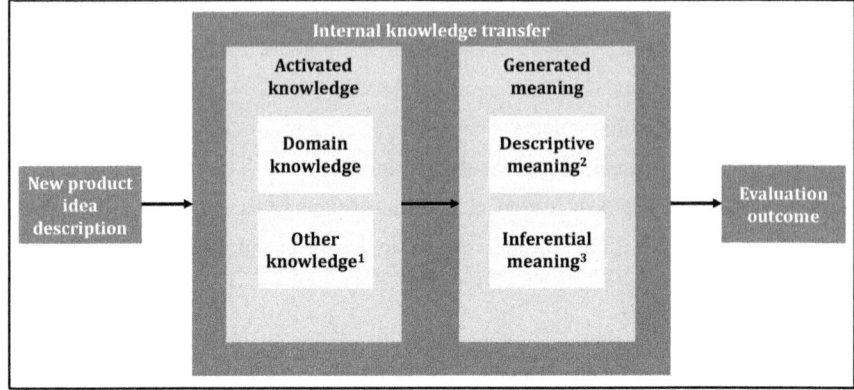

Figure 13: Conceptual model for the influence of domain knowledge on new product idea evaluation outcomes[34,35]

3.6 Research framework and hypotheses development

3.6.1   Research framework

Based on the theories introduced in the previous section, I have constructed a theoretical framework that will guide the further investigation of the proposed research questions. In my theoretical framework, I propose that the individual evaluator's domain knowledge has an impact on a new product idea's perceived originality, user value, feasibility, and the overall impression it creates (H1-4). I further propose that the degree of innovativeness of the product idea under evaluation moderates domain knowledge's influence (H5-8). Finally, I propose that an evaluator's comprehension mediates the influence of domain knowledge on idea evaluation outcomes and that the degree of innovativeness of the

---

[34] Author's illustration, based on Graeff and Olson (1994: 203).
[35] Explanation of footnotes: (1) other knowledge might include relevant knowledge from adjacent or distant domains or functional knowledge obtained from professional experience in M&S or R&D. The influence of other types of knowledge are intentionally excluded from the scope of this dissertation; (2) the ability to discern an appropriate meaning of the idea description (external knowledge transfer); (3) ability to form goal-relevant inferences based on relational mappings (internal knowledge transfer).

product idea under evaluation moderates this indirect domain knowledge effect (H9-14). When investigating the influence of domain knowledge on idea evaluation outcomes in the next section, it is important to understand that evaluators' perceptions rather than their grasp of an objective reality explain the outcomes of their evaluations. Dimensions, such as originality, user vale, feasibility, and overall impression, are – in the light of evaluators' past experiences and impressions – always assessed on the basis of subjective perceptions (Christiaans, 2002). The reasoning behind this framework is set out below.

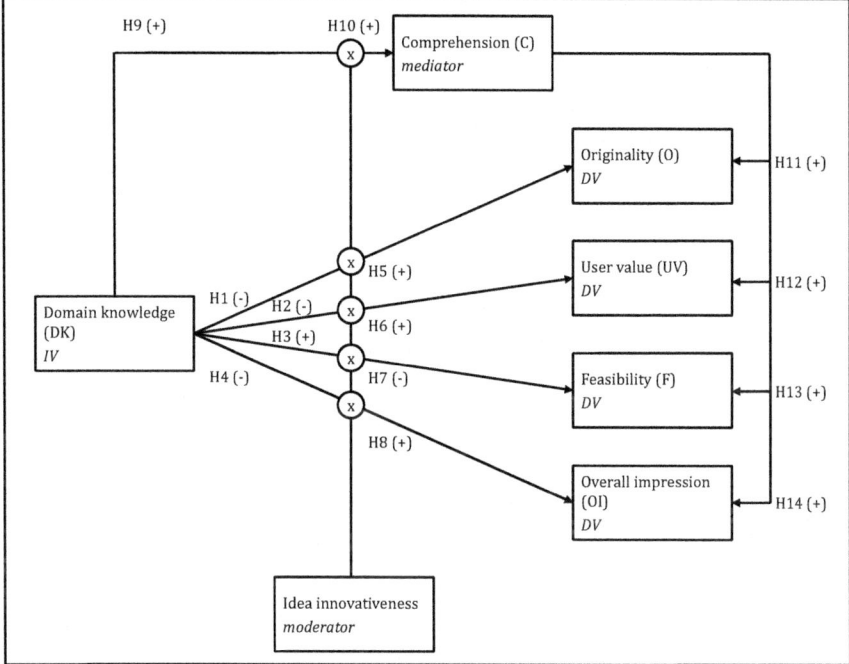

Figure 14: Research framework[36]

---

[36] Author's illustration. Control variables not included in the illustration.

3.6.2   The direct effects of domain knowledge

Section 3.5.3 explained the theoretical concept that domain knowledge can influence new product evaluations by affecting comprehension, attribute interpretations, inferences, and, thus, the overall evaluations of new products (Gregan-Paxton et al., 2002; Gregan-Paxton and Roedder John, 1997; Meyers-Levy and Tybout, 1989; Peracchio and Tybout, 1996). This is premised on the idea that individuals with higher domain knowledge develop schemas that are fundamentally different from the schemas of individuals with lower domain knowledge (Bédard and Chi, 1992). The schemas of individuals with higher domain knowledge are therefore more complex, and relatively more detailed and accurate (Dane, 2010). These complex schemas provide a useful structure for the evaluation of information that an individual can leverage as input to reach a decision (Wyer and Srull, 1994).

Based on this literature, I surmise that evaluators do not only base their evaluations of a new product idea on the examination of its attributes as presented in its description (external knowledge transfer). Evaluators also resort to schemas stored in their memories in order to interpret the information provided, and to deduce inferences about the new product idea's benefits and shortcomings (internal knowledge transfer).

In this context, individuals with high domain knowledge, who have developed more complex schemas in the particular domain, can be expected to function better than individuals with low domain knowledge who possess no schema, or only an inadequate one, to interpret new information (Driscoll, 1994). That is, individuals with higher domain knowledge readily form goal-relevant inferences (Gregan-Paxton and Roedder John, 1997) of the functioning of a potential future product, its application, and whether or not it has relationships with other products on the market (Graeff and Olson, 1994), even though only limited external information might have been provided. By transferring internal knowledge, individuals with higher domain knowledge can, accordingly, establish a frame of reference and overcome uncertainties related to the new product idea's conceptual attributes and the benefits these attributes offer (Hoeffler, 2003). In contrast, individuals with lower domain knowledge are less able to apply internal knowledge, and rely more exclusively on the external information that the idea description provides (Gregan-Paxton and Roedder John, 1997).

The ability to apply internal knowledge is especially influential during the initial evaluation of new product ideas, because early-stage ideas are often intangible, incomplete, ill-defined, unspecific, and vague (Hatchuel and Weil, 2009). Consequently, evaluators need to base their assessments even more stringently on existing knowledge to discern appropriate meaning and reach informed decisions. I thus propose that it is logical to expect evaluators' domain knowledge to have a substantial influence on their perceptions of a new product idea's perceived originality, user value, and feasibility, as well as its overall impression. In this context, perceived comprehension plays a vital role in the relationship between domain knowledge and idea perceptions by indicating how well the individual could leverage existing knowledge.

In terms of assessing a new product idea's originality and user value, individuals with higher domain knowledge have broader frames of reference, including insight into numerous comparable products, as well as current and envisaged trends that determine the customer needs in the domain's current and future markets (Alexy, George, and Salter, 2013; von Hippel, 1988). Individuals with higher domain knowledge can leverage their understanding of consumers' needs and wants to estimate whether or not there might be a potential market for the innovation. They should also readily recognize whether or not a new product idea might manifest as "one more me-too, ho-hum, tired and vanilla product, much the same as competitors" (Cooper, 2011: 27) without originality and/or without creating significant additional benefits for future customers. As such, evaluators with higher domain knowledge are likely to have higher judgment standards (Kaufman et al., 2008), leading to overall lower assessments of the originality and user value of a new product idea. I, thus, propose:

H1: Domain knowledge has a negative effect on the perceived originality of early-stage new product ideas.

H2: Domain knowledge has a negative effect on the perceived user value of early-stage new product ideas.

Contrary to assessing an idea's originality and user value, which reflect the potential benefits of a new product idea from a market perspective, an idea's feasibility could primarily be considered as reflecting a risk assessment from a technological perspective. Consequently, it is possible that domain knowledge could exert a different effect on originality and user value. In a feasibility assessment, broader frames of reference allow individuals with higher domain knowledge to build on their abstract and general understanding of the technologies in the domain when assessing whether or not existing technologies from other products might be leveraged to develop the idea (Danneels, 2007). They can augment their knowledge of the design and manufacture of a new product based on the many different established technologies in the domain, many of which are unknown to individuals who do not possess similar domain knowledge (Kudrowitz and Wallace, 2013). It is therefore possible that individuals with higher domain knowledge will experience less uncertainty with regard to the evaluation of ideas' feasibility and, consequently perceive less risk. Therefore, I expect higher domain knowledge to generally lead to a more positive attitude towards a new product idea's feasibility:

H3: Domain knowledge has a positive effect on the perceived feasibility of early-stage new product ideas.

Regarding the influence of domain knowledge on an overall impression, it is important to recall that such judgment can be considered a holistic evaluation task (see chapter 3.2.2.3). That is, the evaluator is not provided with any specific guidance or criteria to reach a judgment. Therefore, the evaluator has to decide which criteria to take into account in the evaluation, and will thus be the person determining which aspects define the success of a new product idea. Furthermore, the evaluator has to choose the relative weights to be assigned to each of these aspects in order to reach a decision (Magnusson, Netz, and Wästlund, 2014). Such holistic judgment is a highly complex decision-making task based on limited, and sometimes ambiguous, information, thus involving a high degree of uncertainty. Research has established that individuals prefer to use their intuition for these kind of decisions (Agor W.H., 1984).

Such intuitive rather than rational decisions rely more strongly on domain knowledge (Salas, Rosen, and DiazGranados, 2010). Consequently, it can be assumed that individuals have to rely even more on internal knowledge transfer in a holistic judgment task than in a criteria-based evaluation task. Following the line of argumentation that applied to the influence of domain knowledge on perceived originality and perceived user value, domain knowledge can be considered as having a negative influence on an overall impression if the evaluator mainly takes these two criteria into account. On the other hand, based on the influence that domain knowledge exerts on the perception of feasibility, one can expect domain knowledge to have a positive influence on an overall impression if the evaluator considers the idea's feasibility to be the decisive criterion. However, in this context, a study by Magnusson, Netz, and Wästlund (2014) supports the conclusion that perceived user value may be the most decisive criterion in a holistic judgment task. Thus, I propose:

H4: Domain knowledge has a negative effect on the overall impression of early-stage new product ideas.

3.6.3   The interaction effects between domain knowledge and idea innovativeness

Prior research studies allow the conclusion that individuals' domain knowledge might influence their perceptions of a new product idea and that the idea's degree of innovativeness moderates this influence (Alba and Hutchinson, 1987; Gregan-Paxton et al., 2002; Peracchio and Tybout, 1996).

Highly innovative (i.e., radical) ideas are based on new technology components and principles that surpass the existing limitations within the domain, and which aim to fulfill consumers' currently still unmet needs, or even create new needs (Schultz, Salomo, and Talke, 2013; Garcia and Calantone, 2002). Thus, new product ideas with higher innovativeness are likely to have attributes that are very different from those of existing products in the domain (Mugge and Dahl, 2013) and, hence, more difficult to directly match to existing schemas stored in evaluators' memories (Moreau, Markman, and Lehmann, 2001). Accordingly, individuals experience greater difficulty with leveraging existing knowledge as idea innovativeness increases. Individuals with lower domain knowledge may specifically find themselves unable to utilize any prior knowledge and may thus have to rely more exclusively on external information provided in the idea description (Gregan-Paxton and Roedder John, 1997).

Given that such external information is often vague and unspecific in respect of early-stage new product ideas, individuals with lower domain knowledge may perceive the information provided in the idea description of radical ideas as simply reflecting a list of unrelated facts (Alba and Hutchinson, 1987). As such, they may experience a high level of uncertainty regarding the product's benefits and risks when evaluating more innovative ideas (Veryzer, 1998b), which may potentially lead to incorrect evaluations of radical new product ideas in terms of their higher originality, higher user value, and lower feasibility.

Conversely, individuals with higher domain knowledge may be able to overcome the distortion of the internal knowledge transfer by either employing their more complex schemas (Dane, 2010), or by developing new schemas (Gregan-Paxton and Roedder John, 1997). These schemas may help these individuals better understand the link between the radical idea's attributes and form inferences about its benefits and shortcomings "... that 'go beyond' the information given [to] construct more complete and more coherent meanings than is possible by only representing the literal information given" (Graeff and Olson, 1994: 202). This ability can be presumed to ensure that individuals with high domain knowledge are more likely to more accurately assess highly innovative new product ideas due to their superior frame of reference, thereby transcending the uncertainties of evaluating radical new product ideas.

An evaluator with higher domain knowledge is thus better positioned to correctly perceive the higher originality, higher user value, and lower feasibility, and, thus, the higher overall quality of a highly innovative idea in comparison with existing products in the marketplace. This is expected to lead to the opposite evaluation behavior than that proposed in respect of the direct effects of domain knowledge on idea evaluation outcomes. That is, the negative influence of domain knowledge on the perceived originality, user value, and overall impression, as well as the positive influence of domain knowledge on feasibility, is likely to diminish with increasing idea innovativeness. Thus, I propose that:

H5: Idea innovativeness diminishes the negative effect of domain knowledge on the perceived originality of early-stage new product ideas.

H6: Idea innovativeness diminishes the negative effect of domain knowledge on the perceived user value of early-stage new product ideas.

H7: Idea innovativeness diminishes the positive effect of domain knowledge on the perceived feasibility of early-stage new product ideas.

H8: Idea innovativeness diminishes the negative effect of domain knowledge on the over-all impression of early-stage new product ideas.

3.6.4 The mediating effect of comprehension

Comprehension describes the process during which individuals interpret new information based on their prior knowledge. In other words, comprehension reflects the capability of individuals to discern appropriate meaning (Smith and Taffler, 1992).

Based on the research findings presented in section 3.5.3, it can be assumed that individuals with high domain knowledge can more easily leverage their complex domain-specific schemas to form meaningful goal-relevant inferences and relational-mappings in order to complete the missing information that is needed for comprehension. This differential ability to leverage existing knowledge should enable individuals with high domain knowledge to more readily discern appropriate meanings, even when provided with limited information, whereas individuals with low domain knowledge may only perceive this information as being a list of unrelated facts provided in the idea description (Alba and Hutchinson, 1987). Thus, individuals may even encounter difficulties with comprehension in instances when, "objectively," the idea provides sufficient information in its description. However, when evaluators lack domain knowledge, this will prevent them from deducing meaningful information. Based on the argumentation above, I propose:

> H9: Domain knowledge has a positive effect on the perceived comprehension of early-stage new product ideas.

Acknowledging that it is more difficult to match radical new product ideas to existing schemas stored in memory (Moreau, Markman, and Lehmann, 2001), it is likely that by evaluating highly innovative ideas, individuals with lower domain knowledge may become unable to discern any appropriate meaning at all. Individuals with higher domain knowledge, on the other hand, should be able to overcome the distortion of internal knowledge transfer to better understand the link between a radical idea's attributes, and the benefits and risks associated with these attributes (see section 3.6.3). Consequently, domain knowledge may be even more important in the comprehension of radical new product ideas. Thus, I propose:

> H10: Idea innovativeness strengthens the positive effect of domain knowledge on the perceived comprehension of early-stage new product ideas.

The literature has shown that comprehension plays a vital role in how individuals perceive and evaluate new products. Studies have shown that difficulties with comprehending new products lead to lower perceived net benefits (Moreau et al., 2001). That is, if evaluators find it difficult to discern appropriate meaning in relation to the information provided, i.e., they fail to comprehend the new product idea, they face high uncertainty during the evaluation, which is likely to lead to an underestimation of the idea's benefits and an overestimation of its shortcomings (Mukherjee and Hoyer, 2001; Veryzer, 1998b; Mugge and Dahl, 2013; Meyers-Levy and Tybout, 1989). Thus, I propose:

> *H11: Comprehension has a positive effect on the perceived originality of early-stage new product ideas.*
>
> *H12: Comprehension has a positive effect on the perceived user value of early-stage new product ideas.*
>
> *H13: Comprehension has a positive effect on the perceived feasibility of early-stage new product ideas.*
>
> *H14. Comprehension has a positive effect on the overall impression of early-stage new product ideas.*

Acknowledging that domain knowledge has a positive influence on comprehension, on the one hand (H 10), and that comprehension has a positive influence on the perception of new product ideas (H11-14), on the other hand, domain knowledge could indirectly influence idea perceptions through its influence on comprehension. I consequently propose that comprehension acts as a mediator between domain knowledge and perceived originality, user value, feasibility, and overall impression.

> *H15: Comprehension mediates the effects of domain knowledge on the perceived originality of early-stage new product ideas.*
>
> *H16: Comprehension mediates the effects of domain knowledge on the perceived user value of early-stage new product ideas.*
>
> *H17: Comprehension mediates the effects of domain knowledge on the perceived feasibility of early-stage new product ideas.*
>
> *H18. Comprehension mediates the effects of domain knowledge on the overall impression of early-stage new product ideas.*

4 Research design

This chapter starts with a brief introduction to the research setting to justify my reasons for choosing the 3D printing domain (also referred to as additive manufacturing) for the empirical study (section 4.1). I subsequently provide a detailed description of the quantitative online survey used to collect the data (section 4.2). This portrayal covers the layout and sequence of the online survey (section 4.2.1), the selection and manipulation of the new product ideas to be evaluated (section 4.2.2), as well as the operationalization of the theoretical constructs and their transformation into concrete items and measures (section 4.2.3). Subsequently, I describe the data collection and sampling procedure for the online survey (section 4.2.4). The chapter closes with an explanation of the process followed for the data cleansing and the preparation of the data for further analysis (section 4.3).

4.1 Research setting

In order to increase the likelihood of achieving my research objectives, I considered several requirements when selecting an appropriate domain for my data collection. To identify this domain, I compared different domains in terms of the following three criteria:

1. My research setting would include laymen, ordinary users, knowledgeable users, and domain experts in the sample (see section 4.2.4.2). The research field would therefore be one that allows producers, as well as users, to build domain knowledge in terms of need knowledge and solution knowledge. Consequently, I needed to investigate a research field in which not only producers, but also users, innovate. Research has found that a field with intensive and extensive use, moderate technological complexity, and high product involvement favors this kind of environment (Raasch, Herstatt, and Lock, 2008).

2. I would investigate a research field with a high likelihood of successfully identifying users who developed very high degrees of domain-specific need and solution knowledge. Research has established that this condition is favored in markets in which (i) users have to rely on technical equipment to practice their hobbies, (ii) the majority of users need to evolve their skills in line with market trends, and (iii)

leading-edge status is easily noticeable and the users can be expected to report their knowledge base relative to that of others (Schreier and Prügl, 2008).

3. In addition to the other sources recruited for the study, my data collection method comprised inviting 3D printing online community members to participate in a survey, because they are a suitable target group for large-scale data gathering. Therefore, the research field had to be one in which active online communities are are present and easily accessible.

In the light of these criteria, I compared different industries and markets, such as the fields of remote control models, fishing, rowing sport equipment, bicycle equipment, car connectivity technology and services, and 3D printing. However, the 3D printing research field seemed to be best suited to fulfill the outlined prerequisites.

4.2 Quantitative online survey

Research methods in social science can generally be divided into qualitative and quantitative research methods (Walliman, 2006). Qualitative research methods are usually used in research fields with few or no previous studies to provide a theoretical basis for well-grounded hypotheses. These research methods are aimed at developing a theory to contribute to an emerging research field. Quantitative research methods are used to test rather than develop a theory. Therefore, quantitative research methods require deductive research to develop hypotheses and a theoretical framework, which can then be tested and verified. The advantage of quantitative research is that – based on standardized measures and high sample sizes – it may be possible to generalize the results (Bryman, 2008).

I conducted a quantitative research study, as it was my goal to test and verify the theoretical framework that I developed in chapter 3.6. Therefore, I gathered empirical data via a survey that I designed to represent a setting as it may occur in practice. I chose this research approach to ensure the results' external validity, i.e., to ensure that the effects revealed do not just occur in an artificial setting, but can be generalized to occur in practice as well (Mitchell and Jolley, 2001). Furthermore, I decided to undertake the primary data collection by means of a standardized, web-based online survey. This form of data collection enables the gathering of data cheaply, speedily, and interactively, as well as the data's easy storage and processing (Berekhoven, Eckert W., and Ellenrieder P., 2004). In addition, this form of data collection allows access to online community participants, who would otherwise have been difficult to survey (Garton, Haythornthwaite, and Wellman, 2011).

4.2.1 Layout and sequence of the online survey

I structured the online survey into five parts (see Figure 15, the full survey is included in the appendix B). In the first part, I introduced the participants to the sequence of the survey and provided them with task framing. In the task framing, I encouraged the participants to imagine being senior managers in a multinational company with the responsibility to evaluate new product ideas:

"Imagine you just started in a new job as a senior manager in a multinational company. Among other things, it is your responsibility to evaluate various new product ideas from different business units. Your evaluation will be taken into account in deciding which ideas should be taken further in future development processes and eventually be brought to market. Therefore your decisions can have a significant impact on the firm's future success.

Today you are requested to evaluate ideas in the domain of 3D printing. Although you are new to the job and might not possess deep expertise in 3D printing, you are requested to evaluate the ideas to the best of your knowledge."[37]

I used this task framing to ensure that the participants would think about the new product ideas from a managerial point of view rather than from a consumer's perspective. The reasoning behind this is that consumers – who represent a significant share of the intended respondents – might have the "tendency to think primarily about issues relevant to them at the time – in their current life or business situation context" (Veryzer, 1998b: 143). I tried to counteract this tendency with the chosen task framing.

In part II and part III of the survey, I asked the participants to evaluate several new product ideas in the domain of 3D printing. I intentionally manipulated these product ideas to represent different degrees of innovativeness (see section 4.2.2). In part II, I asked the respondents to state their overall impression of the ideas. This task reflects a holistic idea evaluation task (see chapter 3.2.2.3). Subsequently in part III, I asked the participants to use the following evaluation criteria: originality, user value, and feasibility to again evaluate

---

[37] Description as provided in the survey (see appendix B).

the same ideas (see chapter 3.2.2.2). In these two rounds of idea evaluations, I randomized the order of the ideas for each participant in order to avoid the sequence of the evaluation potentially leading to unwanted effects (Field and Hole, 2003). Part IV and part V of the survey included the scientific measures. Part IV focused on the measures intended to measure the participants' knowledge of the 3D printing domain, whereas part V included the measures intended as control variables (see section 4.2.3).

Figure 15: Sequence of the online survey[38]

4.2.2 Selection and manipulation of new product ideas

The new product ideas included in the survey were real-world new product ideas from the domain of 3D printing. In the extensive search for these ideas, I screened numerous 3D printing magazines, blogs, and communities, as well as crowdfunding platforms, such as kickstarter.com and Indiegogo.com. During this search, I gathered a shortlist of 14 new product ideas that I considered suitable for the purpose of this study. When describing the ideas, I either used the original description that the idea generator provided, or adapted the description to allow for limited space and a uniform description of the ideas.

Subsequently, I interviewed three 3D printing experts to validate the ideas from the shortlist in terms of their comparability and suitability for the purpose of my research. As the result of these interviews, I selected eight of the 14 ideas to be used in the online survey (see Table 9). The rationale for this selection was that the experts had confirmed that these ideas were not being launched in the market at the time of the data collection and that they exhibited an adequate spread of more incremental and more radical new product ideas in the domain of 3D printing.

---

[38] Author's illustration.

To investigate the moderating effect of the ideas' innovativeness, I had to find a valid measurement to objectively determine the degree of innovativeness. I contacted nine independent experts in the domain of 3D printing, asking them to assess the innovativeness of the eight selected new product ideas. I selected these experts on the basis of their outstanding knowledge of the market with respect to consumer needs and the latest products on the market, as well as for their solid understanding of the technical aspects related to 3D printers and their components.

The experts evaluated the ideas' innovativeness by means of an online survey in which I requested them to assess each idea's innovativeness against six items that I had adapted from the optimized scale of innovativeness developed by Schultz, Salomo, and Talke (2013). These six items are based on prior work in the field on the measurement of product innovativeness and capture the market-related dimension of innovativeness and the technology-related dimension of innovativeness (see chapter 2.1.1).

I thereafter followed several steps to ensure the reliability and validity of the innovativeness measure. First, I calculated the idea innovativeness construct's intraclass correlation coefficient (ICC), corrected the item-to-total correlation (CITC), and calculated Cronbach's alpha in order to determine the construct's internal consistency and reliability of the construct for each idea (Hair et al., 2014a; Weiber and Mühlhaus, 2010). With an ICC of 0.50 and a Cronbach's alpha of 0.51, idea #3 (lithography-based ceramic 3D-Printer) did not pass the recommended threshold of 0.7 (Nunally and Bernstein, 1994; Peterson, 1994). Consequently, I had to exclude this idea from further data analysis, because its innovativeness could not be reliably determined. For all other ideas, Cronbach's alpha, the ICC, and the CITC exceeded the recommend thresholds (see Table 10).[39]

Subsequently, I conducted an exploratory factor analysis (EFA) based on principal axis factoring with promax rotation in order to confirm the unidimensionality of the six-item construct (the reasoning behind an EFA is explained in more detail in section 4.3.2.1.1). All six items displayed sufficient factor loadings and the resulting unidimensional construct accounted for more than 50 percent of the total variance (see Table 11). With all the ideas (after excluding idea #3 from further analysis) exceeding the recommended reliability and

---

[39] Although the ICC of idea #8 reached only 0.66, the idea was still included in the further analysis, because a threshold of 0.6 has been argued as being acceptable by Hair et al. (2014a).

validity thresholds, I concluded that the six items that I had adapted from the optimized scale of innovativeness construct are a reliable measure of idea innovativeness (Hair et al., 2014a).

Next, I merged all six items into a single reflective measure of innovativeness in respect of each idea and each rater. As a last step, I confirmed that there was sufficient interrater agreement in the raters' innovativeness scores in order to accept the average of the individual innovativeness scores as a reliable measurement for my study (see Table 12).

Table 9: New product ideas used in the survey

#	Idea title	Idea description as provided in the survey
1	Triple-jetting 3D printer	The triple-jetting 3D printer will combine up to three base resins to print a range of material properties from rubber to rigid, transparent to opaque, neutral to vibrantly colored and standard to biocompatible in pre-set configurations to produce more than 50 materials in a single build.[40]
2	Wood, stone and metal filament	The idea is to create a wood, stone, or metal PLA-based filament that contains tiny particles of wood, limestone or metal resulting in 3D printed products that can mimic the finish of limestone or bronze.[41]
	Lithography-based Ceramic 3D-Printer	This printer will allow the production of functioning ceramic parts as green bodies that can be further processed to obtain a completely dense ceramic part. The idea is based on the selective curing of a photosensitive resin, which contains homogeneously dispersed ceramic particles. The centerpiece of the process is a specifically designed imaging system, which enables the transfer of the layer information by means of the latest LED-technology.[42]
3	Chocolate printhead for 3D printer	The chocolate printhead will be a nozzle that is customized to print low viscous material, i.e., chocolate. This nozzle will not require proprietary materials, the goal is, that chocolate found in the local supermarkets can be used[43].
4	Conductive graphene filament	This filament will incorporate highly conductive nano-carbon platelets to enhance the properties of standard PLA filament, allowing a variety of new applications, including the 3D printing of conductive traces, capacitive touch sensors, electromagnetic and radiofrequency shielding and production of high-strength mechanical and functional parts.[44]
5	3D electronics printer	The idea is to create the first 3D desktop printer that can co-print matrix materials such as thermoplastics and highly conductive silver inks enabling to print customized electronic devices like quadcopters, electromagnets and fully functional 3D electromechanical assemblies.[45]
6	All-In-One 3D Printer, mill, & Laser Engraver	The all-in-one 3d printer will combine a 3D Printer, mill, and Laser Engraver in one compact cube. By utilizing quick-change heads, the user will be able to shape a block of aluminum, hardwood, or plastic into intricate designs, 3D print complex plastic shapes, or laser engrave into objects made of wood, leather or plastic with a single machine.[46]
7	Continuous liquid interface production printer	This printer will use light and oxygen to continuously grow objects from a pool of resin instead of printing them layer-by-layer. The idea is to use a photochemical process by carefully controlling the interaction of UV light, which creates the photopolymerization, and oxygen, which inhibits the reaction to create 3D printed products.[47]

[40] Description adopted from stratasys (2015).
[41] Description adopted from fastcodesign.com (2015).
[42] Description adopted from lithoz (2015).
[43] Description adopted from SunP Biotech (2015).
[44] Description adopted from Wheeler (2015b).
[45] Description adopted from Voxel8 (2015).
[46] Description adopted from BoXZY (2015).
[47] Description adopted from Wheeler (2015a).

Table 10: Scale items, measures and reliability of idea innovativeness

Item	Measure	Corrected Item-Total Correlation							
		Idea #1	Idea #2	Idea #3	Idea #4	Idea #5	Idea #6	Idea #7	Idea #8
M1	The idea offers a new customer value not offered before by any other product	.857	.927	.702	.885	.866	.744	.785	.532
M2	The idea creates a totally new market	.729	.692	.462	.800	.900	.440	.348	.464
M3	The idea changes the way the market functions	.779	.782	-.619	.649	.900	.320	.707	.446
T1	The idea is based on new technological principles	.512	.776	.584	.590	.932	.497	.374	.225
T2	The technology that is needed to develop this idea allows significant performance enhancement	.160	.753	.172	.692	.925	.523	.777	.614
T3	The idea can be characterized as being based on very new technological components	.780	.491	.791	.836	.776	.700	.665	.421
	Cronbach's Alpha	.831	.897	.509	.872	.961	.758	.831	.700
	Intraclass Correlation	.822	.865	.499	.775	.949	.738	.799	.659

Note: All items are measured on a 5-point Likert scale ("strongly disagree" / "strongly agree"); ICC is calculated based on a two-way mixed effects model and absolute agreement

Table 11: Factor analysis for idea innovativeness construct

Item	Measure	Factor loadings	Total variance extracted
M1	The idea offers a new customer value not offered before by any other product	.730	53.93%
M2	The idea creates a totally new market	.699	
M3	The idea changes the way the market functions	.656	
T1	The idea is based on new technological principles	.728	
T2	The technology that is needed to develop this idea allows significant performance enhancements	.762	
T3	The idea can be characterized as being based on very new technological components	.820	

Note: All items are measured on a 5-point Likert scale ("strongly disagree" / "strongly agree"); Principal axis factoring with promax rotation

Table 12: Interrater agreement for idea innovativeness

	Rater #1	Rater #2	Rater #3	Rater #4	Rater #5	Rater #6	Rater #7	Rater #8	Rater #9	Average
Idea #1	3.33	3.17	4.33	3.00	1.50	2.33	3.00	3.83	3.17	3.07
Idea #2	3.17	2.00	2.67	1.00	1.50	1.00	2.33	3.17	2.00	2.09
Idea #4	1.33	2.50	1.50	1.17	1.00	2.83	2.17	2.33	3.00	1.98
Idea #5	4.33	2.00	2.67	1.00	1.50	4.33	3.00	2.83	4.67	2.93
Idea #6	4.50	4.17	3.33	3.00	2.50	3.50	4.17	3.50	3.67	3.59
Idea #7	3.67	2.17	2.33	3.00	2.67	3.17	3.33	1.17	3.67	2.80
Idea #8	4.00	4.33	3.50	3.67	3.33	3.67	2.50	2.17	3.17	3.37
									Cronbach's alpha	.82
									Intraclass correlation	.79

Note: Innovativeness is measured with a six-item construct on a 5-point Likert scale ("strongly disagree" / "strongly agree"); ICC is calculated based on a two-way mixed effects model and absolute agreement.

4.2.3 Operationalization of measures

In general, a researcher has the following options when selecting appropriate measures: (i) taking theoretical considerations into account, (ii) conducting exploratory research, (iii) drawing from experience or practice, and (iv) applying existing constructs from previous research studies. I decided to use measures from previous research in the published literature whenever possible. This approach has several advantages. First, the published measures were already confirmed in previous studies as highly reliable and valid. Second, using existing measures avoids the creation of a plethora of different constructs. Third, this approach allows a comparison of the results across different studies (Homburg and Giering, 1996).

Since the survey was concerned with a specific product domain, I had to adjust most of the measures to fit the 3D printing domain. Consequently, the validity and reliability could not be taken for granted and needed to be ensured before the final data analysis (see section 4.3.2). Furthermore, all measures in the survey were based on self-ratings. Self-ratings have been acknowledged as the most commonly used data collection method in social sciences (Malhotra, Kim, and Patil, 2006) and have been extensively used in innovation research (e.g. Franke, Poetz, and Schreier, 2014; Franke, von Hippel, and Schreier, 2006). Nonetheless, several shortcomings of self-ratings have been comprehensively discussed in the literature (e.g. Conway and Huffcutt, 1997). A major point of concern is that common method variance may reduce the validity of the data obtained from self-ratings (Podsakoff, 1986). I therefore took several precautions in the study's design to reduce this risk (see section 4.3.3.).

4.2.3.1 Dependent variables

Perceived originality, user value, feasibility, and overall impression. The participants rated originality, user value, and feasibility for each idea on 7-point Likert scales (strongly disagree / strongly agree) according to the following descriptions:

"*Originality*: determines how novel, unusual and unique you consider the idea to be";

"*User value*: can offer new forms of usage, new and/or more features, or in a broader sense, offer an experience or something else that provides the user with added value";

"*Feasibility*: concerns questions such as whether it is feasible to develop, produce, and successfully commercialize the product within 'reasonable time' and under 'reasonable investments'";

"*Overall impression*: for your evaluation, you are free to consider all potential benefits and shortcomings of the product ideas as you feel is best." [48]

I presented the ideas in random order to avoid unwanted effects due to the ideas' sequencing (Field and Hole, 2003). I provide my reasons for choosing these four criteria in chapter 3.2.2.

4.2.3.2   Independent variable

Domain knowledge. Research scholars have acknowledged that there is no formal system for identifying experts. In a research context, self-report measures of knowledge are thus generally used to assess expertise (see e.g. Park, 1976). As outlined in chapter 3.5.1, I established domain knowledge as reflecting the evaluators' need knowledge and solution knowledge. This is in line with the suggestion in the literature that the process of identifying expert knowledge should never rely on a single method to deduce an individuals' knowledge or expertise (Hoffmann, 1998).

Based on an extensive review of the innovation and general management literatures, I identified two constructs that I deemed appropriate to reflect these two dimensions. First, I used the 7-item consumer domain knowledge scale (Mitchell and Dacin, 1996) to capture the participants' need knowledge. Second, I applied the 7-item technical expertise scale (Franke, von Hippel, and Schreier, 2006) to capture the participants' solution knowledge. These scales are designed to be domain-specific, therefore I adapted the wording to the context of 3D printing (see Table 13). Subsequently, I combined all the items from both scales into a direct, reflective measure of domain knowledge as a first-order latent construct[49]. Given that these two scales had not been combined before, I confirmed the unidimensionality, validity, and reliability of the domain knowledge construct with the established procedures (see section 4.3.2.1.1).

---

[48] Description as provided in the survey (see appendix B).
[49] The approach of combining two different scales into one construct is an established procedure, e.g., the lead user construct is also a combination of two scales in a first-order latent construct (see lead userness construct on the following pages).

Table 13: Operationalization of domain knowledge

Items 'domain knowledge'
Consumer domain knowledge scale
CDK1   Compared to the average person, I do not know much about 3D Printing
CDK2   I am very familiar with 3D printing
CDK3   I am not skilled at utilizing 3D printing technology
CDK4†   I am very interested in 3D printing
CDK5   I use 3D printing products and services a lot
CDK6†   My friends use 3D printing products and services a lot
CDK7   I read articles related to 3D printing all the time
Technical expertise scale
TE1   I can repair 3D printing equipment
TE2   I always try to keep up to date with regard to the materials, innovations, and possibilities with regard to 3D printing
TE3   I can help other users solve problems with 3D printers
TE4   I can make technical changes to 3D printers on my own
TE5   I am a huge fan of the technical aspects of 3D printing
TE6†   I am handy and enjoy tinkering
TE7†   I come from a technical background in my profession or education (e.g. engineering)

Note: All items are measured on a 7-point Likert scale ("strongly disagree" / "strongly agree"); † Excluded after factor analysis.

Lead Userness. Anticipating the probability that some difficulties might arise when measuring domain knowledge directly, I decided to include a measure in the survey that might indirectly represent different degrees of domain knowledge. I therefore included a measure of the participants lead userness in the survey. I based this decision on several research studies, in which innovation management scholars posited that individuals displaying a high degree of lead userness also carry high domain knowledge (von Hippel, 1986, 1994; Faullant et al., 2012).

I measured lead userness with a seven-item scale adapted from Faullant et al. (2012). These measures follow the operationalization of typical lead user characteristics as proposed by Lüthje (2000). Lead userness was therefore measured using two subscales: (i) "ahead of the trend," measured by four items and (ii) "high expected benefit," measured by three items. Despite lead userness originally being conceptualized as a two-dimensional construct (Franke, von Hippel, and Schreier, 2006), it has become most researchers' common practice in the field to include all the items of both scales as a direct reflective measure of lead userness as a first-order latent construct (Schreier and Prügl, 2008; Morrison, Roberts, and Midgley, 2004). I thus decided to follow common practice and measured lead userness as a single construct with seven items.

Table 14: Operationalization of lead userness

Items 'lead userness'
Lead Userness - (Faullant et al. 2013)
AT1   I usually find out about new 3D printing products and solutions earlier than others
AT2   I have benefited significantly from the early adoption and use of 3D printing
AT3   I am regarded as being on the 'cutting edge' in the field of 3D printing
AT4   I have a comprehensive knowledge of the 3D printing equipment available on the market
HEB1   I have often noticed technical problems with 3D printers
HEB2†   I have needs which are not satisfied by existing 3D printing equipment
HEB3†   I am dissatisfied with the existing 3D printing equipment offered on the market

Note: All items are measured on a 7-point Likert scale ("strongly disagree" / "strongly agree"); † Excluded after factor analysis

4.2.3.3 Moderating variable

Idea innovativeness. To achieve different levels of idea innovativeness, I used seven new product ideas offering different degrees of innovativeness (see section 4.2.2). Nine independent experts in the domain of 3D printing validated these different degrees of innovativeness by assessing each idea's innovativeness against six items on a five-point Likert scale (strongly disagree / strongly agree), which I adapted from prior research (Schultz, Salomo, and Talke, 2013). Three of these items were aimed at capturing the market-related dimension and the other three items aimed at capturing the technology-related dimension of idea innovativeness (see chapter 2.1.1).

4.2.3.4 Mediating variable

Comprehension. The participants indicated their understanding of each idea on a seven-point Likert scale (strongly disagree / strongly agree) reflecting the following description:

"*Comprehension:* indicates how well you understood the idea, e.g. did the relationship between an addressed user need and the recommended solution became clear to you?"[50]

I based this description on the proposition that, at the core of new product idea evaluation, the evaluator has to assess the technology that is presented as a solution to a specific need, while simultaneously assessing the market potential created due to the new product fulfilling this need (chapter 3.5.1: 65).

---

[50] Description as provided in the survey (see appendix B).

4.2.3.5   Control variables

I included several control variables in the survey to account for additional factors that may affect evaluation behavior in order to control for undesired factors and to capture possible interdependencies in my research model (Bortz and Schuster, 2010).

Risk aversion. Individuals' risk aversion has been found to fundamentally influence their decision making, as many decisions depend on how individuals assess probabilities and predict values in judgmental decision making (Tversky and Kahnemann, 1974; Conchar, 2004). In other words, the participants' *willingness to take risk* may influence their evaluations of new product ideas. I controlled for this potential effect by measuring risk aversion with six items adapted from the top management risk aversion scale (Jaworski and Kohli, 1993).

Table 15: Operationalization of risk aversion

Items 'risk aversion'
Top management risk aversion scale - (Jaworski and Kohli, 1993)
R1†   I believe that higher financial risks are worth taking for higher rewards
R2†   I accept occasional new product failures as being normal
R3*   I only implement plans if I am certain that they will work
R4†   I like to take big financial risks
R5†   I would encourage the development of innovative new product ideas, knowing well that some will fail
R6*   I like to "play it safe" in regard to product development projects

Note: All items are measured on a 7-point Likert scale ("strongly disagree" / "strongly agree"); † Excluded after factor analysis; * Reverse coded

Professional experience (R&D, Sales, Marketing tenure). Research has shown that the extent to which individuals have developed expertise in an area, tends to cause them to put greater emphasis on criteria that relate to that expertise (Behrens, Ernst, and Shepherd, 2014; Melone, 1994). In addition, prior research has shown that professional experience in certain functions leads to a significant difference in how individuals perceive and interpret information (Dougherty, 1992). For example, research has found that marketing experts value the impact of innovation differently than the way technology rofessionals do (Schultz, Salomo, and Talke, 2013). I controlled for this effect by asking participants for their years of professional experience in R&D, Sales, and Marketing (< 1 year; 1-2 years; 2-3 years; 3-4 years; 4-5 years; 5-10 years; 10-15 years; > 15 years). I subsequently coded the tenure as a binary dummy variable with a threshold of five years' professional experience (1 = high tenure; 0 = low tenure).

Top management position. Top managers tend to process information and reach decisions in a different way than others do. For example, senior managers focus more strongly on strategic aspects when assessing innovation project exploitation decisions (Behrens, Ernst, and Shepherd, 2014) and are also more likely to exhibit a bias towards being overconfident. Such bias has been shown to increase the likelihood of pursuing risky ventures (Simon, Houghton, and Aquino, 1999). I controlled for this influence by asking the participants to state their responsibility level within the company (no managerial responsibility, low-level management, middle-level management, top-level management, and owner of the company). I subsequently coded the top management position as a binary dummy variable (1 = top manager, 0 = not).

Demographics. To control for effects resulting from demographics, I asked the participants to state their gender (male/female), age, and their highest educational degree (middle school, high school, bachelor's degree, master's degree, PhD or doctorate, and professor). I subsequently coded education as a binary dummy variable (1 = bachelor's degree or higher, 0 = middle school or high school). 3D printing can be seen as a new and complex technology that may be more popular among young and/or educated participants and thus, age and education may specifically influence the evaluation behavior of participants.

Native English speaker. As the survey was conducted in English only, I controlled for potential language problems affecting the idea evaluations by asking the participants for their country of origin and coding a binary dummy variable (1 = native, 0 = non-native speaker). For this coding, I considered participants from the United States, United Kingdom, Canada, Australia, and New Zealand as native English speakers.

4.2.4 Data collection and sample

4.2.4.1 Pre-test

Having decided on the sequence of the survey, the ideas to be evaluated, and how to operationalize the measures of the variables, I followed the best practice approach in research and conducted pre-tests of the full survey (Weiber and Mühlhaus, 2010). In the first pre-test, I asked three 3D printing experts to provide feedback on the survey. I instructed the experts to especially focus on the clarity of the idea descriptions. The experts stated that the ideas used in the survey were very clear and they affirmed their positive overall impression of the survey.

In the second pre-test, I asked 22 participants (one professor, six innovation management peers and 16 laymen) to complete the full survey. This allowed me to assess the overall structure of the survey, the comprehensibility of questions, and the idea descriptions, as well as the time required to complete the survey under realistic conditions. The completion of the survey took the participants less than 16 minutes on average, which I considered appropriate for the research purpose. Except for some minor changes with regard to the wording (e.g. replacement of some domain-specific abbreviations), I encountered no problematic elements.

4.2.4.2   Sources of recruitment

A structured and purpose-built procedure guided the selection of suitable participants to ensure an appropriate sample was generated to address the research question. I aimed to include participant groups with (medium) high domain knowledge and participants groups with (medium) low, or no, domain knowledge by recruiting participants from various sources (see Figure 16). Presuming that different target samples may have different degrees of need knowledge and solution knowledge (von Hippel, 1986, 1994; Lüthje, 2004; Magnusson, Wästlund, and Netz, 2016), I chose to include 3D printing industry professionals, 3D printing online community members, general NPD professionals, and laymen with no affiliation to the domain of 3D printing, nor to new product development, in the sample.

In the following paragraphs, I describe how I approached the various sources recruited to participate in the study.

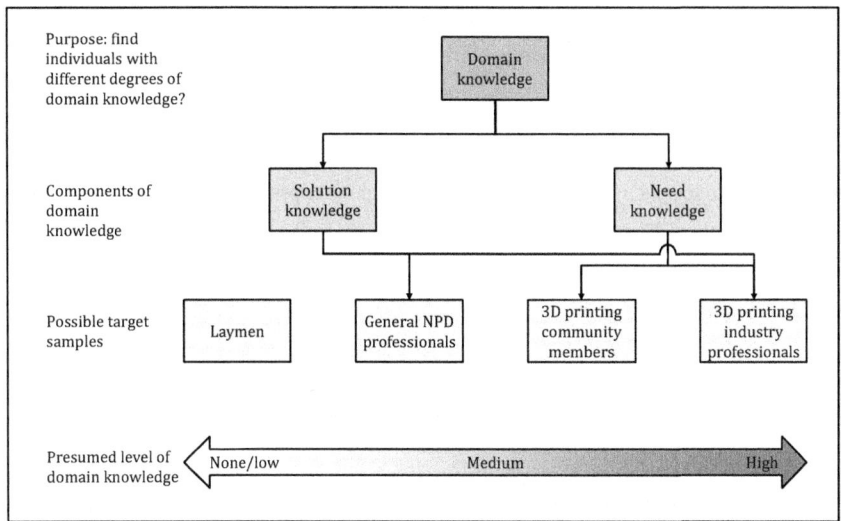

Figure 16: Sample recruitment logic[51]

3D printing industry professionals: I conducted an online search and screened indices of exhibitors of 3D printing trade shows (e.g. Inside 3D printing) to identify relevant 3D printing firms. My search resulted in the identification of 23 3D printing companies and four research centers. I contacted all the firms and research centers telephonically, asking them to support the research project. Five 3D printing companies and two research centers were willing to participate. In each of the participating firms, my points of contact agreed to complete the survey themselves and to send the link to their colleagues by email.

Furthermore, I discovered the consortium AGENT-3D during my online search. At the time of the data collection, this consortium comprised 12 leading research organizations and 28 companies that formed a strategic alliance in the field of additive manufacturing under the leadership of Frauenhofer IWS. This project follows the guiding idea of advancing additive manufacturing procedures based on the belief that this technology is about to become the key technology of Industry 4.0 (Agent3D, 2015). I contacted the office manager of the

---

[51] Author's illustration.

consortium, asking for support for my research project. The office manager agreed to send the link of the survey to all consortium members by email, requesting their participation.

3D printing community members: I identified nine suitable 3D printing communities and contacted all community administrators via social networks, the contact forms on the communities' websites, or email addresses to ask their support for my research project. One administrator (3D-drucken.de) allowed me to advertise the survey directly on their community website and actively helped me promote the survey on the website's main news slider (see Figure 17).

Figure 17: Call for participation on www.3d-drucken.de[52]

The other eight communities (3Dprintingforbeginners.com, 3Dprintingindustry.com, 3DPrintboard.com 3Druck.com, 3Dhubs.com, thingiverse.com, soliforum.com, and reprap.org) did not allow me to post directly on their websites, but encouraged me to post

---

[52] Source: www.3d-drucken.de, retrieved September 3rd 2015.

the survey link in their discussion forums and on their social media pages. I therefore posted an encouraging invitation, in combination with a raffle for a EUR 50 Amazon gift certificate, on their discussion forums and relevant social pages. I provide an example of such a posting in Figure 18.

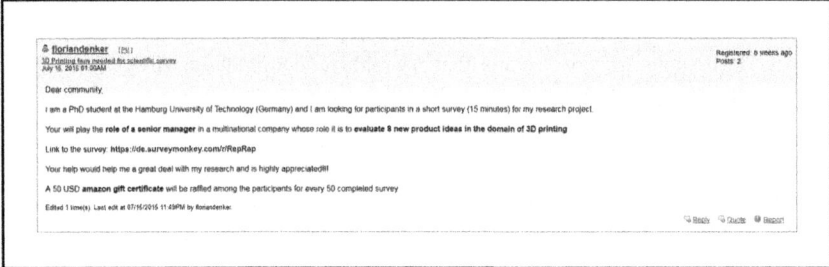

Figure 18: Call for participation on www.reprap.org[53]

General NPD professionals: I leveraged several sources to recruit general NPD professionals for my survey. In addition to leveraging my personal network, I posted invitations to the survey in relevant communities in professional online networks (i.e., Xing and LinkedIn). In addition, I sent personalized emails inviting members of the German Product Development Management Association (PDMA) and the "Verband deutscher Industriedesigner (VDID)" to participate in the survey.

Laymen: To include a sizable number of laymen in the sample, I decided to recruit and compensate respondents through Amazon Mechanical Turk (www.MTurk.com). This platform is described as "a novel, open online marketplace for getting work done by others. [In other words,] MTurk functions as a one-stop shop for getting work done, bringing together the people and tools that enable task creation, labor recruitment, compensation, and data collection [...]. Requesters can create and post virtually any task that can be done at a computer (i.e., surveys, experiments, writing, etc.) using simple templates or technical scripts or linking workers to external online survey tools (e.g., SurveyMonkey)" (Buhrmester, Kwang, and Gosling, 2011: 4). Amazon's Mechanical Turk is a useful source

---

[53] Source: www.reprap.org, retrieved July 15th 2015.

to collect online survey data, because the platform's audience represents a reasonably fair representation of the general public (Buhrmester, Kwang, and Gosling, 2011; Paolacci and Chandler, 2014). I decided to pay participants USD 1.50 for completing the survey, which corresponds to about USD 6 per hour, which constitutes adequate compensation for the task compared to previous studies (Berg, 2016).

In addition, I decided to recruit students from the Hamburg University of Technology. I asked the students to take the survey during an innovation management class of master's students. These students were also included in a raffle for a EUR 50 Amazon gift certificate to encourage them to participate.

The data collection period lasted for four months, starting July 14 and ending November 23, 2015. I approached all the sources in parallel during that time. In respect of the data collection in the online communities, I posted a reminder on the corresponding platforms each month after starting the data collection. Within four months, I had collected a total of 409 responses from the aforementioned sources (see Table 16).

4.3 Data cleansing and preparation

4.3.1 Treatment of missing data and outliers

I prepared the data set for the statistical analysis in order to conduct a meaningful analysis. During this preparation, I discarded 63 incomplete surveys according to the rule of thumb that cases with more than 10 percent missing data should be excluded (Hair et al., 2014a). Furthermore, I eliminated 10 data sets in which the respondents took less than five minutes to complete the survey (lowest percentile of all 409 responses). Eliminating these 73 cases resulted in a data set of 336 valid answers, with no missing data, for further analysis.

The literature on statistics gives rise to serious concern regarding extreme outliers in a data set, because these can significantly impact the reliability of statistical analysis (Hair et al., 2014a). Although the literature suggests eliminating all illegitimate outliers; however, the identification of outliers and assessing whether or not they are illegitimate or legitimate, have proven to be very difficult (Osborne and Overbay, 2008).

Nonetheless, I used two methods that have been proven reliable regarding the identification of outliers. First, I used the "outlier labeling rule" (Hoaglin, Iglewicz, and

Tukey, 1986) with a revised multiplier of 2.2 instead of 1.5 (Hoaglin and Iglewicz, 1987). The revised rule suggests multiplying the Interquartile Range (IQR) by a factor of 2.2. Thereafter, the product is subtracted from the lower 25-percentile value to determine the lower cut-off value and added to the higher 75 percentile value to determine the higher cut-off value. Having analyzed all variables against this rule, I could not identify any outliers. Second, I used the non-recursive procedure described by Selst and Jolicoeur. The procedure suggests a cut-off value of 2.5 SD from the mean if the sample size exceeds 100 (van Selst and Jolicoeur, 1994). The application of the procedure led to the detection of three outliers. These outliers occurred in the evaluation of the new product ideas' perceived user value and feasibility. Since these variables serve as dependent variables in the model, I decided to delete the three outliers from the sample. The elimination of the outliers led to a data set with a final sample size of N = 333. A detailed breakdown of the sample by source is provided in Table 16.

Table 16: Composition of final sample

Target group	Source	Responses total	Responses used in data analysis*
3D printing industry professionals	Advance3D	1	1
	AntoniusKöster GmbH & Co. KG	1	1
	Direct manufacturing research center	7	6
	Frauenhofer IPT	3	3
	Materialise GmbH	1	1
	SLM solutions GmbH	1	1
	Voxeljet AG	1	1
	Consortium "Projekt AGENT-3D"	15	13
3D printing community members	3D Hubs	17	14
	3D Print Board	9	9
	3D-drucken.de	20	14
	3dprintingindustry	3	2
	RepRap	29	20
	soliforum	136	97
General NPD professionals	LinkedIn - Product Design Group	1	1
	LinkedIn - Product Management Group	5	3
	Personal network**	13	10
	Product Development Management Association (PDMA)	12	12
	Verband deutscher Industriedesigner (VDID)	8	7
	Xing - Product Design Group	2	2
	Xing - Product Management Group	1	0
Laymen	Amazon mechanical turk	84	77
	Students from Hamburg University of Technology	39	38
Total		409	333

Note: *After removing respondents with missing values and outliers; **Individuals recruited through personal contacts include product development professionals from, e.g. Airbus, Beierdorf AG, Claas AG, Google AG.

4.3.2 Reliability and validity evaluation of constructs

I obtained the measures introduced in section 4.2.3 from the published literature. However, as these constructs are applied in a different research setting and have been adapted to the specific domain of 3D printing, the quality of the constructs needed to be confirmed in terms of their reliability and validity. For this purpose, different criteria are applicable in respect of reflective and formative constructs (Hair, Ringle, and Sarstedt, 2011). In my study, all variables are single-item scales, or are measured as multi-item reflective constructs. Thus, before using the reflective constructs in the data analysis, I ensured their reliability and validity by means of well-known first generation (section 4.3.2.1) and second-generation methods (section 4.3.2.2), as suggested by Hair et al. (2014a) and

Weiber and Mühlhaus (2010). A summary of the criteria that I used to assess the constructs
is provided in Table 17.

Table 17: Validity and reliability criteria used to assess the multi-item reflective constructs

Criteria	Critical values	Sources for critical values
First generation criteria		
Measure of sampling adequacy	≥ .50	Cureton and D'Agostino, 1993; Hair et al., 2014a
Bartlett's test of sphericity	p ≤ .05	Backhaus et al., 2011; Hair et al., 2014a
Communalities	≥ .50	Weiber and Mühlhaus, 2010; Hair et al., 2014a
Factor loadings	≥ .35	Weiber and Mühlhaus, 2010; Hair et al., 2014a
Kaiser criterion	Single factor with eigenvalue > 1	Weiber and Mühlhaus, 2010; Hair et al., 2014a
Cumulative variance extracted	≥ 50 %	Hair et al., 2014a
Cronbach's alpha	≥ .70	Nunally and Bernstein, 1994; Peterson, 1994
Inter-item correlation	≥ .30	Robinson et al., 1991
Corrected item-to-total correlation	≥ 0.5	Zaichkowsky, 1985
Second-generation criteria		
Outer item loadings	≥ .70*	Hair et al., 2014
Dillon-Goldstein's rho	≥ .70	Weiber and Mühlhaus, 2010
Fornell-Larcker criterion	AVE > .50; correlations between constructs ≤ AVE²	Fornell and Larcker, 1981; Hair et al., 2011

Note: *Items should only be rigorously eliminated when their loadings are lower than 0.4. If item loadings range between 0.4 – 0.7, the decision should be made on a case-by-case basis (Hair et al., 2014).

4.3.2.1   First generation methods

4.3.2.1.1   Assessing the constructs unidimensionality with exploratory factor analysis

The primary purpose of an Exploratory Factor Analysis (EFA) is to define the underlying structure of the variables used in the data analysis (Hair et al., 2014a). Thus, the EFA enabled me to test for the unidimensionality of the reflective constructs and to confirm the relationship between the items and their underlying constructs.

I conducted the EFA for various reasons. First, I captured the respondents' domain knowledge along two dimensions – need knowledge and solution knowledge – respectively using the consumer domain knowledge scale and technical expertise scale (see section 4.2.3). I could therefore use the EFA to determine whether I could integrate the items of both scales into one reflective first-order construct. Second, the literature has suggested that it is very difficult to capture an individual's domain knowledge as a direct self-reported measure. Therefore, I decided to also measure domain knowledge indirectly. For this purpose I measured the participants' lead userness (see section 4.2.3.2). If the composite domain knowledge construct were to prove unreliable, I could use the lead user construct as a replacement. Consequently, these two constructs – domain knowledge and lead userness – have a high probability of overlapping, which the EFA would reveal. Third, even though I relied on employing existing and well-published constructs, their items have not before been adapted to the domain of 3D printing. By means of the EFA, I could test whether or not the adapted items would load on their respective constructs as intended, and if excluding single items might be beneficial in order to increase a specific construct's measurement model (Weiber and Mühlhaus, 2010).

However, in performing an EFA, it is necessary to take the following steps: (i) test the assumptions for the EFA, (ii) choose an extraction method, (iii) choose an appropriate factor rotation method, and (iv) interpret the results (Weiber and Mühlhaus, 2010; Hair et al., 2014a).

Testing the assumptions for the EFA: To undertake a meaningful EFA, there needs to be an assumption of at least some correlation between the items, which will allow the coherent factors to be extracted. The Kaiser-Meyer-Olkin criterion (KMO-criterion) and the Bartlett's test of sphericity can be used to test whether or not the data set is appropriate in terms of this assumption (Hair et al., 2014a; Backhaus et al., 2011). The KMO-criterion indicates the extent of the correlation among the items and should be > 0.5 (Cureton and D'Agostino, 1993). The "Bartlett's test of sphericity" is a statistical significance test to determine whether the correlation matrix has significant correlations among at least some variables (Backhaus et al., 2011), and should thus reach at least a significance level of < 0.05 to confirm that the items are appropriate to conduct an EFA (Hair et al., 2014a).

Furthermore, a meaningful factor analysis requires an adequate sample size. According to Hair et al. (2014a), the minimum sample size should be at least 50 observations or five times the number of items to be analyzed. With a sample size of N = 333 and a maximum of 20 items to be analyzed (see Table 21), this requirement is met.

Choice of extraction method: Choosing either the common factor analysis or the component analysis as method of extraction, depends on (i) the objective of the EFA, and (ii) the researcher's prior knowledge of the variance in the variables (Hair et al., 2014a). The component analysis is deemed appropriate if data reduction is a primary concern and the researcher's prior knowledge suggests that specific and error variance is only a small proportion of the total variance. Common factor analysis, on the other hand, is appropriate if the identification of the latent dimensions or constructs represented in the original items is the researcher's primary objective. This is also appropriate if the researcher has little knowledge of the extent of the specific error variance and thus wants to eliminate this variance. Although there has been an ongoing debate in the literature on the more appropriate method, empirical research studies have demonstrated that, in many instances, both methods yield similar results (Hair et al., 2014a). Nonetheless, the literature suggests that common factor analysis yields the best results in well-specified theoretical applications, and/or in the case of non-normal distributed data (Osborne, Costello, and Kellow, 2008; Weiber and Mühlhaus, 2010). Since the selected constructs were adapted from the established literature and my data are largely non-normally distributed (see chapter 5.2.2.1), I selected common factor analysis to determine the EFA.

Choice of factor rotation method: The major option is to choose either an orthogonal rotation approach, or an oblique rotation approach. The objective of both approaches is to obtain theoretically meaningful factors and the simplest factor structure. Although similar, the difference between orthogonal and oblique rotation is that oblique rotations allow correlated factors instead of maintaining the independence between the rotated factors

(Hair et al., 2014a). Scholars in the field have noted that, in reality, there are hardly any factors that are completely uncorrelated (Weiber and Mühlhaus, 2010). Thus, oblique rotation methods "are best suited to the goal of obtaining several theoretically meaningful factors or constructs" (Hair et al., 2014a: 114). I herefore used an oblique rotation approach. When selecting a specific oblique rotation method (i.e., "Oblimin" or "Promax"), "no specific rules have been developed to guide the researcher in selecting a particular orthogonal or oblique rotational technique" (Hair et al., 2014a: 114). I consequently decided to follow Weiber and Mühlhaus's suggestion to use the "Promax" rotation method (Weiber and Mühlhaus, 2010).

Interpretation of results. I assessed and interpreted the EFA's results by using the commonly accepted cut-off values for the items' measures of sampling adequacy (MSA), communalities, factor loadings, and the Kaiser criterion (see Table 17). The measure of sampling adequacy (MSA) determines the one-dimensionality of the factor by analyzing the intercorrelation of an item against that of the other items. This index varies from 0 to 1, where 1 is achieved if each variable is perfectly predicted, without error, by the other variables (Hair et al., 2014a). The following guideline has been widely accepted for interpretation of the MSA: > .80, meritorious; > .70 middling; > .60 mediocre; > .50, miserable; < .50 unacceptable (Kaiser, 1970; Kaiser and Rice, 1974). Thus, items with MSA values < .50 should be deleted (Hair et al., 2014a).

The communality indicates the extent of variance in the item that the underlying factor can explain. Items with a communality < .50 should be excluded in the determination of the underlying factors (Hair et al., 2014a; Weiber and Mühlhaus, 2010). In terms of factor loadings, Hair et al., 2014a argue that the cut-off value is dependent on the sample size. Given the sample size of N = 333, factor loadings of at least .35 are needed to be regarded as significant (Hair et al., 2014a). The Kaiser criterion can be used to determine the number of extracted factors. By using this criterion, a factor is extracted if its eigenvalue is greater than one, because eigenvalue > 1 indicates that a factor's explained variance is higher than the explained variance of any single item included in that factor (Weiber and Mühlhaus, 2010).

a) EFA results – domain knowledge

As outlined before, a key reason for conducting the EFA was to test if domain knowledge can be measured by combining the items of the consumer domain knowledge scale (Mitchell and Dacin, 1996) and the technical expertise scale (Franke, von Hippel, and Schreier, 2006). As shown in Table 18, the KMO measure (.949 > .50) and the Bartlett's test of sphericity confirm that the data can be used to conduct an EFA.

The initial results of the EFA indicate that there might be two distinct factors with Eigenvalues > 1. However, a closer investigation reveals four items (TE6, TE7, CDK4, and CDK6) that have communalities below the cut-off value of .50. Following suggestions in the literature, I decided to delete those items from further analysis (Hair et al., 2014a). After excluding the four critical items, the EFA shows a single-factor solution with a variance of 68.26 percent extracted. I thus concluded that the combination of the five remaining items from the technical expertise scale, and the five remaining items from the consumer domain knowledge scale, are valid to represent the respondents' domain knowledge as a first-order latent construct.

b) EFA results – lead userness

As shown in Table 19, the KMO measure (0.906 > 0.5) and the Bartlett's test of sphericity confirm that the data can be used to conduct an EFA. The results of the EFA indicate a one-factor solution with an Eigenvalues > 1. However, I deleted two items (HEB1 and HEB2) with communalities below the cut-off value of .50 to increase the validity of the construct. After excluding these critical items, the AVE increased from 60.8 percent to 71.4 percent.

c) EFA results – risk aversion

As shown in Table 20, the KMO measure (.722 > .50) and the Bartlett's test of sphericity confirm that the data can be used to conduct an EFA. The results of the EFA indicate that there are two distinct factors with Eigenvalues > 1. A closer investigation reveals three items (R2, R4, and R5) that have communalities below the cut-off value of .50, but I decided not to eliminate those items. The subsequent EFA, excluding items R2, R4, and R5, results in a single-factor solution. However, item R1 still falls below the cut-off values for communality and factor loading. I subsequently decided to exclude R1 as well. The final

EFA – including R3 and R6 – yields a one-factor solution in which both items show sufficient communality and factor loadings with an acceptable cumulative variance of 59.36 percent.

d) EFA across all selected items

In order to assess the discriminant validity between the constructs for domain knowledge, lead userness, and risk aversion, I conducted an EFA, including all the items of the final constructs. Table 21 shows the combined quality criteria for all selective items of the reflective constructs. Both the KMO measure (.956 > .50) and the Bartlett's test of sphericity confirm the appropriateness of the data for an EFA.

All the MSA scores, communalities, and factor loadings are well above their respective cut-off values. The EFA extracted two factors with Eigenvalues > 1 and a cumulative explained variance of 68.1 percent. Not surprisingly, all the items for domain knowledge (technical expertise items and consumer domain knowledge items) and lead userness (ahead of trend and high expected benefits) load on the same factor. This is in line with the initial intention to use the lead user construct as a backup construct if the measure of domain knowledge would fail to prove itself as a valid and reliable construct.

Since all the items of the domain knowledge construct and the lead user construct seemed to reflect the same underlying factor, it seemed appropriate to either use one of the two constructs in the further analysis, or to build a summated scale, including all the items from both constructs in one extended composite measure (Hair et al., 2014a). In undertaking the further analysis, I proceeded as originally intended by measuring domain knowledge by means of the items from the consumer domain knowledge scale and the items from the technical expertise scale. The lead user construct was thus excluded from further analysis.[54]

---

[54] It should be noted that the composite measure of domain knowledge and lead userness, as well as the lead userness construct by itself, could be used interchangeably in the further regression analysis. Testing these constructs yielded the same results.

Table 18: EFA results – domain knowledge

Domain knowledge before item deletion

		MSA	Communality	Pattern matrix	
Kaiser-Meyer-Olkin Measure of Sampling Adequacy				.949	
Significance of Bartlett's Test of Sphericity				.000	
				Factor 1	Factor 2
Items	Critical value	>.50	>.50	> .35	
TE1		.931	.845	.987	-.093
TE2		.950	.740	.249	.657
TE3		.937	.910	.924	.038
TE4		.932	.878	1.028	-.125
TE5		.957	.602	.091	.704
TE6		.962	.425	.357	.339
TE7		.958	.345	.253	.373
CDK1		.948	.628	.276	.563
CDK2		.958	.772	.279	.649
CDK3		.958	.686	.611	.264
CDK4		.942	.466	-.201	.821
CDK5		.962	.756	.702	.208
CDK6		.933	.151	.169	.245
CDK7		.950	.642	.010	.794
Initial Eigenvalue				8.411	1.048
Rotation sums of squared loadings				8.108	.739
Cumulative variance explained				63.191	

Domain knowledge after item deletion

		MSA	Communality	Factor 1
Kaiser-Meyer-Olkin Measure of Sampling Adequacy				.965
Significance of Bartlett's Test of Sphericity				.000
Items	Critical value	> .50	> .50	> .35
TE1		.929	.731	.855
TE2		.938	.704	.839
TE3		.928	.851	.923
TE4		.920	.737	.858
TE5		.963	.503	.709
CDK1		.936	.590	.768
CDK2		.945	.732	.856
CDK3		.954	.689	.830
CDK5		.970	.758	.871
CDK7		.943	.531	.728
Initial Eigenvalue				7.130
Rotation sums of squared loadings				6.826
Cumulative variance explained				68.264

Note: Extraction method: principal axis factoring; rotation method: promax with Kaiser-normalization.

Table 19: EFA results – lead userness

Lead Userness before item deletion				
Kaiser-Meyer-Olkin Measure of Sampling Adequacy			.906	
Significance of Bartlett's Test of Sphericity			.000	
	MSA	Communality	Factor 1	
Items Critical value	> .50	> .50	> .35	
AT1	.941	.634	.796	
AT2	.926	.658	.811	
AT3	.910	.756	.870	
AT4	.893	.743	.862	
HEB1	.931	.711	.843	
HEB2	.868	.489	.700	
HEB3	.836	.264	.514	
Initial Eigenvalue			4,608	
Rotation sums of squared loadings			4.255	
Cumulative variance explained			6.790	
Lead Userness after item deletion				
Kaiser-Meyer-Olkin Measure of Sampling Adequacy			.903	
Significance of Bartlett's Test of Sphericity			.000	
	MSA	Communality	Factor 1	
Items Critical value	> .50	> .50	> .35	
AT1	.927	.643	.802	
AT2	.914	.705	.840	
AT3	.885	.776	.881	
AT4	.875	.800	.894	
HEB1	.926	.647	.805	
Initial Eigenvalue			3,853	
Rotation sums of squared loadings			3.572	
Cumulative variance explained			71.434	

Note: Extraction method: principal axis factoring; rotation method: promax with Kaiser-normalization.

Table 20: EFA results – risk aversion

Risk aversion				
Kaiser-Meyer-Olkin Measure of Sampling Adequacy			.722	
Significance of Bartlett's Test of Sphericity			.000	
			Pattern matrix	
	MSA	Communality	Factor 1	Factor 2
Items Critical value	> .50	> .50	> .35	
R1	.734	.621	.836	-0,115
R2	.810	.296	.550	-0,012
R3	.619	.487	-.070	0,728
R4	.761	.317	.537	0,052
R5	.794	.375	.518	0,165
R6	.665	.748	.077	0,826
Initial Eigenvalue			2.622	1,169
Rotation sums of squared loadings			2.124	.720
Cumulative variance explained			47.415	
Risk aversion after 1st round of item deletion				
Kaiser-Meyer-Olkin Measure of Sampling Adequacy			.536	
Significance of Bartlett's Test of Sphericity			.000	
	MSA	Communality	Factor 1	
Items Critical value	> .50	> .50	> .35	
R1	.639	.080	.283	
R3	.527	.379	.615	
R6	.523	.920	.959	
Initial Eigenvalue			1.728	
Rotation sums of squared loadings			1.379	
Cumulative variance explained			45.965	
Risk aversion after 2nd round of item deletion				
Kaiser-Meyer-Olkin Measure of Sampling Adequacy			.500	
Significance of Bartlett's Test of Sphericity			.000	
	MSA	Communality	Factor 1	
Items Critical value	> .50	> .50	> .35	
R3	.500	.594	.770	
R6	.500	.594	.770	
Initial Eigenvalue			1.595	
Rotation sums of squared loadings			1.187	
Cumulative variance explained			59.364	

Note: Extraction method: principal axis factoring; rotation method: promax with Kaiser-normalization.

Table 21: EFA across all selected items

EFA across all selected items					
Kaiser-Meyer-Olkin Measure of Sampling Adequacy				.956	
Significance of Bartlett's Test of Sphericity				.000	
				Pattern matrix	
		MSA	Communality	Factor 1	Factor 2
Construct	Items	> .50	> .50	loading > .35	
	TE1	.949	.713	**.848**	-.036
	TE2	.968	.738	**.851**	.061
	TE3	.952	.839	**.920**	-.063
	TE4	.943	.735	**.861**	-.044
Domain	TE5	.977	.548	**.726**	.087
knowledge	CDK1	.951	.613	**.757**	.135
	CDK2	.967	.745	**.857**	.046
	CDK3	.966	.705	**.841**	-.017
	CDK5	.982	.772	**.882**	-.046
	CDK7	.960	.615	**.756**	.144
	AT1	.963	.716	**.810**	.174
	AT2	.976	.756	**.873**	-.140
Lead userness	AT3	.953	.693	**.837**	-.074
	AT4	.967	.750	**.868**	-.030
	HEB1	.985	.686	**.832**	-.130
Risk aversion	R3	.515	.748	-.031	**.868**
	R6	.558	.798	.033	**.889**
Initial Eigenvalue				10,514	1.656
Rotation sums of squared loadings				1.510	1.795
Cumulative variance explained				71.595	

Note: Extraction method: principal axis factoring; rotation method: promax with Kaiser-normalization.

4.3.2.1.2   Assessing construct and indicator reliability

After having established the one-dimensionality of the domain knowledge and risk aversion constructs to be used in the further analysis, the final constructs needed to be checked for sufficient reliability before they could be used for data analysis purposes. I checked the constructs' reliability by taking into account Cronbach's alpha, inter-item-correlation (IIC), and the corrected item-to-total-correlation (CITC) as suggested by the established literature (Weiber and Mühlhaus, 2010).

Cronbach's alpha reflects the average correlation between all the items for a specific construct and thus measures the degree of communality between items (Cronbach, 1951). A well-accepted cut-off value for Cronbach's alpha is .70; levels higher than .70 therefore suggest an acceptable level of reliability (Nunally and Bernstein, 1994; Peterson, 1994). The inter-item-correlation calculates the average correlation between items and should at least be .30 (Robinson, Shaver, and Wrightsman, 1991). The corrected item-to-total correlation refers to the correlation of each single item to the construct (Nunally and Bernstein, 1994) and measures the correlation of an indicator to the sum of all other indicators by means of its theoretical construct (Weiber and Mühlhaus, 2010). Thus, a high item-to-total correlation supports high convergent validity (Hair et al., 2014a). If a construct does not achieve the required Cronbach's alpha threshold, items with a CITC below .50 should be removed from the construct (Zaichkowsky, 1985). As shown in Table 22, the reflective constructs for domain knowledge and risk aversion, and their respective items, all exceed the relevant thresholds.

Table 22: First generation reliability assessment of constructs

Construct	Items	Criterion Critical value	Cronbach's alpha > .70	IIC > .30	CITC > .50
Domain knowledge	TE1		.954	.678	.838
	TE2				.817
	TE3				.903
	TE4				.842
	TE5				.692
	CDK1				.748
	CDK2				.832
	CDK3				.809
	CDK5				.851
	CDK7				.707
Risk aversion	R3		.764	.595	.595
	R6				.595

4.3.2.2 Second-generation methods

Conducting the EFA has led to the elimination of several items in order to increase the validity of the underlying constructs (see previous section). In addition, I conducted a first discriminant validity and reliability check of the final constructs by using established first-generation methods. However, research scholars have detected several weaknesses with regard to the first-generation methods and criteria. The restrictive assumptions underlying these approaches led to most of the criticism. There has also been criticism of the threshold values for the assessment of reliability and validity being based on rules of thumb, rather than on statistic inferences (Gerbing and Anderson, 1988).

The literature has developed second-generation methods and criteria based on confirmatory factor analysis (CFA) in order to overcome these shortcomings. Consequently, I used these second-generation methods to assess the reflective constructs with their remaining items in respect of their indicator reliability, internal consistency reliability, convergent validity, and discriminant validity (Hair, Ringle, and Sarstedt, 2011; Hair et al., 2012). The second-generation methods can only by carried out with the help of structural equation models (Weiber and Mühlhaus, 2010). I followed established examples in the literature and used a PLS-based structural equation model for this purpose (Wellner, 2014; Schweisfurth, 2012). The results of the second-generation methods are explained in the following paragraphs.

4.3.2.2.1 Indicator reliability

The indicator reliability shows the extent of the item's variance that can be explained by the variance of the underlying latent variable (MacKenzie, Podsakoff, and Podsakoff, 2011). It is assessed by checking each item's absolute standardized loading and significance (Hair et al., 2012). Acceptable values for these loadings should exceed .70 (Hair et al., 2014b). Despite this cut-off value, only items with loadings lower than .40 should be rigorously eliminated. If item loadings range between .40 – .70, the decision should be made on a case-by-case basis (Hair, Ringle, and Sarstedt, 2011).

In addition to the absolute standardized loadings, I checked the significance of each item for the underlying latent variable. As depicted in Table 23, all the remaining items load on their respective latent variables with loadings well above the suggested cut-off value. These loadings are significant at, at least, a 5 percent-level of significance.

4.3.2.2.2 Internal consistency reliability

The internal consistency reliability describes whether or not all items of a construct measure the same aspect. Thus, it refers to the average correlation among the items (Nunally and Bernstein, 1994). The internal consistency reliability has already been assessed with first-generation methods, such as Cronbach's alpha (see section 4.3.2.1.2). However, Cronbach's alpha has been criticized, because it assumes that all items have equal reliabilities. This assumption results in an inability to provide a differentiated assessment of individual items and their respective measurement errors' reliability (Gerbing and

Anderson, 1988). Using Dillon-Goldstein's rho for the evaluation of the internal consistency reliability can mitigate this problem, because Dillon-Goldstein's rho, also known as composite reliability, does not assume equal reliability in respect of all items (Hair, Ringle, and Sarstedt, 2011). Thus, this method is superior to Cronbach's alpha when assessing internal consistency (Chin, 1998a; Hair et al., 2012). For the assessment of the items, I used the suggested cut-value for Dillon-Goldstein's rho of .7 (Hair, Ringle, and Sarstedt, 2011). Table 23 shows that all constructs meet this requirement.

4.3.2.2.3 Convergent validity

The convergent validity shows to what extent the items converge on their theoretical construct (Campbell and Fiske, 1959). The average variance extracted (AVE), which measures how much of the item's variance the underlying theoretical construct explains, can be examined to assess this matter. A construct is suggested to show a sufficient convergent validity if it explains at least 50 percent of the item's variance, i.e., the AVE must be higher than .50 (Fornell and Larcker, 1981; Hair, Ringle, and Sarstedt, 2011). Table 23 shows that all the constructs exceed this threshold.

Table 23: Indicator reliability, internal consistency reliability and convergence validity of measurement model

		Indicator reliability		Internal consistency reliability	Convergence validity
	Criterion	Standardized outer item loadings λ	T-value	Dillon-Goldstein's ρ	Average variance extracted (AVE)
	Critical values	$\lambda \geq .70$	$\geq 1.96; p < .05$ $\geq 2.58; p < .01$ $\geq 3.29; p < .001$	$\rho \geq .70$	$AVE \geq .50$
Construct	Items				
Domain knowledge	TE1	.870	67.324	.961	.713
	TE2	.855	51.526		
	TE3	.922	123.595		
	TE4	.872	67.048		
	TE5	.742	29.790		
	CDK1	.798	3.772		
	CDK2	.871	57.782		
	CDK3	.850	4.180		
	CDK5	.884	67.946		
	CDK7	.762	29.644		
Risk	R3	.835	5.095	.879	.785
	R6	.939	7.399		

Note: Bootstrapping conducted with 333 cases and 5.000 samples.

4.3.2.2.4 Discriminant validity

Discriminant validity evaluates whether or not the relationship between selected items, and their respective theoretically derived construct is higher than those of any other latent construct used in the study (Campbell and Fiske, 1959). First, I applied the Fornell/Larcker criterion to assess the discriminant validity (Hair, Ringle, and Sarstedt, 2011). According to the Fornell-Larcker criterion, discriminant validity is given if the correlations between constructs is lower than the square root of each construct's AVE (Fornell and Larcker, 1981). Table 24 shows that the criterion is met in all the cases. The lowest square root of AVE is .888, while the highest construct correlation is .128.

In addition, I examined the cross-loadings at the item level to determine discriminant validity. Sufficient discriminant validity is given when all items load highest on their respective theoretically derived constructs (Chin, 1998b). Table 25 shows that this requirement is fulfilled for all the constructs.

Table 24: Correlations and discriminant validity

	DK	Risk
DK	**.844**	
Risk	.128	**.888**

Note: Bold numbers represent the squared root of the AVE.

Table 25: Cross-loadings

	DK	Risk
CDK1	**.798**	.168
CDK2	**.871**	.115
CDK3	**.850**	.092
CDK5	**.884**	.072
CDK7	**.762**	.164
TE1	**.870**	.090
TE2	**.855**	.120
TE3	**.922**	.069
TE4	**.872**	.091
TE5	**.742**	.127
R3	.084	**.835**
R6	.135	**.939**

4.3.2.3 Summary of reliability and validity tests

This study's constructs are all taken from the literature. However, the specific research setting required me to adapt most of the constructs' items to the 3D printing domain. Consequently, the validity and reliability could no longer be taken for granted and I thus employed first-generation and second-generation methods to ensure the validity and reliability of the constructs (see Table 17). During this assessment, I adhered to suggestions in the literature and therefore excluded some items from the constructs in order to increase the validity and the reliability (Hair et al., 2014a; Weiber and Mühlhaus, 2010). After the items' deletion, all the constructs exceed all the recommended thresholds. Consequently, I assumed that the reflective constructs to measure participants' domain knowledge and risk aversion can be considered valid and reliable when conducting the further analysis.

4.3.3 Common method bias test

The use of a single method of data collection based on self-reported, cross-sectional data is argued to potentially cause a bias due to a shared covariance among the variables (Podsakoff, 1986). The choice of study design and statistical procedures can help control for common-method bias (Podsakoff et al., 2003).

I tried to avoid a potential common method bias by including several mitigating steps in the study's design. First, the survey was pre-tested to ensure that clear language is used and to thus minimize item ambiguity and problems of interpretation. Second, I decided to use only measurement scales from published research studies, as the use of concrete constructs mitigates common variance (Malhotra, Kim, and Patil, 2006). Third, I guaranteed all the participants complete anonymity to reduce a potential tendency to give socially desirable answers (Podsakoff et al., 2003). Fourth, I constructed the study's design in such a way that the idea innovativeness variable is based on the judgment of nine independent experts who did not participate in the survey. All the other variables stemmed from the responses of the 333 survey participants. Consequently, a common method bias between the moderator variable, idea innovativeness, and the other independent, dependent, and control variables, is logically impossible.

In addition to these preventive countermeasures, I used statistical remedies to further control for a potential common method bias. I calculated Harman's single-factor test by applying a factor analysis without rotation to check for the fit of a single-factor model (Podsakoff et al., 2003; Malhotra, Kim, and Patil, 2006). The test revealed more than one factor, with all the factors showing a cumulative variance extracted of well below the threshold of 50 percent (39.58 percent). Of those, the largest factor provided an explanation for only 12.67 percent. Furthermore, I checked the correlations between the constructs. Bivariate correlations above .90 can be interpreted as an indicator of a common method bias (Pavlou, Liang, and Xue, 2007). The highest value in my data is .688. Based on these two tests, I assumed that a potential common method bias is of no concern for the data analysis.

5 Empirical findings

The objective of this chapter is to present the study's empirical findings. The chapter begins with a descriptive analysis of the data gathered in the survey and a first interpretation of the proposed hypotheses (section 5.1). Subsequently, multiple regression modeling is introduced as the method of choice to statistically test the proposed hypotheses (section 5.2).

5.1 Descriptive analysis

The following sections aim to provide a descriptive analysis of the key results based on the response in the online survey. The section starts with an overview of the sample characteristics in terms of demographics and professional experience (section 5.1.1). In the next section, I provide a detailed examination of the participants' domain knowledge in the field of 3D printing as the key variable in the context of this study (section 5.1.2). I subsequently present my first insights into the influence of domain knowledge on idea evaluation outcomes, based on a descriptive analysis of the evaluation results (section 5.1.3). A short discussion of the correlations between the study's most relevant variables (section 5.1.4) precedes the last section, which closes with a summary of the descriptive results and their indicative implications with regard to the proposed hypotheses (section 5.1.5).

5.1.1 Sample analysis – demographics and professional experience

Of the 333 participants in the final sample (see Table 16 in chapter 4.3.1), the average survey participant is 35.87 years old (SD 12.20) and predominantly male (82 percent). About 50 percent of the participants are native English speakers from either the United States or the United Kingdom. Most of the participants (74 percent) received a higher form of education, i.e., hold at least a Bachelor's degree. A more detailed breakdown of the demographic data by participant group is provided in Table 26.

Table 26: Sample descriptives – demographics

		3D printing professionals		Community members		NPD professionals		Laymen		Total	
	Sample size	27		156		35		115		333	
Age	Mean	39.93		34.08		42.71		34.78		35.87	
	SD	11.49		13.13		10.54		11.20		12.20	
Gender	Male	23	85%	151	97%	28	80%	72	63%	274	82%
	Female	4	15%	5	3%	7	20%	43	37%	59	18%
Nationality	Germany	22	81%	32	21%	17	49%	14	12%	85	26%
	USA/UK	1	4%	78	50%	10	29%	75	65%	164	49%
	Other	4	15%	46	29%	8	23%	26	23%	84	25%
University degree		26	96%	102	65%	33	94%	84	73%	245	74%

Note: University degree = bachelor's degree or higher.

Several participants stated that they have relevant professional experience (> 5 years) in the fields of research and development (n = 74), marketing (n = 39), or sales (n = 41). This corresponds to 22 percent of the participants having worked at least five years in R&D and 12 percent of the participants having worked at least five years in marketing and/or sales. Furthermore, seven percent of the participants (n = 24) are employed in a top-level management position. Not surprisingly, the share of participants with long-lasting professional experience was highest in the 3D printing professional group and lowest in the laymen group. Table 27 provides a breakdown of professional experience by sample group.

Table 27: Sample descriptives – professional experience

	3D printing professionals		Community members		NPD professionals		Laymen		Total	
Sample size	27		156		35		115		333	
R&D experience > 5 years	17	63%	35	22%	19	54%	3	3%	74	22%
Marketing experience > 5 years	7	26%	16	10%	12	34%	4	3%	39	12%
Sales experience > 5 years	7	26%	19	12%	6	17%	9	8%	41	12%
Top management position	2	7%	10	6%	8	23%	4	3%	24	7%

Note: Top management = top-level management responsibility in current employment.

5.1.2 Sample analysis – domain knowledge

In the context of this study, it is important to understand the participants' characteristics with regard to their levels of domain knowledge. It is also important to ensure that the participants in the overall sample do indeed represent various levels of domain knowledge, in order to investigate the influence of domain knowledge on the evaluation behavior.

The domain knowledge histogram shows that domain knowledge seems to be roughly normally distributed across the sample (Figure 19). The distribution has a slight negative skew of -.297 and is flatter than a perfect normal distribution, with a negative kurtosis of -1.161. This indicates that the sample might include participants who are more knowledgeable about the 3D printing domain than the general population. Nonetheless, the purposive sampling procedure that I had chosen for sample recruitment achieved its purpose by including individuals with low, moderate, and high level domain knowledge (see chapter 4.2.4.2).

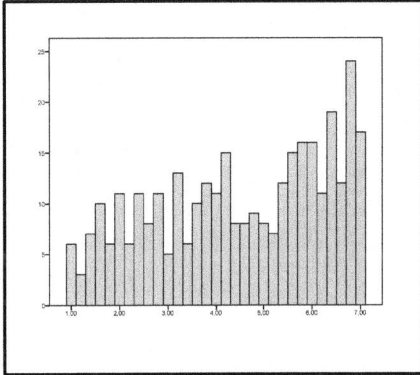

Figure 19: Domain knowledge histogram for the overall sample[55]

In assessing how domain knowledge is distributed between the various sources of recruitment, substantial differences are observed (Table 28). Community members mentioned the highest level of domain knowledge (mean = 5.87; SD = 1.06), followed by 3D printing professionals (mean = 4.81; SD = 1.06). On average, most of the NPD professionals mentioned having moderate knowledge of the 3D printing domain (mean = 3.72; SD = 1.29),

---

[55] Illustration generated with IBM SPSS statistics 23.

whereas most laymen stated that they had limited or no knowledge at all (mean = 2.73; SD = 1.05).

Table 28: Sample descriptives – domain knowledge indicators

		3D printing professionals	Community members	NPD professionals	Laymen	Total
	Sample size	27	156	35	115	333
Domain knowledge	Mean	4.81	5.87	3.72	2.73	4.47
	SD	1.06	1.01	1.29	1.05	1.78
Need knowledge	Mean	5.23	5.90	4.31	3.11	4.72
	SD	1.22	5.84	1.49	1.28	1.72
Solution knowledge	Mean	4.40	5.84	3.12	2.34	4.22
	SD	1.14	1.13	1.24	1.01	1.95
Lead userness	Mean	4.92	5.15	3.76	2.54	4.08
	SD	0.91	1.16	1.30	1.19	1.66

Note: All constructs measured on a 7-point Likert scale (strongly disagree / strongly agree).

A detailed analysis of the self-stated responses reflecting the participants' need knowledge (see Figure 20) and solution knowledge (see Figure 21) – representing the two major constituents of domain knowledge defined in the context of this study (see chapter 3.5.1) – provides further insight into the root causes of the differences in these groups' levels of domain knowledge.

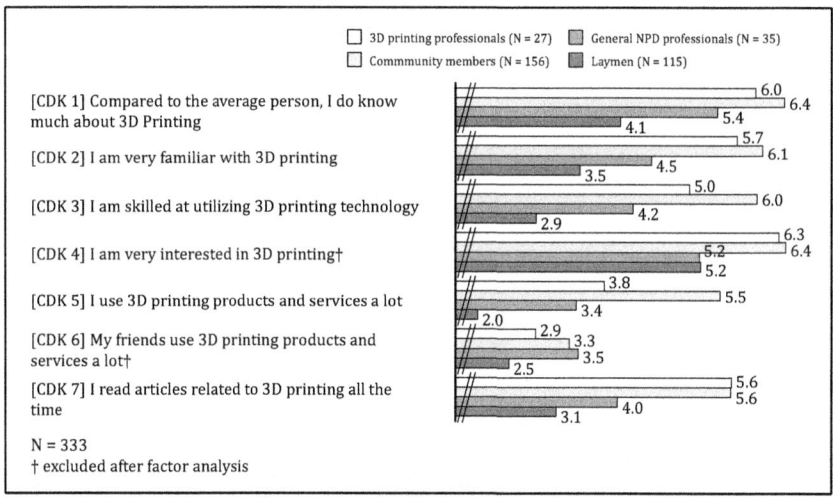

Figure 20: Need knowledge comparison by participant-group[56]

All the participants seemed to be generally interested in 3D printing [CDK 4], but the 3D printing professionals and community members specifically reported very high levels of interest. They also stated that they actively try to stay informed by means of frequently reading 3D-printing-related articles [CDK 7]. The actual usage of 3D printing products accounts for an even bigger difference between the participant groups. Community members seem to use 3D printing products and services substantially more often than participants in the other groups [CDK 5], and reported being more skilled in utilizing 3D printing technologies [CDK 3]. This combination of information seeking behavior and actual usage may also explain why 3D printing professionals and community members seem to be substantially more familiar with 3D printing products in general [CDK 2]. On average, community members have higher reported need knowledge than 3D printing professionals, which is in line with the established literature. Research scholars have argued that users typically possess more need knowledge than industry professionals do (Poetz and Schreier, 2012; Magnusson, 2009).

---

56 Author's illustration.

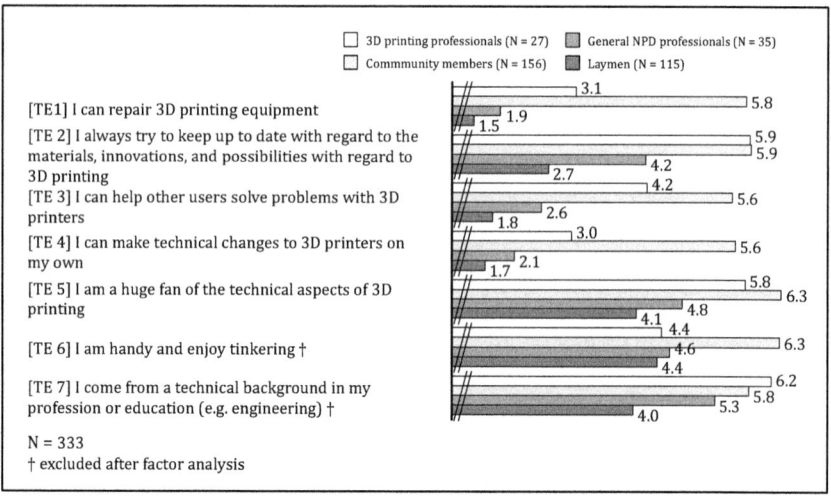

Figure 21: Solution knowledge comparison by participant-group[57]

The level of differences in knowledge between the groups seems to be even more severe in respect of the reported solution knowledge. The community members reported the highest level of solution knowledge by far, even higher than those of the 3D printing professionals. This difference seems to be rooted in community members' abilities to make technical changes to 3D printing equipment on their own [TE 4], to help other users to solve problems with 3D printers [TE 3], and to repair 3D printers [TE 1]. Furthermore, a very high proportion of community members appear to have a technical background due to their professions [TE7]. Not surprisingly, the responses of NPD professionals and laymen show that these groups do not possess any substantial solution knowledge in the domain of 3D printing.

Whereas most domains have largely assumed that producers are predominantly the ones with solution knowledge (Poetz and Schreier, 2012; Magnusson, 2009), the distribution of solution knowledge in this study seems to deviate from this pattern. However, taking the sources of recruitment that I have used in my study into account, this is understandable. The online communities that I have targeted for recruitment are forums where users

---

exchange ideas on how to modify, enhance, and repair 3D printing equipment. Research has shown that, in markets in which users rely on technical equipment to practice their hobbies, they are also likely to develop high level domain-specific solution knowledge (Schreier and Prügl, 2008). The 3D printing community members are likely to regularly and actively seek out modifications to and technical improvements of their 3D printing equipment, whereas 3D printing industry professionals are likely to focus on their specific areas of functional expertise in the domain. Therefore, it seems plausible to me that the 3D printing community members might have developed more solution knowledge than the industry professionals.

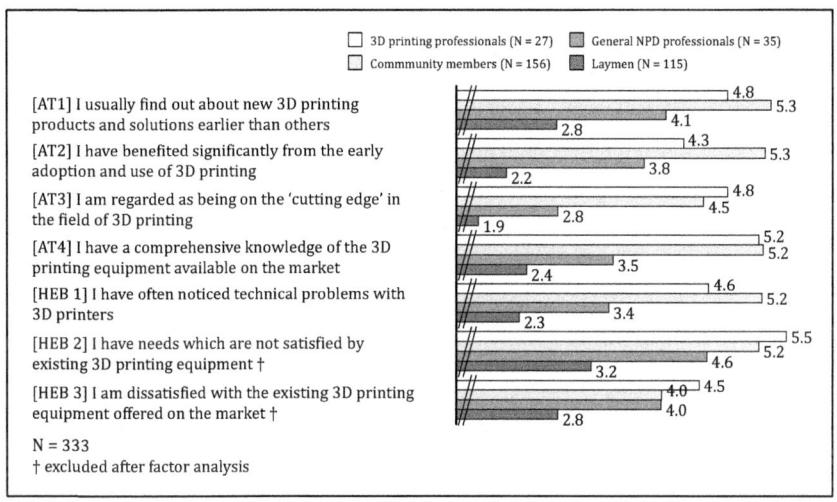

Figure 22: Lead userness comparison by participant-group[58]

Taking into consideration the definition of domain knowledge in the context of this study (see chapter 3.5.1), the participants' degree of reported lead userness may also be an indicator of their level of domain knowledge. As has been described and empirically shown in the literature, lead users usually possess high-level need knowledge and solution knowledge (von Hippel, 1986; Faullant et al., 2012). The responses to the various questions

---

posed on an individual's degree of lead userness, largely confirm the findings with regard to domain knowledge. Community members stated the highest level of lead userness (mean = 5.15; SD = 1.16), followed by the 3D printing professionals (mean = 4.92; SD = .91). As expected, general NPD professionals are placed third (mean = 3.76; SD = 1.30), and laymen placed last in terms of their reported lead userness (mean = 2.54; SD = 1.19).

To summarize, as intended by the study's research setting, the sample includes individuals who differ strongly in terms of their 3D printing domain knowledge. The participants' reported domain knowledge ranges from almost none (predominantly within the laymen group) to very high levels of domain knowledge (mostly within the community members and 3D printing professionals groups). On average, community members reported having the highest domain knowledge, which is mainly due to their higher solution knowledge.

Therefore, the overall sample achieves the study's imperative requirement of investigating individuals with different levels of domain knowledge. Thus, the sample gathered seems to be highly suitable for the intended research purpose of uncovering the role of domain knowledge in new product idea evaluation.

Furthermore, the core of this study to endeavoring to understand how individuals with different levels of domain knowledge evaluate new product ideas that are more incremental or more radical by nature (see chapter 2.1.1). Thus, for the purpose of further descriptive analysis, I decided to divide the overall sample into four groups according to the participants' level of domain knowledge. I followed the established approach of grouping the sample with cut-off values at +1 SD and -1 SD from the mean (Aiken and West, 1991). This division yields four groups with the groups' average domain knowledge ranging from none to low (group 1; DK (mean) = 1.85; SD = .48), to very high domain knowledge (group 4: DK (mean) = 6.65; SD = .24). A detailed breakdown of the four groups is provided in Table 29.

Table 29: Domain knowledge groups for descriptive analysis

		Group 1: "none to low DK" [DK >-1 SD]	Group 2: "low to moderate" [DK <-1 SD]	Group 3: "moderate to high DK" [DK <+1 SD]	Group 4: "very high DK" [DK >+1 SD]	Total
	Sample size	68	91	102	72	333
Domain knowledge	Mean	1.85	3.60	5.46	6.65	4.47
	SD	.48	.52	.49	.24	1.78
Need knowledge	Mean	2.12	4.10	5.66	6.62	4.72
	SD	.72	.52	.65	.35	1.72
Solution knowledge	Mean	1.58	3.11	5.26	6.68	4.22
	SD	.50	.72	.73	.31	1.95
Lead userness	Mean	1.86	3.42	4.88	5.89	4.08
	SD	.84	1.01	.82	.72	1.66

Note: All constructs measured on a 7-point Likert scale.

5.1.3 Evaluation outcomes analysis

In chapter 3, I proposed several hypotheses on how domain knowledge may influence idea evaluation outcomes in a holistic and a criteria-based evaluation task. According to these hypotheses, domain knowledge influences the overall impression of new product ideas, as well as the perceived originality, user value, and feasibility (see chapter 3.6.1). Furthermore, I suggested that an idea's degree of innovativeness may moderate this influence. Finally, these two effects (direct and interaction) are likely to be mediated by means of the individual's ability to understand the new product idea. Consequently, in the following descriptive analysis of the evaluation outcomes, I present the evaluation scores of the seven different new product ideas' evaluation scores in the dimensions overall impression, originality, user value, feasibility, and comprehension by comparing the average results of the domain knowledge groups (see Table 30). This comparison is aimed at deriving the first indicative insights into how domain knowledge influences idea evaluation behavior.

Table 30: Average idea evaluation scores by domain knowledge groups

Average ratings across ideas		Group 1: "none to low DK" [DK >-1 SD]	Group 2: "low to moderate" [DK <-1 SD]	Group 3: "moderate to high DK" [DK <+1 SD]	Group 4: "very high DK" [DK >+1 SD]	Total
	Sample size	476	637	714	504	2331
Overall impression	Mean	5.04	5.27	5.26	5.17	5.20
	SD	1.49	1.49	1.55	1.63	1.54
Originality	Mean	5.10	4.99	4.41	4.17	4.66
	SD	1.32	1.48	1.48	1.96	1.69
User value	Mean	4.89	5.01	5.00	4.90	4.96
	SD	1.56	1.48	1.57	1.69	1.57
Feasibility	Mean	4.25	4.60	4.72	5.01	4.65
	SD	1.52	1.47	1.57	1.57	1.58
Comprehension	Mean	4.55	5.03	5.37	5.65	5.17
	SD	1.72	1.44	1.37	1.38	1.52

Note: All constructs are measured on a 7-point Likert scale.

According to Figure 23, groups with lower, rather than higher domain knowledge perceive new product ideas' originality very differently. As expected, individuals with higher domain knowledge have, on average, given the new product ideas lower ratings than those given by individuals with lower domain knowledge. Furthermore, when comparing the ratings that the groups allocated to the more incremental rather than the more radical new product ideas, individuals with none to low DK (group 1) seem to perceive all ideas to be somewhat original, irrespective of the ideas' degree of innovativeness. In contrast, individuals with moderate to high DK (group 3), as well as with very high DK (group 4), seem to clearly differentiate between more incremental and more radical new product ideas by assigning substantially higher originality scores to the more radical new product ideas.

Thus, the descriptive results support the proposition that evaluators generally become more conservative in their originality ratings as their domain knowledge increases. Furthermore, as proposed, the descriptive analysis indicates that this effect seems to diminish in respect of more radical new product ideas.

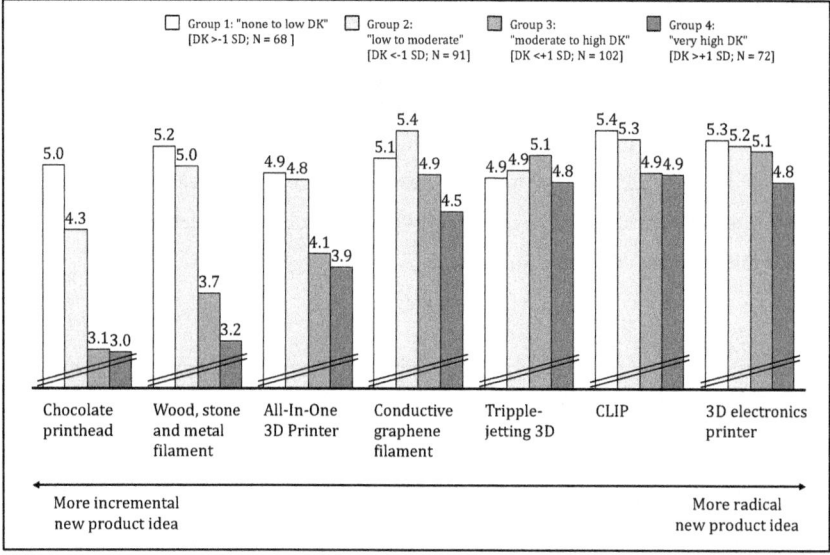

Figure 23: Idea evaluation outcomes – originality[59]

Based on the descriptive results presented Figure 24, it is difficult to identify a clear difference between the groups with regard to their average user value evaluations. Across all ideas, group 2 and group 3 on average evaluated the ideas with a score of about 5.0, whereas group 1 and group 4 on average assigned a score of about ~ 4.9 to the new product ideas (see Table 30). Thus, the results show no general tendency towards higher or lower user value assessments. However, by taking the ideas' degree of innovativeness into account, the groups with lower domain knowledge (group 1 and 2) assigned higher user value scores to the more incremental ideas, and lower scores to the more radical ideas than the scores given by the groups with higher domain knowledge. For example, the more incremental idea, an "all-in-one 3D printer," scored an average of 5.6 in group 1 and 5.7 in group 2, compared to 5.1 in group 3 and 4.8 in group 4. A similar pattern is observed in respect of the other more incremental ideas, such as the "chocolate printhead" and the "wood, stone, and metal filament." Interestingly, this pattern is reversed in respect of the more radical product ideas. For example, group 1 assigned "CLIP" an average user value

---

59 Author's illustration.

score of 3.8, and group 2 scored it 4.5, whereas groups 3 and 4 assigned a score of about 4.7 to this idea.

These findings support the proposition that domain knowledge may have a negative effect on the perception of incremental new product ideas. However, the effect of domain knowledge on more radical new product ideas seems to be positive. Nonetheless, the descriptive data do not support the proposed effect that evaluators generally become more critical at higher levels of domain knowledge.

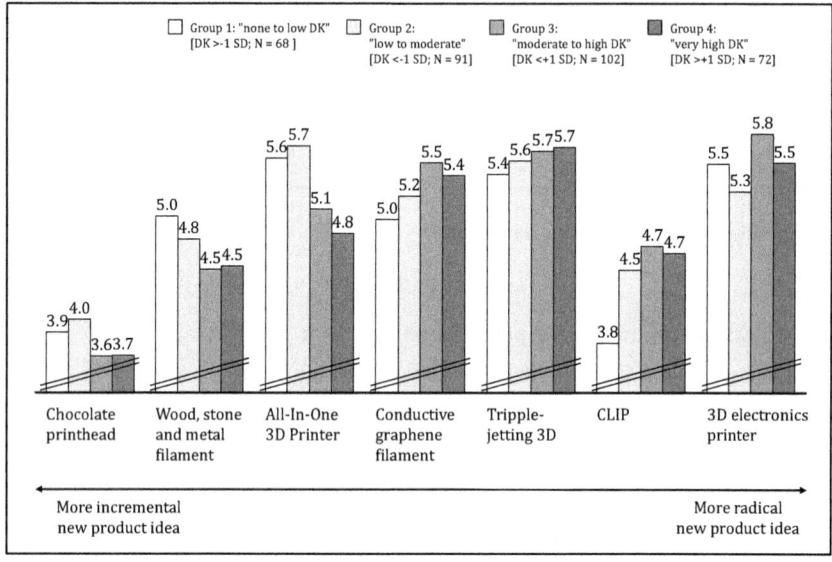

Figure 24: Idea evaluation outcomes – user value[60]

Figure 25 shows that individuals with higher domain knowledge (group 3 and group 4) have generally perceived new product ideas to be more feasible compared to the perceptions of their counterparts with lower domain knowledge (group 1 and group 2). Furthermore, the more positive perception of feasibility seems to be higher for the more incremental ideas and seems to decrease when ideas' innovativeness increases. This

---

[60] Author's illustration.

observation supports the proposed relationship between domain knowledge and perceived feasibility. First, domain knowledge seems to have a positive influence on perceived feasibility and, second, this positive influence is likely to decrease in respect of more innovative new product ideas.

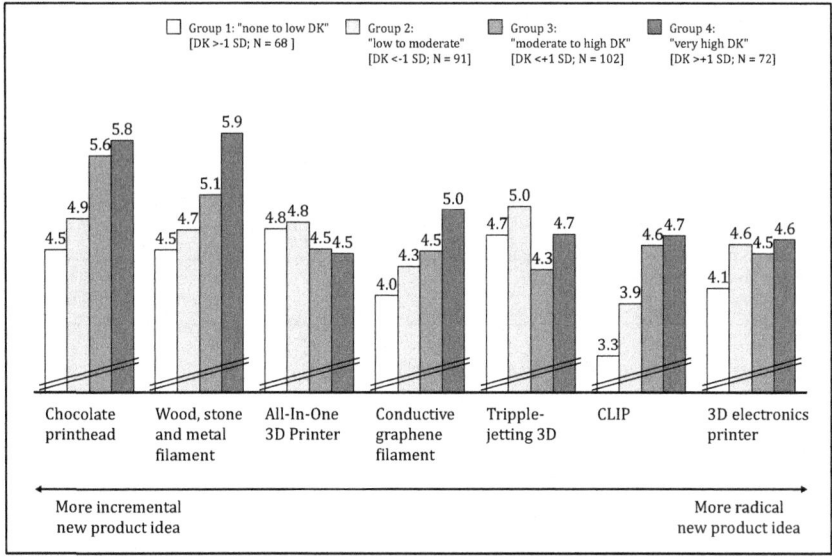

Figure 25: Idea evaluation outcomes – feasibility[61]

Figure 26 reveals that the groups' different evaluation patterns of overall impression are somewhat similar to the evaluation pattern of user value. Whereas the scores of the groups do not seem to reflect a general tendency towards higher or lower assessments between the groups, there are differences with regard to their perceptions of more incremental and more radical new product ideas. Individuals with higher domain knowledge (group 3 and 4) assigned higher ratings to more radical ideas and lower ratings to the more incremental ideas, compared to the ratings of individuals with lower domain knowledge (group 1 and 2).

---

[61] Author's illustration.

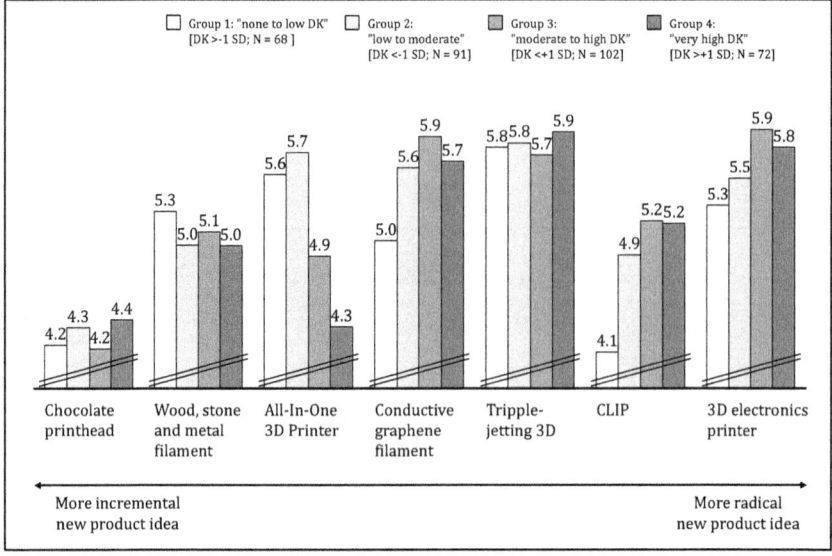

Figure 26 Idea evaluation outcomes – overall impression[62]

According to Figure 27, the descriptive results reveal that domain knowledge has a very clear effect on comprehension. First, individuals with higher domain knowledge (group 3 and 4) showed higher comprehension across all ideas on average than individuals with lower domain knowledge (group 1 and 2). Second, group 4 reported the highest comprehension, followed by group 3 and group 2. Group 1 reported the lowest comprehension. Third, the more radical new product ideas show larger differences in comprehension than those of the more incremental new product ideas.

In summary, the descriptive results support the proposition that domain knowledge increases comprehension and that this effect is even stronger in respect of more radical new product ideas.

---

62 Author's illustration.

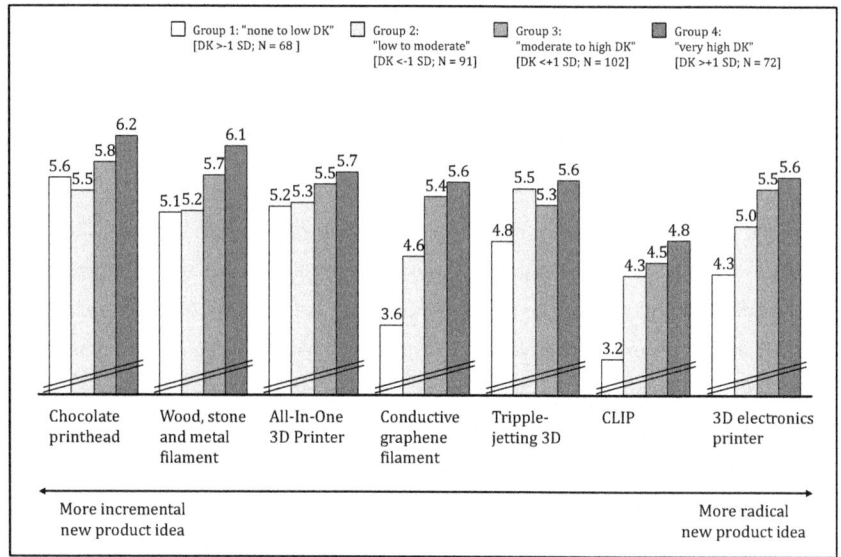

Figure 27: Idea evaluation outcomes – comprehension[63]

5.1.4 Correlation analysis

The correlations yield several indicative insights into the relationships between the variables. First, the correlations between domain knowledge and the independent variables support the findings of the descriptive analysis. Domain knowledge is significantly negatively correlated with perceived originality and significantly positively correlated with perceived feasibility. There is no significant correlation for the dependent variables' perceived user value and perceived overall impression.

Second, domain knowledge is significantly positively correlated with comprehension and, in turn, comprehension is significantly positively correlated with all four independent variables. This provides a first indication that comprehension might mediate the effects of domain knowledge (see sections 5.2.3.3 and 5.2.3.4).

Third, as expected, idea innovativeness is significantly positively correlated with perceived originality, user value, and overall impression. It is also significantly negatively correlated

---

[63] Author's illustration.

with perceived feasibility and perceived comprehension. Based on the definition of innovativeness, these results were anticipated. More radical ideas should, in general, be perceived as more original and having a higher user value, while, simultaneously, individuals should perceive them as less feasible and more difficult to understand (see chapter 2.1.1).

Fourth, the correlation analysis reveals a significant correlation between the four dependent variables (perceived originality, user value, feasibility, and overall impression). This is in line with findings in prior studies (Kudrowitz and Wallace, 2013). For example, as outlined above, a more innovative idea is expected to usually being perceived as more original, while at the same time being perceived as being less feasible. Furthermore, in line with prior research on intuitive decision making, the correlations between the overall impression and the criteria of originality, user value, and feasibility indicate that individuals are likely to intuitively take these three criteria into account when evaluating new product ideas in holistic judgments (Magnusson, Netz, and Wästlund, 2014).

Finally, the correlations between the control variables and the dependent variables show that almost every control variable (except native English speaker) is significantly correlated with at least one of the dependent variables. This indicates that controlling for these effects is beneficial.

Table 31: Descriptives and correlations between the study's variables

	Variables	Mean	SD	1	2	3	4	5	6	7	8	9	10	11	12	13	14	15
1	Age	35,710	12,374	1,000														
2	Native speaker	,520	,500	,126 **	1,000													
3	University degree	,740	,441	,173 **	-,290 **	1,000												
4	R&D tenure > 5 years	,220	,416	,441 **	-,108 **	,189 **	1,000											
5	Marketing tenure > 5 years	,120	,322	,327 **	-,005	,112 **	,344 **	1,000										
6	Sales tenure > 5 years	,120	,329	,301 **	,049 *	,079 **	,261 **	,688 **	1,000									
7	Top-level management	,070	,259	,131 **	,012	,141 **	,186 **	,224 **	,108 **	1,000								
8	Risk aversion	4,050	1,343	,033	,024	,070 **	,239 **	,070 **	,037	,055 **	1,000							
9	Idea innovativeness	2,833	,562	,000	,000	,000	,000	,000	,000	,000	,000	1,000						
10	Domain knowledge	4,473	1,773	-,102 **	-,083 **	-,064 **	,200 **	,051 *	,052 *	,023	,122 **	,000	1,000					
11	Perceived originality	4,660	1,695	-,056 **	-,001	-,054 **	-,151 **	-,081 **	-,091 **	-,010	-,135 **	,263 **	-,208 **	1,000				
12	Perceived use value	4,960	1,570	-,042 *	,003	-,016	-,064 **	-,032	-,015	-,062 **	-,024	,249 **	,016	,396 **	1,000			
13	Perceived feasibility	4,650	1,581	-,049 *	,011	,048 *	-,044 *	,002	,025	-,040	-,020	-,199 **	,159 **	-,132 **	,217 **	1,000		
14	Perceived overall impression	5,200	1,545	-,072 **	-,001	,060 **	-,085 **	-,054 **	-,036	-,082 **	-,022	,206 **	,032	,346 **	,601 **	,240 **	1,000	
15	Comprehension	5,170	1,519	-,049 *	-,015	-,007	,065 **	,009	,020	-,005	,054 **	-,218 **	,262 **	-,078 **	,293 **	,522 **	,221 **	1,000

Note: n = 2.331; * p ≤ ,05; ** p ≤ ,01; *** p < ,001

5.1.5 Summary of descriptive analysis

The descriptive analysis of the evaluation outcomes indicates support for the proposed hypotheses (see Table 32). However, multivariate data analysis techniques have to be employed to test whether, or not, the influence of domain knowledge on perceived originality, user value, feasibility, overall impression, and comprehension can also be considered statistically significant when controlling for other possible effects (Hair et al., 2014a).

Table 32: Support of hypotheses based on the descriptive analysis

Hypotheses	Indicative support*
Direct effects of domain knowledge	
H1: Domain knowledge has a negative effect on the perceived originality of early-stage new product ideas.	Yes
H2: Domain knowledge has a negative effect on the perceived user value of early-stage new product ideas.	No
H3: Domain knowledge has a positive effect on the perceived feasibility of early-stage new product ideas.	Yes
H4: Domain knowledge has a negative effect on the overall impression of early-stage new product ideas.	No
Interaction effects between domain knowledge and idea's innovativeness	
H5: Idea innovativeness diminishes the negative effect of domain knowledge on the perceived originality of early-stage new product ideas.	Yes
H6: Idea innovativeness diminishes the negative effect of domain knowledge on the perceived user value of early-stage new product ideas.	Yes
H7: Idea innovativeness diminishes the positive effect of domain knowledge on the perceived feasibility of early-stage new product ideas.	Yes
H8: Idea innovativeness diminishes the negative effect of domain knowledge on the overall impression of early-stage new product ideas.	No
Moderated mediation effects	
H9: Domain knowledge has a positive effect on perceived comprehension of early-stage new product ideas.	Yes
H10: Idea innovativeness strengthens the positive effect of domain knowledge on perceived comprehension of early-stage new product ideas.	Yes
H11-18 are not observable through descriptive analysis	

*The indicative support represents a first observation based on the descriptive analysis. The final validation or falsification of hypotheses is undertaken through multiple regression analysis

5.2 Multiple regression analysis

The goal of this section is to test the hypotheses with regard to the effects of domain knowledge on idea evaluation outcomes as proposed in the context of this study (see chapter 3.6). I statistically tested the influence of the independent variables (domain knowledge and control variables), the moderating variable (idea innovativeness), and the mediating variable (comprehension) on the four dependent variables (originality, user value, feasibility, and overall impression). Multiple linear regression analysis with ordinary least squares (OLS) estimation was used to test the hypotheses, because I designed the survey to measure all central variables on interval scales and the hypotheses propose a linear relationship between the variables (Hair et al., 2014a; Backhaus et al., 2011; Aiken and West, 1991; Cohen et al., 2003). The hypotheses related to the four dependent variables (DVs) were tested in four separate models, each representing one DV (model A – originality, model B – user value, model C – feasibility, and model D – overall impression).

5.2.1 Data set

Following a purposive sampling procedure, I invited different participant groups (3D printing professionals, 3D printing community members, NPD professionals, and laymen; for details see chapter 4.2.4.2) to participate in the survey. I based this sampling procedure on the assumption that the individuals within these groups would display different levels of domain knowledge in the field of 3D printing (Magnusson, Wästlund, and Netz, 2016; Poetz and Schreier, 2012). In the survey, each participant was asked to evaluate seven new product ideas in a two-step process. First, the participants stated their overall impression, followed by an assessment of the ideas' originality, user value, and feasibility (for more details on the sequence of the survey see chapter 4.2.1).

This approach resulted in a final data set with 333 participants, each evaluating seven ideas by means of the four dimensions. Each individual participant's rating of an idea's criterion thus yields a value for a dependent variable. Following an established approach (Girotra, Terwiesch, and Ulrich, 2010), I based the regression analysis on the data in its long form. Therefore, the data set used for analysis includes 333 (# participants) times seven observations (# ideas), resulting in N = 2.331 observations for each DV. Table 33 exemplifies the structure of the data set.

Table 33: Exemplary structure of the final data set

Partici-pant	Idea	Domain know-ledge	Idea inno-vative-ness	Com-prehen-sion	Origin-ality	User value	Feasi-bility	Overall impres-sion	N
#1	#1	4.6	3.1	6	6	6	4	6	1
#1	#2	4.6	2.1	5	6	6	4	5	2
#1	#3	4.6	2.0	3	5	5	4	3	3
#1	#4	4.6	2.9	4	6	6	4	4	4
#1	#5	4.6	3.6	5	6	6	6	5	5
#1	#6	4.6	2.8	6	6	6	6	6	6
#1	#7	4.6	3.4	5	5	3	5	5	7
...	...	...	...	...	...	...	...	...	...
#333	#1	3.2	3.1	5	4	6	6	6	2325
#333	#2	3.2	2.1	5	4	6	6	5	2326
#333	#3	3.2	2.0	3	5	5	5	3	2327
#333	#4	3.2	2.9	3	6	7	7	6	2328
#333	#5	3.2	3.6	6	4	6	6	7	2329
#333	#6	3.2	2.8	3	6	6	6	6	2330
#333	#7	3.2	3.4	1	6	5	5	4	2331

Note: N = 2.331, 333 participants with seven evaluations each; example values are taken from the original data set

In such a data set it is highly likely that a single evaluator's evaluation scores for the seven new product ideas may not be independent. In terms of regression analysis, this could lead to the violation of an underlying assumption – the independence of the error terms. Consequently, I thoroughly checked whether or not the results were subjected to such an effect, which was shown not to be the case (see section 5.2.2.4).

5.2.2 Test of underlying assumptions

The standard works on multivariate analysis demand testing the underlying assumption of an OLS regression analysis to prevent potential inaccuracies occurring in the results. These inaccuracies may include (i) inappropriate tests of significance and/or biased and (ii) inaccurate predictions of the dependent variable. Thus, there are important assumptions that need to be met to conduct a meaningful regression analysis. These assumptions include: normality, homoscedasticity, linearity, and the independence of error terms (Hair et al., 2014a; Backhaus et al., 2011). In addition to these assumptions, there are two issues that – while not OLS regression assumptions – can be of great concern for the analysis and should be checked as well: (i) the absence of multicollinearity, i.e., predictors that are highly linearly related and (ii) the absence of unusual and influential data (Hair et al., 2014a).

Consequently, in order to prevent possible inaccuracies in my analysis, I applied established methods from the literature to test my data before conducting the regression analysis.

5.2.2.1 Normality

Multivariate data analysis generally requires the independent and dependent variables in the model to be normally distributed. A violation of this assumption can affect the level of significance and/or power (Hair et al., 2014a). A graphical inspection of the variables' data distribution (e.g. normal probability plots) can check the normality of the variables. This can be done by exploring the data distributions' skewness and kurtosis and/or by applying two commonly used tests that check for normality – the Kolmogorov-Smirnov test and the Shapiro-Wilk test.

Assessing the data distributions' skewness and kurtosis, and the results of the statistical tests, reveals that all variables have a statistically significant deviation from the normality assumption (see Table 34). However, the deviations are rather small, with the highest skewness being -.749 and the highest kurtosis being -1.209. Furthermore, research scholars have argued that, in respect of OLS regression, it is only the normality of residuals, rather than the normality of variables, that is important to derive meaningful results (Cohen et al., 2003). Consequently, I checked whether the residuals of the four regression models met the assumption with regard to normality.

Table 34: Normality tests for key variables

	Skewness		Kurtosis		Test of normality		
	Statistic	z value*	Statistic	z value*	KS-test	SW-test	Description of the distribution
Independent variable							
Domain knowledge	-.294	-5.765	-1.161	-11.495	.000	.000	Flatter, negative skew
Moderator variable							
Innovativeness	-.337	-6.608	-1.209	-11.970	.000	.000	Flatter, negative skew
Mediator variable							
Comprehension	-.698	-13.686	-.183	-1.812	.000	.000	Flatter, negative skew
Dependent variables							
Originality	-.476	-9.333	-.607	-6.010	.000	.000	Flatter, negative skew
User value	-.560	-10.980	-.425	-4.208	.000	.000	Flatter, negative skew
Feasibility	-.327	-6.412	-.639	-6.327	.000	.000	Flatter, negative skew
Overall impression	-.749	-14.686	-.155	-1.535	.000	.000	Flatter, negative skew
Control variables**							
Age	.555	10.882	-.527	-5.218	.000	.000	Flatter, positive skew
Risk aversion	.030	.588	-.669	-6.624	.000	.000	Flatter

Notes: N = 2.331;

* The z values are derived by deviding the statistics by the appropriate standard errors of .051 (skewness) and .101 (kurtosis);

Significance levels are +/- 1.96 (p = 0.05) and +/- 2.58 (p = 0.01). (Hair et al. 2014a)

** Nominal control variables (R&D tenure, sales tenure, top management position, university degree and native speaker) excluded from analysis

Table 35: Normality tests for the error term distributions

	Skewness		Kurtosis		Test of normality		Description of the distribution
	Statistic	z value*	Statistic	z value*	KS-test	SW-test	
Studentized Residuals (Model A - originality)	-.294	-5.765	-.440	-4.356	.000	.000	Flatter, negative skew
Studentized Residuals (Model B - use value)	-.597	-11.706	.126	2.471	.000	.000	Steeper, negative skew
Studentized Residuals (Model C- feasibility)	-.666	-13.059	.416	8.157	.000	.000	Steeper, negative skew
Studentized Residuals (Model D - overall impression)	-.797	-15.627	.403	7.902	.000	.000	Steeper, negative skew

Notes: N = 2.331;

* The z values are derived by deviding the statistics by the appropriate standard errors of .051 (skewness) and .101 (kurtosis);

Significance levels are +/- 1.96 (p = 0.05) and +/- 2.58 (p = 0.01). (Hair et al. 2014a)

Table 36: Normal probability plots of error term distributions

	Regression models			
	Model A - Originality	Model B - User value	Model C - Feasibility	Model D - Overall impression
Normal P-P Plots				

Like the analysis of the variables, the assessment of the residuals' skewness and kurtosis, as well as the statistical tests, indicates that the residuals are not normally distributed (see Table 35). However, according to the visual inspection of the normal probability plots, this deviation seems to be minor (see Table 36). In addition to the visual inspection, several arguments support the conclusion that the deviation from normality, as found in my data, does not need to be a major concern in respect of further data analysis.

First, research scholars have pointed out that the KS-Test and SW-Test are overly conservative and especially sensitive to large sample sizes (Huang, Yeo, and Li, 2007). Since my sample size (N = 2.331) is quite large, it is not surprising that these tests indicate a significant deviation from normality.

Second, although the exploration of the data distribution has indicated that the distribution is, in almost all cases, flatter, with a negative skew, the values for the skewness and kurtosis are rather small. According to commonly accepted best practices, values of -2 to +2 for skewness and kurtosis can be ignored when assessing the normality of data distributions (George and Mallery, 2012).

Third, research scholars have advised on the rule of thumb that, in general, normality is only relevant for small sample sizes. For sample sizes > 200 non-normality does not constitute a problem (Hair et al., 2014a). Given that the regression models are calculated with N = 2.331, this threshold is exceeded by more than factor ten.

Based on this argumentation, I assumed that the slight deviations from normality did not pose a problem regarding the correct estimation of the coefficients or the significance tests in the four models.

5.2.2.2 Homoscedasticity

Heteroscedasticity (the presence of unequal variances of the error terms) is one of the most common assumption violations in OLS regressions. A violation of this assumption can produce significance tests and confidence intervals that are too liberal or too conservative (Hayes and Cai, 2007). There are two common statistical tests to check whether or not heteroscedasticity is present: (i) White's test of general heteroscedasticity (White, 1980) and (ii) the Breusch-Pagan test (Breusch and Pagan, 1979). As shown in Table 37, both statistical tests rejected the null-hypothesis in all four models and the alternative hypothesis – that the variance is not homogenous – must therefore be accepted.

However, these tests are very sensitive to deviations from normality as they appear in the four models (see section 5.2.2.1). According to the literature, it is accepted common practice to combine statistical tests with a visual inspection of the diagnostic plots to judge whether or not the severity of heteroscedasticity calls for correction. These diagnostic plots are created by plotting the predicted dependent value by means of the residuals and comparing them to the null plot. If the residuals show a consistent pattern, the variance is not constant. Common patterns that indicate heteroscedasticity are triangle-shaped or diamond-shaped (Hair et al., 2014a). The visual inspection of the scatterplots provided in Table 37 does not display any of these consistent patterns.

Table 37: Analysis of homoscedasticity assumption

	Model A - Originality	Model B - User value	Model C - Feasibility	Model D - Overall impression
Scatter-plot (standardized predicted value/ residuals)				
White-Test	Prob. > chi² = .000	Prob. > chi² = .000	Prob. > chi² = .000	Prob. > chi² = .000
Breusch-Pagan-Test	Prob. > chi² = .000	Prob. > chi² = .000	Prob.> chi² = .000	Prob. > chi² = .000

Furthermore, I ensured that heteroscedasticity has no significant influence on the models by employing heteroscedasticity-consistent standard error (HCSE) estimators of OLS parameter estimates (White, 1980) as a robustness check. This alternative method of estimating the standard errors does not assume homoscedasticity. Following the suggestion of Hayes and Cai (2007), I applied HC3 and HC4 estimators to all four models to double-check the results of the OLS regression against the results obtained with the HC estimators. With this approach, I was able to ensure that heteroscedasticity did not compromise my results. The models based on the HC3 and HC4 estimators show that neither the coefficient nor the significance levels change recognizably (see appendix D). I therefore assumed that heteroscedasticity does not pose a problem in my models.

5.2.2.3 Linearity

One of the most basic assumptions of linear regression is that the relationship between the dependent variable and the independent variables is linear. A violation of this assumption leads to a regression model that tries to fit a straight line to data that simply does not fit a straight line. Linearity can be assessed by analyzing the residuals (testing the overall variate) and the partial regression plots of each independent variable in the model (UCLA: Statistical Consulting Group, 2016). Considering that each of the four models includes 12 different independent variables, this analysis required a total of 52 plots. A visual inspection of the plots reveals no nonlinear patterns, not in respect of the independent variables, nor regarding the residuals.[64] I thus assumed that my models meet the assumption of linearity.

5.2.2.4 Independence of error terms

Another assumption of regression analysis is that the observations need to be independent. The predicted value is thus not related to any other prediction. Violations of this assumption can lead to biased standard errors and thus influence the significance tests. Possible violations of this assumptions are most likely to occur in time series, but also in clustered data (Hair et al., 2014a; UCLA: Statistical Consulting Group, 2016). Given that I collected several observations (one for each idea) from the same participants, it is possible that the errors are not independent (see section 5.2.1).

To detect potential violations of this assumption, I followed suggestions in the literature and applied the Durbin-Watson test to all four models (Durbin and Watson, 1950)[65]. This test can achieve values between 0 and 4. The literature suggests that values between 1.5 and 2.5 indicate that the assumption is not violated (Hair et al., 2014a). Applying the test to the four models yields values from 1.871 to 1.999, indicating that independence of error terms is not a severe problem.

Table 38: Durbin-Watson Tests

	Regression models			
	Model A – Originality	Model B – User value	Model C – Feasibility	Model D – Overall impression
Durbin-Watson Test	d = 1.999	d = 1.841	d = 1.977	d = 1.871

In addition to this statistical test, Hair et al. (2014a) suggest that plotting the residuals against any possible sequencing variable will best identify possible violations of the assumption. If the residuals are independent, the resulting pattern should appear random and similar to the null plot. As my data are clustered in participants, I thus decided to plot the residuals against the individual participants as a possible sequencing variable. A visual

---

[64] Owing to limited space, these plots are not included in the dissertation. However, the plots can be provided by the author on request.

[65] Although the Durbin-Watson test is mainly designed for detecting autocorrelation errors in time-series data (Hair et al. (2014a)), it might also help identify a violation of the independence of error terms in clustered data (Backhaus et al. (2011)).

inspection of the scatterplots does not reveal consistent patterns in the residuals (see Table 39). Consequently, I assume that the assumption of the independence of the error terms has not been violated.

However, since tests that rely on visual inspection may be misleading, I conducted further robustness checks and calculated cluster-robust regression models (Colin Cameron and Miller, 2015), as well as random effect regression models (Hedeker and Gibbons, 1994). These robustness checks show that the levels of significance do not change recognizably in comparison to the original OLS (see appendix D).

I thus concluded that a possible violation of the independence of the error terms in my data does not influence the results of the OLS regression.

Table 39: Analysis of independence of error terms

	Model A – Originality	Model B – User value	Model C – Feasibility	Model D - Overall impression
Scatterplot (participant/ residuals)	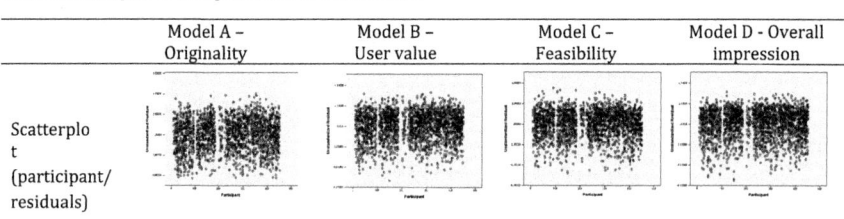			

5.2.2.5 Multicollinearity

Multicollinearity describes a phenomenon in which two or more independent variables in a multiple regression model are highly correlated. This phenomenon can lead – in cases of strong correlation – to inefficient estimates and thus needs to be considered when estimating multiple regression models. If multicollinearity is present, the coefficient estimates of the multiple regressions may change erratically in response to small changes in the model or the data, thus affecting calculations regarding individual independent variables. The estimate of one independent variable's impact on the dependent variable, while controlling for the others, therefore tends to be less precise than if the variables were uncorrelated (Backhaus et al., 2011). I checked for commonly known indicators to detect possible multicollinearity issues in the multiple regression model (Hair et al., 2014a). First,

I investigated the correlation matrix of the independent variables. Correlations around +0.9/-0.9 indicate severe multicollinearity.

The highest correlation is between the nominal variables, marketing tenure and sale tenure, with a correlation of .688. I therefore assumed that multicollinearity was highly unlikely (see Table 31: p. 135). Nonetheless, I calculated the tolerance and variance inflation factor (VIF) as measures that quantify multicollinearity's severity. Multicollinearity becomes problematic with tolerance values below 0.1 or VIFs above 10 (Hair et al., 2014a; UCLA: Statistical Consulting Group, 2016). All the variables are far from these critical values, with a minimum tolerance of .478 and a maximum VIF of 2.093 (see Table 40). All the variables are below even the more restrictive VIF threshold value of 5 (Hair et al., 2014a).

In the light of these results, I conclude that multicollinearity is not an issue in the proposed multiple regression models.

Table 40: Analysis of multicollinearity

Variables	Tolerance	VIF
Age	.684	1.461
University degree	.848	1.179
Native English speaker	.842	1.188
Risk aversion	.644	1.553
R&D tenure > 5 years	.478	2.093
Marketing tenure > 5 years	.514	1.944
Sales tenure > 5 years	.918	1.089
Top management position	.923	1.083
Innovativeness	.844	1.185
Domain knowledge	.949	1.054
Interaction (Inno. x DK)*	.997	1.003
Comprehension	.879	1.138

Note: * Mean-centered product term.

5.2.2.6   Unusual and influential data

Unusual and influential data are observations that are substantially different from all other observations and thus have a disproportionate effect on the regression results. Consequently, should such observations occur, they require further investigation. According to Hair et al. (2014a), there are three ways to classify data as unusual: (i) outliers (observations with large residual values), (ii) leverage points (observations with an extreme value on the predictor variable), and (iii) influential observations (all observations that have a disproportionate effect on the regression results).

Although unusual and influential data are difficult to identify, there are several established procedures that can help spot suspicious data. I followed suggestions in the literature and investigated Cook's D as an overall measure of outliers and leverage points. I applied the conventional cut-off point of 4/n (UCLA: Statistical Consulting Group, 2016). Based on this cut-off value, several influential data points can be observed throughout models A-D. Plotting the squared residuals against their leverage also allows these influential data points to be visualized (see Table 41). The visual inspection of the scatter plots supports the findings by showing several observations with high residuals, high leverage, or a combination of both, in the models.

Table 41: Analysis of unusual and influential data

	Model A – Originality	Model B – User value	Model C – Feasibility	Model D - Overall impression
Scatter-plot (residuals²/ leverage)				

I ran all the models without the critical values in order to assess the influential observations' influence on models A-D. Although deleting these observations from the sample increases the R-square, I retained the influential observations in all the models for three reasons. First, retaining the outliers in the models does not change the significance of the proposed main effects. Second, different influential observations can be identified between models A-D. Consequently, by deleting model-specific observations, the samples for the models would differ, complicating further data analysis. Third, since most variables are measured on the basis of anonymous participants' responses, it is very hard to distinguish between (i) valid, but exceptional, observations that can be explained by means of an ordinary situation, (ii) exceptional observations with no likely explanation, and (iii) whether or not the observations may be ordinary in their individual characteristics, but exceptional in their combinations of characteristics. Whereas the first two reasons call for a deletion of observations, the latter requires the researcher to retain them (Hair et al., 2014a). Consequently, in the context of my study, deleting these outliers would have been an arbitrary act with the purpose of enhancing the models' outcomes. I therefore decided not to follow this method.

5.2.2.7 Interim summary

The extensive examination of the OLS regressions' underlying assumptions revealed minor assumption violations. The normality assumption does not pose a problem due to the large sample size (Hair et al., 2014a). Furthermore, double-checking the results of the OLS regression by means of the results obtained with heteroscedasticity-consistent estimators confirmed that the slight heteroscedasticity that the statistical tests detected did not pose a problem for my models.

Table 42: Overview of assumptions' analysis

Assumption/issues	Guideline/test	Violation	Remedy
Normality	Shapiro-Wilk-Test	Yes	Sample size > 200
	Visual inspection	Yes	
Homoscedasticity	White-Test	Yes	Employing heteroscedasticity-consistent standard error (HCSE)
	Breusch-Pagan-Test	Yes	estimators
	Visual inspection	No	
Linearity	Visual inspection	No	
Independence of error terms	Durbin-Watson-Test	No	
	Visual inspection	No	
Multicollinearity	Correlations > 0.9	No	
	VIF > 5	No	
Unusual/influential data	Cook's D > 4/n	Yes	Robust regression
	Visual inspection	Yes	

Note: The violations apply similarly to all four models

Nonetheless, a potential problem remains with respect to influential observations. Cook's D and a visual inspection of the data reveal that the data include several observations that are worrying. As it is very difficult to decide whether or not these observations are legitimate, I followed a conservative approach and kept all the influential observations in the data set.

To conclude, although I found minor violations with regard to the assumptions, none of these violations is severe enough to have a substantial and significant influence on the outcome of the data analysis. Furthermore, I conducted several robustness checks, which confirmed the validity and reliability of the results (see appendix D)[66]. The robustness of the OLS results is not surprising. The literature states that "the large number of restrictive assumptions of the OLS regression may appear to limit its applicability – but this is not the case. The OLS regression is quite insensitive to minor violations of the assumptions"[67] (Backhaus et al., 2011). Consequently, I proceeded with the original data set – including 333 participants and 2.331 observations – and applied the hypotheses tests based on multiple OLS regression analyses.

5.2.3 Results

Investigating all the hypotheses in my research framework (chapter 3.6.1, Figure 14) required a set of four independent regression models, one for each dependent variable (Model A-D). To test my hypotheses, I followed the same analytic procedure for all four regression analyses and conducted hierarchical multiple regression modeling (Aiken and West, 1991; Cohen et al., 2003). I first set up baseline models that only included the control variables (models A-D (1)). Subsequently, I introduced the independent variable domain knowledge into the models (models A-D (2)), followed by the product term of the mean-centered domain knowledge and innovativeness variables as an interaction effect (models A-D (3)). Lastly, I included the comprehension variable to test potential mediation effects

---

[66] To support this conclusion, I performed several robustness checks, including (i) regression employing heteroscedasticity-consistent standard error (HCSE) estimators to control for potential violations of homoscedasticity and normality; (ii) random effect regression, and (iii) cluster regression to control for potential violations of the independence of error terms. The latter two checks control for the data on 2,331 observations stemming from 333 participants. It is thus possible that the seven different evaluation scores from an individual participant are not independent. Neither of the robustness checks indicates any substantial change with regard to the coefficients or significance tests (see appendix D).

[67] Translated from English by the author.

(models A-D (4)). This procedure allowed me to clearly distinguish the hypothesized total effects, moderation effects, and mediation effects.

The results of the regression analysis are presented in Table 43, Table 44, Table 45, and Table 46. The review presented in the following sections starts with the direct effects of domain knowledge on the perceived originality, user value, feasibility, and overall impression (section 5.2.3.1). This is followed by the interaction effects between domain knowledge and idea innovativeness (section 5.2.3.2), and the mediation effect of comprehension (section 5.2.3.3). Subsequently, I applied conditional process analysis (Hayes, 2013) to investigate all the effects jointly in a moderated mediation model (section 5.2.3.4).

Table 43: Regression results – Model A (originality)

| | Model A (originality) | | | | | | | |
| | Model A-1 | | Model A-2 | | Model A-3 | | Model A-4 | |
	B	Sig.	B	Sig.	B	Sig.	B	Sig.
Constant	3.083	.000 ***	4.048	.000 ***	4.048	.000 ***	3.830	.000 ***
Age	.003	.284	-.002	.488	-.002	.481	-.002	.519
Native English speaker	-.073	.309	-.113	.112	-.113	.106	-.115	.100
University degree	-.127	.119	-.205	.011 **	-.205	.010 **	-.207	.009 **
R&D tenure > 5 years	-.498	.000 ***	-.283	.004 **	-.283	.003 **	-.287	.003 **
Marketing tenure > 5 years	.005	.971	-.004	.979	-.004	.979	-.001	.993
Sales tenure > 5 years	-.321	.023 *	-.263	.057	-.263	.053	-.267	.050 *
Top-level management	.172	.199	.181	.170	.181	.163	.184	.156
Risk aversion	-.130	.000 ***	-.113	.000 ***	-.113	.000 ***	-.114	.000 ***
Idea innovativeness	.793	.000 ***	.793	.000 ***	.793	.000 ***	.815	.000 ***
H1: Domain knowledge			-.181	.000 ***	-.181	.000 ***	-.189	.000 ***
H5:Interaction (Inno. x DK)					.283	.000 ***	.280	.000 ***
H11: Comprehension							.037	.102
R²	.107		.139		.167		.168	
Adjusted R²	.104		.135		.163		.164	
Adj. R² change			.031		.028		.001	
F-statistic	30.911	.000 ***	37.520	.000 ***	42.223	.000 ***	38.956	.000 ***
F change			86.724	.000 ***	76.968	.000 ***	2.683	.102

Note: Hierarchical regression models. (1) controls (2) + independent variable, (3) + interaction effect; (4) + mediation effect (full moderated mediation model); unstandardized regression coefficients reported; * p < .05; ** p <.01; *** p < .001; n = 2.331 (333 respondents with seven idea evaluations each)

Table 44: Regression results – Model B (user value)

| | Model B (user value) | | | | | | | |
| | Model B-1 | | Model B-2 | | Model B-3 | | Model B-4 | |
	B	Sig.	B	Sig.	B	Sig.	B	Sig.
Constant	3.149	.000 ***	3.012	.000 ***	3.012	.000 ***	.667	.008 ***
Age	-.002	.486	-.001	.671	-.001	.670	.001	.792
Native English speaker	.003	.968	.008	.903	.008	.903	-.013	.833
University degree	.011	.883	.022	.774	.022	.773	-.001	.994
R&D tenure > 5 years	-.176	.055	-.206	.028 *	-.206	.028 *	-.250	.004 **
Marketing tenure > 5 years	-.037	.792	-.036	.799	-.036	.798	-.008	.954
Sales tenure > 5 years	.063	.635	.055	.679	.055	.678	.017	.893
Top-level management	-.309	.015 *	-.311	.014 *	-.311	.014 *	-.279	.017 *
Risk aversion	-.011	.655	-.013	.588	-.013	.586	-.021	.356
Idea innovativeness	.697	.000 ***	.697	.000 ***	.697	.000 ***	.932	.000 ***
H2: Domain knowledge			.026	.171	.026	.169	-.060	.001 **
H6: Interaction (Inno. x DK)					.143	.000 ***	.113	.000 ***
H12: Comprehension							.398	.000 ***
R^2	.069		.070		.078		.208	
Adjusted R^2	.066		.066		.074		.204	
Adj. R^2 change			.000		.008		.130	
F-statistic	19.190	.000 ***	17.466	.000 ***	17.905	.000 ***	50.876	.000 ***
F change			1.877	.171	20.804	.000 ***	381.260	.000 ***

Note: Hierarchical regression models. (1) controls (2) + independent variable, (3) + interaction effect, (4) + mediation effect (full moderated mediation model); unstandardized regression coefficients reported; * p < .05; ** p <.01; *** p < .001; n = 2.331 (333 respondents with seven idea evaluations each)

Table 45: Regression results – Model C (feasibility)

| | Model C (feasibility) | | | | | | | |
| | Model C-1 | | Model C-2 | | Model C-3 | | Model C-4 | |
	B	Sig.	B	Sig.	B	Sig.	B	Sig.
Constant	6.584	.000 ***	5.754	.000 ***	5.754	.000 ***	2.673	.000 ***
Age	-.006	.065	-.001	.789	-.001	.788	.002	.487
Native English speaker	.007	.917	.041	.548	.041	.547	.013	.829
University degree	-.124	.116	-.057	.464	-.057	.462	-.087	.199
R&D tenure > 5 years	-.087	.349	-.273	.004 **	-.273	.004 **	-.330	.000 ***
Marketing tenure > 5 years	.004	.979	.012	.934	.012	.934	.049	.691
Sales tenure > 5 years	.244	.073	.194	.147	.194	.146	.144	.217
Top-level management	-.187	.149	-.194	.128	-.194	.127	-.152	.170
Risk aversion	-.013	.590	-.028	.258	-.028	.257	-.038	.078
Idea innovativeness	-.560	.000 ***	-.560	.000 ***	-.560	.000 ***	-.251	.000 ***
H3: Domain knowledge			.156	.000 ***	.156	.000 ***	.043	.011 *
H7: Interaction (Inno. x DK)					-.109	.001 **	-.150	.000 ***
H 13: Comprehension							.523	.000 ***
R^2	.047		.075		.079		.301	
Adjusted R^2	.043		.071		.075		.297	
Adj. R^2 change			.028		.004		.222	
F-statistic	12.765	.000 ***	18.684	.000 ***	11.967	.000 ***	83.026	.000 ***
F change			68.604	.000 ***	18.154	.001 **	733.546	.000 ***

Note: Hierarchical regression models. (1) controls (2) + independent variable, (3) + interaction effect, (4) + mediation effect (full moderated mediation model); unstandardized regression coefficients reported; * $p < .05$; ** $p < .01$; *** $p < .001$; n = 2.331 (333 respondents with seven idea evaluations each).

Table 46: Regression results – Model D (overall impression)

| | Model D (overall impression) | | | | | | | |
| | Model D-1 | | Model D-2 | | Model D-3 | | Model D-4 | |
	B	Sig.	B	Sig.	B	Sig.	B	Sig.
Constant	3.935	.000 ***	3.740	.000 ***	3.740	.000 ***	2.003	.000 ***
Age	-.004	.193	-.003	.366	-.003	.365	-.001	.673
Native English speaker	-.041	.543	-.033	.624	-.033	.623	-.049	.449
University degree	-.137	.074	-.121	.115	-.121	.114	-.138	.061
R&D tenure > 5 years	-.188	.038 *	-.231	.013 **	-.231	.013 **	-.264	.003 **
Marketing tenure > 5 years	-.059	.673	-.057	.683	-.057	.682	-.036	.787
Sales tenure > 5 years	.025	.849	.014	.919	.014	.918	-.015	.905
Top-level management	-.365	.004 **	-.366	.004 **	-.366	.003 **	-.343	.004 **
Risk aversion	-.002	.919	-.006	.809	-.006	.809	-.011	.622
Idea innovativeness	.568	.000 ***	.568	.000 ***	.568	.000 ***	.742	.000 ***
H4: Domain knowledge			.037	.048 *	.037	.048 *	-.027	.141
H8: Interaction (Inno. x DK)					.107	.001 **	.084	.005 **
H14: Comprehension							.295	.000 ***
R^2	.057		.059		.063		.137	
Adjusted R^2	.053		.055		.059		.133	
Adj. R^2 change			.002		.004		.074	
F-statistic	15.606	.000 ***	14.454	.000 ***	14.269	.000 ***	30.687	.000 ***
F change			3.908	.048 *	11.747	.001 **	197.957	.000 ***

Note: Hierarchical regression models. (1) controls (2) + independent variable, (3) + interaction effect, (4) + mediation effect (full moderated mediation model); unstandardized regression coefficients reported; * p < .05; ** p < .01; *** p < .001; n = 2.331 (333 respondents with seven idea evaluations each).

5.2.3.1 Testing for direct effects

In most cases, investigating a research question tries to answer the question: "Does variable X predict or cause variable Y?" (Frazier, Tix, and Barron, 2004). Researchers therefore try to establish a relationship between an independent and a dependent variable. This study focuses on establishing a relationship between domain knowledge and evaluation outcomes (i.e., perceived originality, user value, feasibility, and overall impression). To test these relationships, I applied several multiple regression analyses (models A-D). According to the findings of models A-2, B-2, C-2, and D-2, domain knowledge has a significant negative effect on the perceived originality (b = -.181; p < .001), and a significant positive effect on the perceived feasibility (b = .156; p < .001), as well as on overall impression (b = .037; p = .048). The proposed negative effect of domain knowledge on the perceived user value is not significant (b = .026; p = .171). Therefore, based on these results, H1 and H3 are supported, whereas H2 and H4 have to be rejected. Contrary to the proposed negative effect of domain knowledge on the overall impression (H4), the results show that domain knowledge has a positive effect on the overall impression.

However, it should be acknowledged that these effects just establish a general relationship between domain knowledge and the dependent variables based on the average of all the observations. They do not explain either "when" or "under which conditions," "how" or "why" domain knowledge influences evaluation outcomes. These questions are further investigated in the following moderation and mediation analyses.

5.2.3.2 Testing for moderation effects

Moderation analysis is concerned with the questions of "when" or "under which condition" a variable most strongly predicts or causes an outcome variable. Thus, a moderator is a variable that alters the strength or direction of the relationship between an independent variable and a dependent variable (Baron and Kenny, 1986). Therefore, moderation effects are no more than an interaction whereby the effect of one variable depends on the level of another (Frazier, Tix, and Barron, 2004). In the context of my study, I investigated whether or not the effect of domain knowledge depends on the level of idea innovativeness (H 5-8). If idea innovativeness is a significant moderator, the effect of domain knowledge will be different in respect of ideas with low, moderate, and high innovativeness.

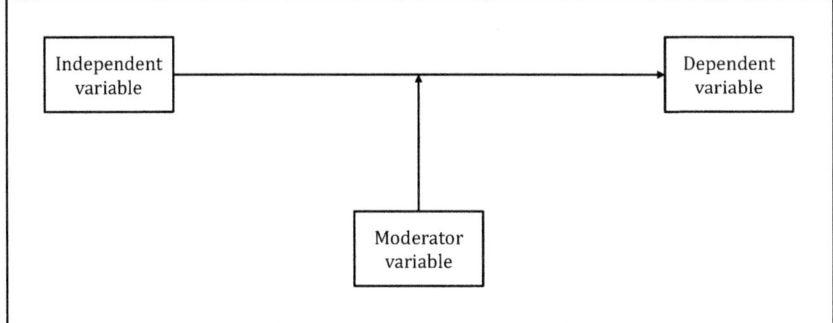

Figure 28: Moderation model diagram[68]

The literature suggests that multiple regression analysis is preferable to the analysis of variance (ANOVA) to test moderation effects. Furthermore, it has been suggested that variables measured on continuous scales should be retained in their continuous form and not artificially grouped by, for example, using median splits. The reason for this is that creating such artificial groupings results in a loss of information (Aiken and West, 1991; Cohen et al., 2003). Research studies have supported this conclusion by showing that hierarchical multiple regression procedures that retain the true nature of continuous variables are superior to those that use artificially grouped variables (Stone-Romero, Alliger, and Aguinis, 1994). Following these findings, I kept the moderator variable idea innovativeness in its continuous form and did not artificially group the ideas into groups of low innovativeness (e.g. incremental ideas) and high innovativeness (e.g. radical ideas).

To test the interaction effect, I adhered to the recommendations in the literature. First, I centered the variables domain knowledge and idea innovativeness in order to avoid multicollinearity problems.[69] Subsequently, I created the product term of the mean-centered variables, domain knowledge and idea innovativeness, to represent the moderator variable to be tested. After creating the moderator variables, I followed the procedure of hierarchical multiple regression analysis by entering the variables into the

---

[68] Author's illustration, based on Frazier, Tix, and Barron (2004: 116).
[69] I used mean-centered variables to build the product term. According to Aiken and West (1991), it makes no difference whether or not the variables are mean-centered or z-centered.

models in a series of steps (Aiken and West, 1991; Cohen et al., 2003). I first set up a baseline model only, which included the control variables (models A-D 1). Subsequently, I introduced the independent variable domain knowledge into the models (models A-D 2), followed by the product term of the mean-centered domain knowledge and innovativeness variables as interaction effects (models A-D 3). The results are presented in Table 43 (model A – originality), Table 44 (model B – user value), Table 45 (model C – feasibility), and Table 46 (model D – overall impression).

The models A-D (3) show that adding the interaction effect as a product term of mean-centered domain knowledge and mean-centered idea innovativeness to the model, leads to a significant change in the explained variance (adj. R^2) in all four models. In order to further probe the interaction effects, I followed Aiken and West's (1991) suggestions and conducted a simple slope analysis between meaningful groups. I did so by applying the common practice of using the "pick-a-point approach" – also referred to as spotlight analysis (Spiller et al., 2013) – to test the moderation effect by comparing the simple slopes at meaningful values of the moderator. I defined these meaningful values by using the most popular approach and choosing the mean, as well as the low (-1 SD) and the high (+1 SD) values, of the moderating variable, idea innovativeness (Cohen et al., 2003). Furthermore, I applied a "floodlight analysis" by following the Johnson-Neyman procedure to provide an estimate and statistical tests of domain knowledge's effect across all of the moderator variable's values (Spiller et al., 2013). I followed this approach, because the simple slope analyses at -1 SD below the mean and +1 SD above the mean of the moderator may be widely used, but this approach is still viewed as arbitrary. Conversely, the floodlight analysis enabled me to show the regions of significance and, thus, indicate the exact ranges of the moderator variable when the simple slopes are significant (Hayes, 2013).

5.2.3.2.1 Interaction effect – Model A (originality)

As depicted in Figure 29, the effect of domain knowledge is significant for ideas with moderate (b = -.181; p <.001) and low (b = -.340; p < .001) innovativeness. In respect of ideas with high innovativeness, it is however not significant (b = -.022; n.s.). Therefore, domain knowledge has a significant negative effect on perceived originality with regard to ideas with low and moderate innovativeness, but there is no association in respect of ideas with high innovativeness. The corresponding floodlight analysis confirms the findings of the simple slope analysis. Domain knowledge has a significantly negative effect on the perceived originality concerning all the innovativeness values ≤ 3.303. Furthermore, this effect shrinks when idea innovativeness increases (see Table 47). These results confirm that the negative effect of domain knowledge on perceived originality is strongest for ideas with a low degree of innovativeness and diminishes with increasing innovativeness of the ideas. In respect of the most innovative ideas, domain knowledge has no significant influence on perceived originality at all. Thus, hypothesis H5 is supported.

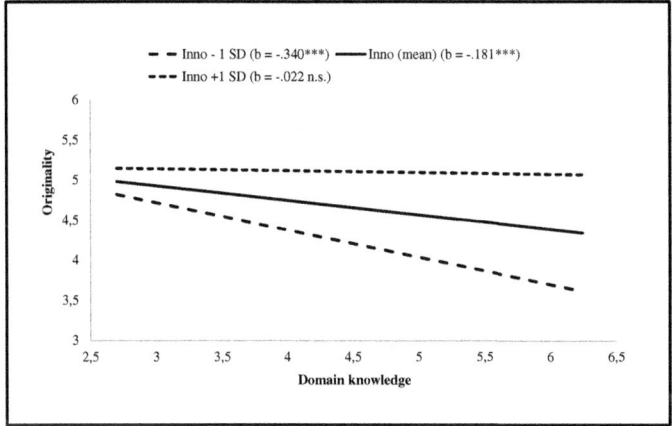

Figure 29: Simple slopes for the interaction effect on perceived originality[70]

Table 47: Conditional effect of domain knowledge on perceived originality at values of the
moderator (Johnson-Neyman Technique)

Moderator:	Effect of independent:	
Innovativeness, measured on a 5-point Likert scale	Effect of domain knowledge on *originality*	Sig.
1.982	-.422	.000
2.062	-.399	.000
2.143	-.376	.000
2.223	-.354	.000
2.304	-.331	.000
2.384	-.308	.000
2.465	-.285	.000
2.545	-.262	.000
2.626	-.240	.000
2.707	-.217	.000
2.787	-.194	.000
2.868	-.171	.000
2.948	-.148	.000
3.029	-.126	.000
3.109	-.103	.000
3.190	-.080	.000
3.270	-.057	.016
3.303	-.048	.050
3.351	-.034	.176
3.432	-.012	.671
3.512	.011	.698
3.593	.034	.273

Johnson-Neyman significance region:
Value=3.30; % below=71.43; % above=28.57

5.2.3.2.2 Interaction effect – Model B (user value)

Figure 30 shows domain knowledge has a significant negative effect on the perceived user
value with regard to ideas with low innovativeness (b = -.055; p = .032) and a significant
positive effect on ideas with high innovativeness (b = .106; p < .001). However, in respect
of ideas with moderate innovativeness, the effect of domain knowledge is not significant (b
= .023; n.s.). The corresponding floodlight analysis confirms these findings. Domain
knowledge has a negative effect on perceived user value with regard to ideas with lower
innovativeness (innovativeness ≤ 2.317). Conversely, with regard to highly innovative
ideas (innovativeness ≥ 2.912), domain knowledge has a positive effect on perceived user
value. However, in respect of ideas of moderate innovativeness (innovativeness 2.384 –
2.868), domain knowledge has no significant influence on perceived user value (see Table
48). These results support the finding that the negative effect of domain knowledge on the

perceived user value is strongest when ideas have a low degree of innovativeness. This negative effect disappears when ideas have moderate innovativeness and actually turns into a positive effect for highly innovative ideas. Thus, hypothesis H6 is supported.

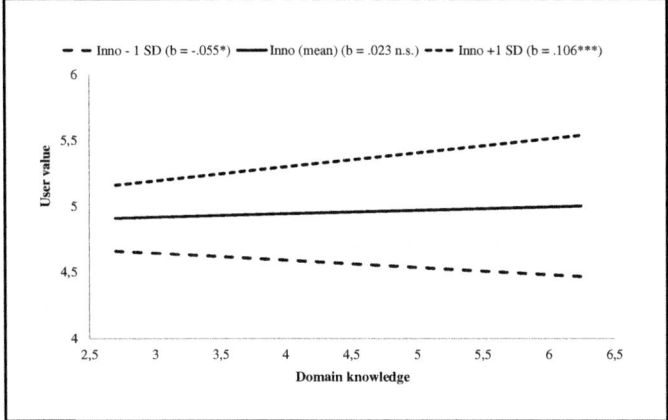

Figure 30: Simple slopes for the interaction effect on perceived user value[71]

---

[71] Author's illustration.

Table 48: Conditional effect of domain knowledge on perceived user value at values of the moderator (Johnson-Neyman Technique)

Moderator: Innovativeness, measured on a 5-point Likert scale	Effect of independent: Effect of domain knowledge on *user value*	Sig.
1.982	**-.097**	**.003**
2.062	**-.085**	**.006**
2.143	**-.073**	**.010**
2.223	**-.062**	**.021**
2.304	**-.050**	**.044**
2.317	**-.049**	**.050**
2.384	-.039	.097
2.465	-.027	.215
2.545	-.016	.449
2.626	-.004	.835
2.707	.007	.696
2.787	.019	.310
2.868	.031	.102
2.912	**.037**	**.050**
2.948	**.042**	**.027**
3.029	**.054**	**.006**
3.109	**.065**	**.002**
3.190	**.077**	**.000**
3.270	**.088**	**.000**
3.351	**.100**	**.000**
3.432	**.111**	**.000**
3.512	**.123**	**.000**
3.593	**.135**	**.000**

Johnson-Neyman significance region:
Value=2.31; % below=28.57; % above=71.43 - Value=2.91; % below=42.86; % above=57.14

5.2.3.2.3   Interaction effect – Model C (feasibility)

According to Figure 31, the positive effect of domain knowledge is significant for ideas with low (b = .217; p < .001), moderate (b = .156; p < .001), and high (b = .094; p < .001) innovativeness. However, the simple slope analysis indicates that this positive effect diminishes with increasing idea innovativeness. The corresponding floodlight analysis confirms that there are no statistical significant transition points within the observed range of the moderator. Domain knowledge thus has a positive effect on perceived feasibility with respect to all levels of innovativeness and this effect diminishes with increasing levels of the moderator (see Table 49). Based on these results, it can be presumed that the positive effect of domain knowledge on the perceived feasibility is strongest in respect of ideas with a low degree of innovativeness and becomes weaker for ideas with moderate and high innovativeness. Thus, hypothesis H7 is supported.

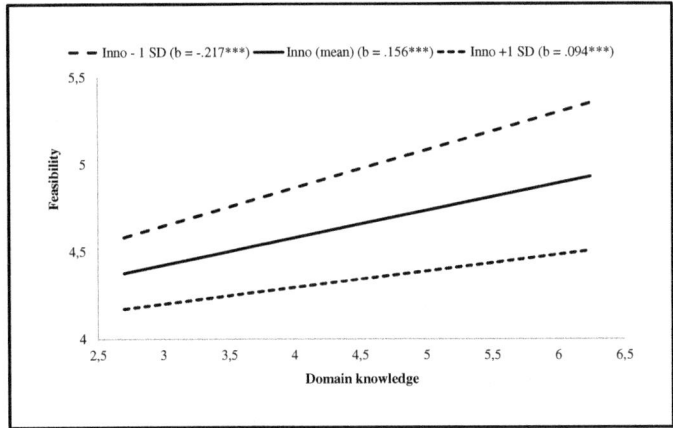

Figure 31: Simple slopes for the interaction effect on perceived feasibility[72]

Table 49: Conditional effect of domain knowledge on perceived feasibility at values of the moderator (Johnson-Neyman Technique)

Moderator:	Effect of independent:	
Innovativeness, measured on a 5-point Likert scale	Effect of domain knowledge on *feasibility*	Sig.
There are no statistical significant transition points within the observed range of the moderator		

5.2.3.2.4 Interaction effect – Model D (overall impression)

As depicted in Figure 32, domain knowledge has a significant positive effect on the overall impression regarding ideas with moderate (b = .037; p = .048) and high (b = .097; p < .001) innovativeness, but it is not significant in respect of ideas with low innovativeness (b = -.023; n.s.). The corresponding floodlight analysis confirms these findings. Domain knowledge has a significant positive effect on the overall impression in respect of all values of innovativeness higher than 2.830. Furthermore, this positive effect increases with higher

---

[72] Author's illustration.

levels of idea innovativeness (see Table 50). Based on these results, it can be concluded that the positive effect of domain knowledge increases with idea innovativeness. Thus, hypothesis H8 is supported.[73]

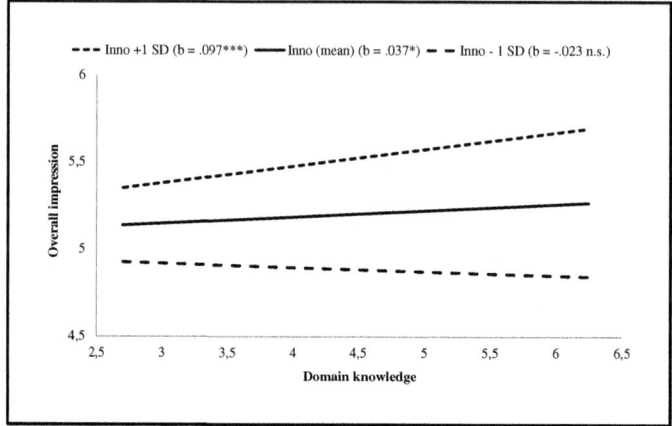

Figure 32: Simple slopes for the interaction effect on overall impression[74]

---

[73] The initial hypothesis presumed that, "idea innovativeness diminishes the negative effect of domain knowledge on the overall impression of early-stage new product ideas," and, thus, a positive interaction effect. Given that domain knowledge was showed to exert a positive effect on the overall impression, the positive interaction effect needs to interpreted as "idea strengthens the positive effect of domain knowledge on the overall impression of early-stage new product ideas."

[74] Author's illustration.

Table 50: Conditional effect of domain knowledge on overall impression at values of the moderator (Johnson-Neyman Technique)

Moderator:	Effect of independent:	
Innovativeness, measured on a 5-point Likert scale	Effect of domain knowledge on *overall impression*	Sig.
1.982	-.054	.093
2.062	-.046	.131
2.143	-.037	.190
2.223	-.029	.281
2.304	-.020	.419
2.384	-.011	.623
2.465	-.003	.898
2.545	.006	.777
2.626	.014	.461
2.707	.023	.223
2.787	.032	.088
2.830	**.036**	**.050**
2.868	**.040**	**.030**
2.948	**.049**	**.009**
3.029	**.057**	**.003**
3.109	**.066**	**.001**
3.190	**.075**	**.001**
3.270	**.083**	**.000**
3.351	**.092**	**.000**
3.432	**.101**	**.000**
3.512	**.109**	**.000**
3.593	**.118**	**.000**

Johnson-Neyman significance region:
Value=2.83; % below=57.14; % above=42.86

5.2.3.3 Testing for mediation effects

A mediation analysis is concerned with the question of "how" or "why" one variable predicts or causes an outcome variable. Thus, a mediator is defined as a variable that explains the relation between an independent variable and a dependent variable and, as such, acts as the mechanism through which an independent variable influences a dependent variable (Baron & Kenny, 1986). In this study, I introduced comprehension as a mediator of the relation between domain knowledge and the perception of originality, user value, feasibility, and overall impression. For example, if comprehension is a significant mediator, individuals with high domain knowledge might have a higher level of comprehension, which explains why individuals with high domain knowledge perceive new product ideas as more feasible. Consequently, mediation analysis could help me test my theories about the causal mechanisms behind the observed relationship between domain knowledge and evaluation outcomes (Judd and Kenny, 1981).

In the past, most studies relied on the "causal steps approach" developed by Baron and Kenny (1986) to test for mediation effects. This method uses four steps to establish that a variable mediates the relation between an independent variable and a dependent variable. First, the researcher needs to show that there is a significant relationship between the independent variable and the dependent variable (path c). Second, the independent variable needs to be shown to be significantly related to the mediator variable (path a). Third, the relationship between the mediator and the dependent variable needs to be checked for significance (path b). In step four, the researcher has to assess the strength of the relationship between the independent variable and the dependent variable. If the effect that the independent variable has on the dependent variable (path c) is significantly reduced after the mediator is added to the model, the mediation effect is confirmed. Thus, if the relationship becomes insignificant, the relationship is fully mediated, but if the relationship becomes significantly smaller, it is partially mediated (Frazier, Tix, and Barron, 2004; Baron and Kenny, 1986). This logic and the paths mentioned are depicted in Figure 33.

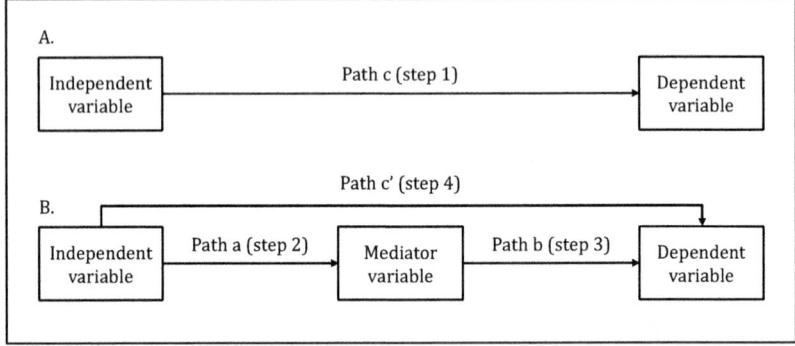

Figure 33: Mediation model path diagram[75]

---

[75] Author's illustration, based on Frazier, Tix, and Barron (2004: 126).

The causal steps approach has been very popular ever since its introduction, because it is simple to understand, can be carried out without the help of sophisticated statistical software, and is easy to describe. However, despite its popularity, the causal steps approach has been subjected to strong criticism and research scholars have argued convincingly against its use (Hayes, 2013: 167): "recognition is growing that this approach is not ideal both statistically and philosophically, and soon it will be difficult to get away with the use of the causal steps strategy. Before long, you won't be able to publish your research if you rely on the causal steps method." (a detailed discussion of the shortcoming of the causal steps approach is provided in Hayes (2013)).

Fortunately, since the causal steps approach was introduced, research scholars have developed more than a dozen approaches to statistically test an indirect effect (mediation) that can be used instead (for a discussion of various approaches see, e.g. MacKinnon et al. (2002)). Since different tests have different benefits and shortcomings, I decided to test the indirect effect with (i) the normal theory approach, also called the Sobel test, and (ii) by constructing bias-corrected bootstrap confidence intervals with 10,000 bootstraps[76] (Hayes, 2013). The results of these tests are presented in Table 51.

The results show that the bias-corrected bootstrap confidence intervals in respect of the indirect effects were entirely above or below zero regarding model B (user value), model C (feasibility), and model D (overall impression), thus supporting the existence of significant indirect effects. Regarding model A (originality), the confidence intervals include zero, thus supporting the indirect effect being insignificant. The Soble test confirmed these findings, yielding significant results regarding models B, C, and D, but not model A. From these tests, it can be concluded that domain knowledge indirectly influences the perceived user value, feasibility, and overall impression through its positive effect on comprehension. Thus, hypotheses H16-18 are supported by the simple mediation analysis and H15 is rejected.[77]

---

[76] A review of the subtle details behind the bootstrapping procedure can be found in e.g. Good (2001) or Wood (2005).

[77] I avoided using the terms "partial mediation" and "complete mediation," because leading research scholars have suggested abandoning this distinction. The reasoning behind this is explained by e.g. Hayes (2013).

Table 51: Statistical tests for mediation effects

	Effect	Sig.	LLCI	ULCI
Total effect of domain knowledge on originality (O) - Model A	-.181	.000	-.219	-.143
Direct effect	-.188	.000	-.228	-.150
Indirect effect through comprehension	.008		-.002	.019
Normal theory tests for indirect effects	.008	.106		
Total effect of domain knowledge on user value (UV) - Model B	.026	.171	-.011	.062
Direct effect	-.061	.001	-.095	-.025
Indirect effect through comprehension	.086		.070	.103
Normal theory tests for indirect effects	.086	.000		
Total effect of domain knowledge on feasibility (F) - Model C	.156	.000	.119	.192
Direct effect	.043	.011	.098	.076
Indirect effect through comprehension	.113		.093	.133
Normal theory tests for indirect effects	.113	.000		
Total effect of domain knowledge on overall impression (OI) - Model D	.037	.048	.000	.073
Direct effect	-.027	.141	-.063	.009
Indirect effect through comprehension	.064		.051	.079
Normal theory tests for indirect effects	.064	.000		

Note: Number of bootstrap samples for bias-corrected bootstrap confidence intervals: 10.000; analysis carried out with Hayes' PROCESS macro Model 4.

5.2.3.4 Testing for moderated mediation

The presence of a moderator (section 5.2.3.2) and a mediator (section 5.2.3.3) in all four models creates the possibility that a moderated mediation model may best explain the models' effects (also referred to as conditional process analysis). Moderated mediation describes a situation in which the mediated relationship between an independent and a dependent variable varies across a moderator's levels (Hayes, 2013). Conceptually, there are many ways that this can happen (for examples, see e.g. Hayes, 2013; Edwards and Lambert, 2007). However the moderated mediation that is best applicable in the context of this study can be depicted as follows:[78]

---

[78] Other models have been tested and rejected. For example, I tested whether or not the relationship between the mediator and the dependent variable might be moderated by innovativeness or domain knowledge. This was not the case.

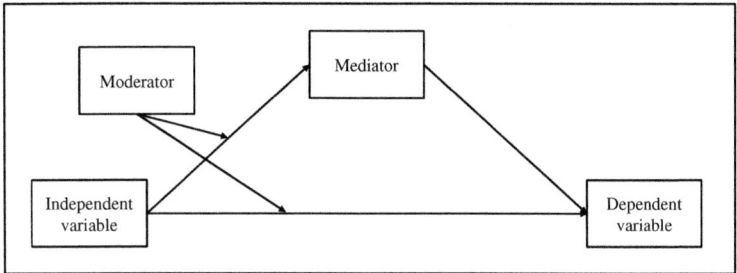

Figure 34: Simplified moderated mediation model[79]

Following the framework presented in Figure 34, I propose that the mediated relationship between domain knowledge and evaluation outcomes (perceived originality, user value, feasibility, and overall impression, see section 5.2.3.3) is moderated by idea innovativeness. More specifically, idea innovativeness moderates (i) the direct effect between domain knowledge and evaluation outcomes (H 5-8), and (ii) the indirect effect by moderating the relationship between domain knowledge and comprehension (H 10). The first moderation effects have already been confirmed in section 5.2.3.2. The latter needed to be tested in a new regression model, with comprehension the dependent variable (see Table 52). This model shows that domain knowledge has a significant positive effect on the perceived comprehension (b = .216; p < .001) and that this effect is strengthened when idea innovativeness increases (b = .078; p = .009). Consequently, H9 and H10 are supported.

---

[79] Author's illustration, based on Hayes (2013: 330).

Table 52: Direct and moderated effect of domain knowledge on comprehension

	Model E (comprehension)								
	Model E-1			Model E-2			Model E-3		
	B	Sig.		B	Sig.		B	Sig.	
Constant	7.047	.000	***	5.895	.000	***	5.895	.000	***
Age	-.012	.000	***	-.005	.075	***	-.005	.074	***
Native English speaker	.007	.915		.054	.399		.054	.399	
University degree	-.035	.643		.057	.432		.057	.432	
R&D tenure > 5 years	.367	.000	***	.110	.213	***	.110	.212	***
Marketing tenure > 5 years	-.083	.548		-.072	.591		-.072	.591	
Sales tenure > 5 years	.165	.201		.097	.440		.097	.439	
Top-level management	-.070	.569		-.080	.502		-.080	.502	
Risk aversion	.039	.101		.019	.410		.019	.409	
Innovativeness	-.591	.000	***	-.591	.000	***	-.591	.000	***
H4: Domain knowledge				.216	.000	***	.216	.000	***
H8: Interaction (Inno. x DK)							.078	.009	**
R^2	.062			.119			.121		
Adjusted R^2	.058			.115			.117		
Adj. R^2 change				.057			.002		
F-statistic	16.902	.000	***	63.728	.000	***	29.064	.000	***
F change				150.190	.000	***	6.833	.009	**

Note: Hierarchical regression models. (1) controls (2) + independent variable, (3) + interaction effect

(4) + mediation effect (full moderated mediation model) ; unstandardized regression coefficients reported;

* $p < .05$; ** $p < .01$; *** $p < .001$; n = 2.331 (333 participants, each evaluating seven ideas).

Testing moderated mediation is a complex procedure that requires several steps and sophisticated statistical software. Fortunately, Hayes (2013) developed the PROCESS macro for SPSS that can be used to test a model, as depicted in Figure 34. The results obtained from the PROCESS tool are presented in Table 53. A close examination of these results confirms that (i) the direct effects and (ii) the indirect effects of domain knowledge on the evaluation outcome variables are dependent on the level of idea innovativeness. However, different effects are revealed across the four models (models A-D). These effects will be discussed in the following section.

Table 53: Results of conditional process analysis

	Effect	Sig.	LLCI	ULCI
Conditional effects of domain knowledge on originality (O) - Model A (4)				
Conditional direct effects				
Idea innovativess (-1SD)	-.346	.000	-.398	-,294
Idea innovativess (mean)	-.189	.000	-.228	-,150
Idea innovativess (+1 SD)	-.031	.244	-.084	,021
Conditional indirect effects				
Idea innovativess (-1SD)	.006		-.002	,015
Idea innovativess (mean)	.008		-.002	,018
Idea innovativess (+1 SD)	.010		-.003	,022
Indirect effect of highest order product	.003		.000	.009
Conditional effects of domain knowledge on user value (UV) - Model B (4)				
Conditional direct effects				
Idea innovativess (-1SD)	-.123	.000	-.171	-,076
Idea innovativess (mean)	-.060	.001	-.095	-,025
Idea innovativess (+1 SD)	.003	.904	-.045	,051
Conditional indirect effects				
Idea innovativess (-1SD)	.069		.050	,089
Idea innovativess (mean)	.086		.070	,104
Idea innovativess (+1 SD)	.103		.081	,127
Indirect effect of highest order product	.031		.007	.054
Conditional effects of domain knowledge on feasibility (F) - Model C (4)				
Conditional direct effects				
Idea innovativess (-1SD)	.127	.000	.082	,172
Idea innovativess (mean)	.043	.011	.010	,076
Idea innovativess (+1 SD)	-.041	.073	-.087	,004
Conditional indirect effects				
Idea innovativess (-1SD)	.090		.066	,115
Idea innovativess (mean)	.113		.093	,133
Idea innovativess (+1 SD)	.136		.107	,165
Indirect effect of highest order product	.041		.010	.071
Conditional effects of domain knowledge on overall impression (OI) - Model D (4)				
Conditional direct effects				
Idea innovativess (-1SD)	-.074	.003	.003	-,026
Idea innovativess (mean)	-.027	.141	.141	,009
Idea innovativess (+1 SD)	.020	.419	.419	,069
Conditional indirect effects				
Idea innovativess (-1SD)	.051		.036	,068
Idea innovativess (mean)	.064		.050	,079
Idea innovativess (+1 SD)	.076		.058	,096
Indirect effect of highest order product	.023		.006	.041

Note: Number of bootstrap samples for bias corrected bootstrap confidence intervals: 10.000;
analysis carried out with Hayes' PROCESS macro Model 8.

5.2.3.4.1 Effects in Model A – perceived originality

The conditional process analysis shows that domain knowledge has a negative total effect on the perceived originality of ideas with low innovativeness (direct effect: b = -.346; LLCI = -.398; ULCI = -.294; indirect effect: b = .006; LLCI = -.002; ULCI = .015). The direct effect diminishes in respect of ideas with moderate innovativeness (direct effect: b = -.189; LLCI = -.228; ULCI = -.150; indirect effect: b = .008; LLCI = -.002; ULCI = .018) and becomes insignificant in respect of ideas with high innovativeness (direct effect: b = -.031; LLCI = -.084; ULCI = .021; indirect effect: b = .010; LLCI = -.003; ULCI = .022). Acknowledging that no significant indirect effect can be observed in the data, the decrease in the effect size is fully accounted for by the weakened negative direct effect of domain knowledge.

5.2.3.4.2 Effects in Model B – user value

The initial moderation analysis showed that domain knowledge has a negative effect on the perceived user value of ideas with low innovativeness, and a positive effect on ideas with high innovativeness. Domain knowledge has not shown a significant relationship in the analysis in terms of ideas with moderate innovativeness. The conditional process analysis reveals that, in respect of ideas with low innovativeness, the negative direct effect (direct effect: b = -.123; LLCI = -.171; ULCI = -.076; indirect effect: b = .069; LLCI = .050; ULCI = .089) dominates domain knowledge's total effect. Regarding ideas with moderate innovativeness, the negative direct effect and the positive indirect effect almost offset one another (direct effect: b = -.060; LLCI = -.095; ULCI = -.025; indirect effect: b = .086; LLCI = .070; ULCI = .104). This may explain the apparent insignificance of the effect of domain knowledge in Model B-3 if comprehension is not introduced. The finding that the negative direct effect is insignificant and the positive indirect effect thus becomes dominant (direct effect: b = .003; LLCI = -.045; ULCI = .051; indirect effect: b = .103; LLCI = .081; ULCI = .127) accounts for the positive effect in respect of ideas with high innovativeness.

5.2.3.4.3 Effects in Model C – feasibility

The initial analysis confirmed that domain knowledge has a positive effect on the perceived feasibility with regard to ideas with low, moderate, and high innovativeness levels. However, this positive effect diminishes with increasing idea innovativeness. Based on the results of the conditional process analysis, this weakening effect can be rooted in a decrease in the positive direct effect, which is not fully compensated for by the increasing indirect effect. Thus, in respect of ideas with low innovativeness, a weaker indirect effect (direct effect: b = .127; LLCI = .082; ULCI = .172; indirect effect: b = .090; LLCI = .066; ULCI = .115) accompanies a strong direct effect. With regard to ideas with moderate innovativeness, the indirect effect increases while the direct effect decreases. This leads to the indirect effect becoming the dominating effect (direct effect: b = .043; LLCI = .010; ULCI = .076; indirect effect: b = .113; LLCI = .093; ULCI = .133). Finally, in terms of ideas with high innovativeness, the direct effect decreases further and becomes insignificant, whereas the indirect effect further increases (direct effect: b = -.041; LLCI = -.087; ULCI = .004; indirect effect: b = .136; LLCI = .107; ULCI = .165). However, with regard to ideas with moderate and high innovativeness, the increase in the indirect effect does not fully compensate for the decrease in the direct effect and, thus, the total effect of domain knowledge on the perceived feasibility diminishes with increasing idea innovativeness.

5.2.3.4.4   Effects in Model D – overall impression

Initial analysis has shown that domain knowledge has a positive effect on ideas with moderate and high innovativeness, but not on the overall impression of ideas with low innovativeness.

The results of the conditional process analysis reveal that, with regard to ideas with low innovativeness, domain knowledge has a negative, but insignificant, direct effect and a positive significant indirect effect on the overall impression (direct effect: b = -0.74; LLCI = .003; ULCI = -.026; indirect effect: b = .051; LLCI = .036; ULCI = .068). Domain knowledge did not show a significant effect in the preceding moderation analysis and a possible explanation may be that the insignificant negative direct effect of domain knowledge dominates the small indirect positive effect. The direct effect is weakened and the indirect strengthened (direct effect: b = -0.27; LLCI = .141; ULCI = .009; indirect effect: b = .064; LLCI = .050; ULCI = .079) in respect of ideas with moderate innovativeness. This trend continues regarding the evaluation of ideas with high innovativeness. The results show that the direct effect actually becomes positive (direct effect: b = 0.20; LLCI = .419; ULCI = .069; indirect effect: b = .076; LLCI = .058; ULCI = .096).

The positive effect of domain knowledge on overall impression is mainly rooted in a positive indirect effect that increases with idea innovativeness and if they dominate. It is also due to a smaller negative direct effect that diminishes with ideas innovativeness and eventually becomes positive for highly innovative ideas.

5.2.3.4.5 Summary of conditional process analysis results

I applied conditional process analysis, which enabled me to show that domain knowledge exerts its total effect on evaluation outcomes (i.e., perceived originality, user value, feasibility, and overall impression) by having a direct effect and an indirect effect (through the mediator comprehension). Furthermore, I have shown that the new product idea's degree of innovativeness moderates the direct effects, as well as the indirect effects, of domain knowledge. Specifically, idea innovativeness has been found to moderate the direct effects by diminishing the negative effects of domain knowledge on the perceived originality, user value, and overall impression, as well as the positive effect on perceived feasibility. In addition, idea innovativeness has also been found to moderate the positive relationship between domain knowledge and comprehension, such that the positive indirect effect on the perceived user value, feasibility, and overall impression increases with idea innovativeness. However, the strength and significance of these effects are quite different across the four models and were examined in more detail in the previous sections. The extent of the effects on different levels of the moderator is depicted in Figure 35 and supports this analysis.

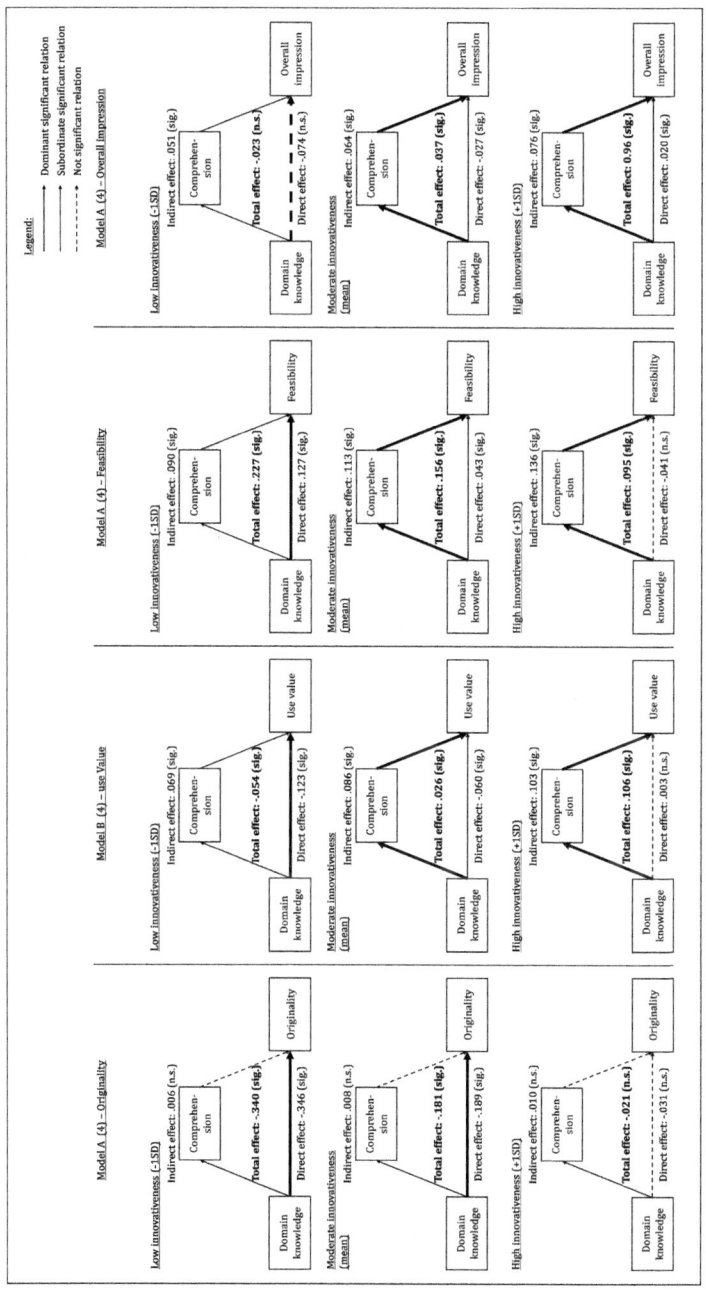

Figure 35: Overview of direct and indirect effects of domain knowledge at different levels of idea innovativeness

6 Discussion of findings and implications

In this last chapter, I discuss the study's findings in the light of the proposed hypotheses, as well as the study's contribution to theory and practice. This chapter closes with the study's limitations and highlights opportunities for future research.

6.1 Discussion

Increasing the proficiency of early-stage new product idea evaluation is an important topic for management research and practice alike (Barczak, 2014). The overarching research goal of this thesis is to enhance our understanding of the role of individuals' domain knowledge in the proficient evaluation of early-stage new product ideas in the front-end of innovation (RQ 1), thus adding value to prior research findings on this topic. Another aim is to answer the question whether or not firms should give more, or less, consideration to domain knowledge as an important factor in selecting appropriate judges – internal and external to the firm – to evaluate early-stage new product ideas (RQ 2).

The study therefore aimed to contribute to the literature in three ways: by (i) investigating the influence of domain knowledge on the evaluation of new product ideas in a criteria-based evaluation task (RQ 1a), (ii) investigating the influence of an individual's domain knowledge on the evaluation of new product ideas in a holistic evaluation task (RQ 1b), and (iii) investigating whether or not the influence of domain knowledge might differ when evaluating more rather than less innovative new product ideas (RQ 1c).

A summary of the study's results is provided in Table 54 and Table 55. The results of the final conditional process model (moderated mediation) are depicted in Figure 36. In the following sections, these results will be discussed in the light of the presented research questions.

Table 54: Summary of results – part I

Hypotheses	Effect	Hypothesis supported	Reference model
Total effects of domain knowledge			
H1: Domain knowledge has a negative effect on the perceived originality of early-stage new product ideas.	b = -.181***	Yes	Model A-2
H2: Domain knowledge has a negative effect on the perceived user value of early-stage new product ideas.	b = .026 (n.s.)	No	Model B-2
H3: Domain knowledge has a positive effect on the perceived feasibility of early-stage new product ideas.	b = .156***	Yes	Model C-2
H4: Domain knowledge has a negative effect on the overall impression of early-stage new product ideas.	b = .037*	No (positive effect)	Model D-2
Interaction effects between domain knowledge and idea's innovativeness			
H5: Idea innovativeness diminishes the negative effect of domain knowledge on the perceived originality of early-stage new product ideas.	b = .283***	Yes	Model A-3
H6: Idea innovativeness diminishes the negative effect of domain knowledge on the perceived user value of early-stage new product ideas.	b = .143***	Yes	Model B-3
H7: Idea innovativeness diminishes the positive effect of domain knowledge on the perceived feasibility of early-stage new product ideas.	b = -.109**	Yes	Model C-3
H8: Idea innovativeness diminishes the negative effect of domain knowledge on the overall impression of early-stage new product ideas.	b = .107**	No (strengthening of positive effect)	Model D-3

Note: * p ≤ .05; ** p ≤ .01; *** p ≤ .001.

Table 55: Summary of results – part II

Hypotheses	Effect	Hypothesis supported	Reference model
Moderated mediation effects			
H9: Domain knowledge has a positive effect on perceived comprehension of early-stage new product ideas.	b = .216***	Yes	Model E-2
H10: Idea innovativeness strengthens the positive effect of domain knowledge on perceived comprehension of early-stage new product ideas.	b = .107**	Yes	Model E-3
H11: Comprehension has a positive effect on the perceived originality of early-stage new product ideas.	b = .037 (n.s.)	No	Model A-4
H12: Comprehension has a positive effect on the perceived user value of early-stage new product ideas.	b = .398***	Yes	Model B-4
H13: Comprehension has a positive effect on the perceived feasibility of early-stage new product ideas.	b = .523***	Yes	Model C-4
H14: Comprehension has a positive effect on the overall impression of early-stage new product ideas.	b = .295***	Yes	Model D-4
H15: Comprehension mediates the effects of domain knowledge on perceived originality of early-stage new product ideas.		No	
H16: Comprehension mediates the effects of domain knowledge on perceived user value of early-stage new product ideas.		Yes	
H17: Comprehension mediates the effects of domain knowledge on perceived feasibility of early-stage new product ideas.		Yes	Mediation analysis
H18: Comprehension mediates the effects of domain knowledge on overall impression of early-stage new product ideas.		Yes	

Note: * p ≤ .05; ** p ≤ .01; *** p ≤ .001.

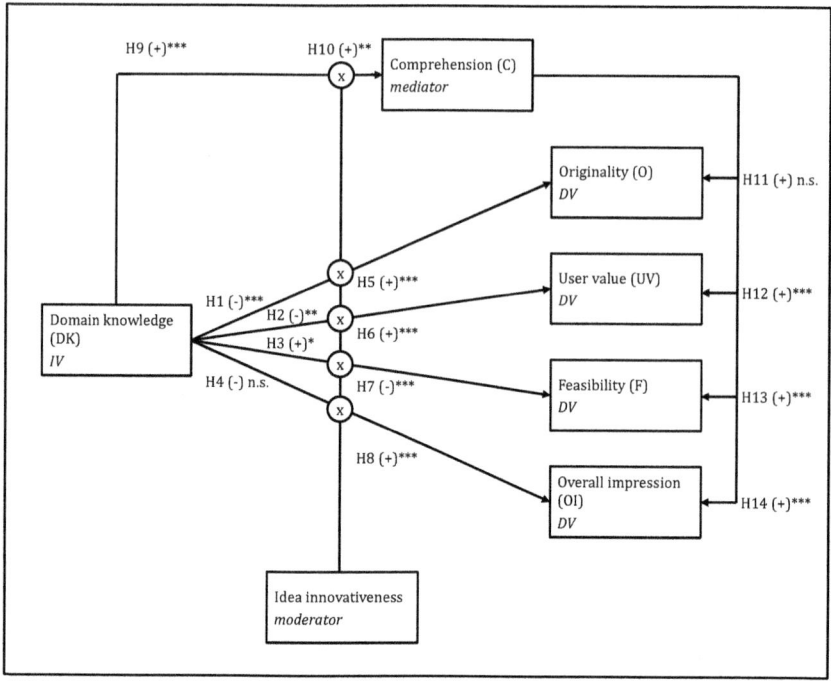

Figure 36: Overview of final results (models A-D (4))[80]

In the criteria-based idea evaluation task (RQ1a), the results show that evaluators with higher domain knowledge generally exhibit more conservative evaluation behavior with regard to the perceived originality. This is arguably the result of their higher judgment standards due to their broader frames of reference, which provide insight into numerous comparable products, as well as into current and envisaged trends that determine customer needs in the domain's current and future markets (Alexy, George, and Salter, 2013; von Hippel, 1986). Domain knowledge's expected negative influence on the perception of user value did not materialize in the data. A possible explanation is that domain knowledge influences the perception of user value very differently in terms of ideas with lower rather than higher degrees of innovativeness, which could cancel the mean effect (see below). Furthermore, the study corroborates that, among evaluators with higher

---

[80] Author's illustration.

domain knowledge, positive perceptions of an idea's feasibility tend to be higher than the perceptions of those with less domain knowledge. This could be attributed to evaluators with higher domain knowledge being more familiar with the current chances and limitations of available technology in the domain (Magnusson, 2009). A further reason could be the proposition that individuals with higher domain knowledge, who also have a general understanding of the technologies available in existing products (Danneels, 2007), are likely to be more positive about a new product idea's feasibility than individuals who do not understand the underlying technologies in the domain.

In the holistic idea evaluation task (RQ 1b), the data do not support domain knowledge's hypothesized negative effect on the perceived overall impression. The data revealed that domain knowledge exerts the opposite effect. Thus, individuals with higher domain knowledge have a more positive perception of new product ideas. At first glance, this is surprising, as one expects an elaborate frame of reference and higher judgment standards to lead to a more negative perception of new product ideas, because individuals with high domain knowledge could perceive ideas as generally less original and less useful (H1 and H2). However, in a holistic idea evaluation task, the evaluators individually decide which criteria to take into account for the evaluation, as well as the relative weight to assign to each criteria (Magnusson, Netz, and Wästlund, 2014). Additional data analyses actually show that all three criteria – perceived originality, user value, and feasibility – have a significantly positive influence on the overall impression and these three criteria thus mediate the effect of domain knowledge on the overall impression. In this respect, conditional process analysis showed that of these three criteria, user value had the strongest influence (see appendix C). In respect of all the ideas, domain knowledge did not show a significant effect on perceived user value, but showed a significant negative effect on the perceived originality and a significant positive effect on the perceived feasibility (see above). The influence on those two criteria might therefore largely explain the positive effect of domain knowledge on the overall impression. Given that individuals seem to specifically prefer ideas that are feasible (Rietzschel, Nijstad, and Stroebe, 2010), the more optimistic view of the idea's feasibility might mainly the more positive effect of domain knowledge on the overall impression.

The results also show that idea innovativeness significantly moderates the influence of domain knowledge on the perceived originality, user value, feasibility, and overall impression (RQ 1c).

In originality assessments, domain knowledge's negative effect diminishes with increasing idea innovativeness. A possible explanation for this effect is that individuals with higher domain knowledge have superior ability to differentiate between ideas of higher and lower innovativeness in terms of these ideas' higher rather than lower originality. This is because individuals with high domain knowledge can access their more complex schemas to better comprehend the benefits and risks associated with an early-stage radical new product idea and to reference the idea in terms of existing concepts and products in the marketplace (Dane, 2010; Mukherjee and Hoyer, 2001; Graeff and Olson, 1994). Evaluators with lower domain knowledge, on the other hand, experience greater difficulty with the uncertainties surrounding early-stage radical new product ideas (Veryzer, 1998b; Peracchio and Tybout, 1996; Alba and Hutchinson, 1987). They are thus less proficient in accurately distinguishing between innovative and less innovative ideas in terms of these ideas' higher originality levels.

User value perceptions' results show that the influence of domain knowledge differs substantially depending on the level of idea innovativeness. I suggest that higher domain knowledge's negative effect diminishes as idea innovativeness increases. However, the data showed that domain knowledge's negative effect on the perceived user value becomes significantly positive when highly innovative (i.e., radical) new product ideas are evaluated. This change in the effect that domain knowledge has on the perceived user value (i) helps explain why there was no proof of domain knowledge having a significantly direct effect on the perceived user value and (ii) indicates that domain knowledge unfolds a counteracting positive effect to the generally more conservative evaluation behavior in respect of the evaluation of radical new product ideas. This positive effect can, again, be linked to the impact that inherent uncertainties play in the evaluation of early-stage radical new product ideas (Veryzer, 1998b; Mugge and Dahl, 2013) and to domain knowledge's contribution in overcoming uncertainty-related evaluation problems (Gregan-Paxton and Roedder John, 1997). Research has shown that individuals perceive it as rewarding when such uncertainties are resolved, which generally leads to more positive evaluations (Meyers-Levy and Tybout, 1989).

Idea innovativeness also significantly moderates the effect of domain knowledge on feasibility assessments. The study substantiates that the overall positive effect of domain knowledge on perceived feasibility is lower when evaluating high rather than less innovative ideas. An examination of this effect shows that evaluators with higher domain knowledge can more accurately distinguish between radical and incremental ideas in terms of their feasibility than those with lower domain knowledge. An explanation might be that correctly assessing the feasibility of early-stage radical new product ideas is more difficult than assessing early-stage incremental ideas. This is because evaluating radical ideas usually requires evaluators to assess an idea's potentially advanced technological capabilities against current, more limited, technologies available in the domain (Schultz, Salomo, and Talke, 2013). Thus, it becomes more difficult to leverage existing knowledge to benefit the evaluation process, and a higher level of uncertainty may arise, especially for those evaluators with lower domain knowledge. This could explain the less accurate feasibility evaluations of evaluators with lower domain knowledge.

Furthermore, I proposed that idea innovativeness would diminish the proposed negative effect of domain knowledge on perceived the overall impression. However, the data analysis revealed that domain knowledge has a positive influence on the perceived overall impression (see above). Thus, it is not surprising that the observed moderation effect does not diminish a negative effect, but significantly strengthens the positive effect of domain knowledge on the overall impression. This strengthening effect is due to the influence of the perceived originality, user value, and feasibility on the overall impression. Conditional process analyses revealed that the negative effects of domain knowledge on the perceived originality and user value diminish with increasing idea innovativeness. Given that the perception of these three attributes largely determines the overall impression, with user value having the strongest influence (see Appendix), it is thus not surprising that the moderation effect of the overall impression follows the same direction as the moderation effect of the perceived user value, i.e., exerting a positive effect on the evaluation of highly innovative ideas.

Based on the preceding discussion, it is clearly demonstrated that there is a significant relationship between an individual's domain knowledge and the perception and evaluation of early-stage new product ideas. Furthermore, the discussion of the moderation effects, i.e., the effect of how idea innovativeness alters the relationship between domain knowledge and evaluation outcomes, helps clarify under which conditions domain knowledge exerts its influence on the perceived originality, user value, feasibility, and overall impression of early-stage new product ideas.

However, in an attempt to not only explain "when" or "under which condition," but also "how" and "why" domain knowledge influences evaluation outcomes, the research framework also considered comprehension as a potential mediator of the relationship between domain knowledge and idea perceptions. The study's results substantiate the proposed mediation effect. In line with prior findings in the literature, the results show that domain knowledge has a significant positive influence on comprehension. Furthermore, comprehension also has a significant positive influence on idea perceptions by exerting a positive influence on the perceived user value, feasibility, and overall impression (Moreau, Lehmann, and Markman, 2001).

Based on this relationship, domain knowledge exerts a positive indirect effect on the perceived user value, feasibility, and overall impression. This indirect effect can be related to the effect of uncertainty in the evaluation of new product ideas. Research scholars have shown that when individuals face uncertainty about the benefits and shortcomings of a new product, their evaluations are likely to develop a more negative attitude (Veryzer, 1998b; Mukherjee and Hoyer, 2001; Mugge and Dahl, 2013). The findings of psychology research studies support the conclusion that individuals generally avoid uncertainty in idea evaluation. These studies concluded that individuals have a general disdain for innovative ideas (Blair and Mumford, 2007) and favor ideas that are familiar and provide tangible short-term benefits (Licuanan, Dailey, and Mumford, 2007). In this context, the study's results support the conclusion that domain knowledge helps overcome such an uncertainty-related bias (Lipshitz et al., 2001). The data show that domain knowledge helps discern appropriate meaning (i.e., comprehension). Thus, the study's data support the theory that individuals with high domain knowledge can leverage their complex schemas to build goal-relevant inferences (Gregan-Paxton and Roedder John, 1997) which provide them with anchoring points for the evaluation. They are therefore able to transfer existing knowledge to the evaluation object to establish comprehension and reduce uncertainty about the idea's potential (Gregan-Paxton et al., 2002). In addition, the study's data support prior findings that higher comprehension leads to more positive perceptions of new product ideas (Moreau, Lehmann, and Markman, 2001; Mugge and Dahl, 2013).

Furthermore, corroborating the mediation effect of comprehension by means of conditional process analysis shows that the positive indirect effect of domain knowledge becomes stronger with increasing idea innovativeness. This finding suggests that individuals with low domain knowledge have difficulties with discerning appropriate meaning from the idea description provided, especially in respect of the evaluation of more radical ideas. Therefore it can be assumed that evaluators with low domain knowledge are more likely to have a "bias against originality" (Blair and Mumford, 2007; Licuanan, Dailey, and Mumford, 2007) and, consequently, to underestimate the value of highly innovative ideas, because they face higher uncertainty during evaluation (Veryzer, 1998b). It can thus be argued that the ability of individuals with high domain knowledge to more easily discern appropriate meaning from the given idea description by means of transferring internal knowledge, helps these individuals identify the true value of highly innovative ideas.

In conclusion, although participants in the overall sample were able to – to some extent – correctly evaluate radical new product ideas by assigning higher scores in respect of the overall impression, originality, user value, and lower feasibility to the more innovative ideas, domain knowledge seems to have an important influence on the proficiency of the evaluation outcomes. Individuals with higher domain knowledge appear to be more capable of distinguishing between highly innovative and less innovative ideas. Conversely, individuals with lower domain knowledge tend to overestimate the originality and user value of ideas with lower innovativeness and specifically undervalue the user value of more innovative ideas. This is also why individuals with low domain knowledge seem to undervalue radical new product ideas in holistic assessments. These findings support the central proposition of this study that domain knowledge plays a significant role in proficient new product idea evaluation. This proposition is particularly true during the initial evaluation of early-stage new product ideas at the front-end of innovation where individuals are likely to resort to schemas stored in their memories to interpret the information provided and to make inferences about the new product idea's benefits and shortcomings (Broniarczyk and Alba, 1994; Gregan-Paxton and Roedder John, 1997; Graeff and Olson, 1994). More specifically, by providing the ability to form goal-relevant inferences, domain knowledge helps evaluate early-stage new product ideas, because it (i) provides evaluators with an appropriate frame of reference and (ii) helps discern appropriate meaning even when the evaluators are given limited and ambiguous information. The latter helps evaluators overcome uncertainty-related biases that especially arise when evaluating radical new product ideas.

In summary, evaluators with higher domain knowledge seem to be better positioned to evaluate early-stage new product ideas on the basis of their abilities to:

- Judge the originality of early-stage ideas with reference to existing products, concepts, and trends in the market.
- Assess the user value of early-stage ideas based on an understanding of consumers' current and future needs and wants and by transferring existing knowledge to the evaluation object to reduce the uncertainty about the idea's user benefits.
- Evaluate an idea's feasibility in the light of a general understanding about the changes and boundaries of the technologies in the domain.

Therefore, employing individuals with high domain knowledge in the evaluation of early-stage ideas is likely to also increase idea selection proficiency. Such individuals can help decision makers more effectively reduce the likelihood of selecting too many incremental ideas by overestimating their values (false positives), and rejecting too many radical ideas by underestimating their values (false negatives). Overall, the results of this study strongly support the premise that evaluators with high domain knowledge cannot simply be replaced with those with low domain knowledge (Kaufman et al., 2008) when aiming to effectively identify high potential new product ideas.

6.2 Theoretical implications

Prior research aimed at increasing proficiency in idea evaluation was largely focused on process design aspects such as (i) formal vs. informal evaluation processes (Eling, Griffin, and Langerak, 2016), (ii) intuition-based rather than criteria-based idea evaluation (Eling, Langerak, and Griffin, 2015; Netz, Sukhov, and Magnusson, 2015), (iii) evaluation criteria (Dean et al., 2006; Hart et al., 2003; Carbonell-Foulquié, Munuera-Alemán, and Rodriguez-Escudero, 2004), (iv) rating scale design (Riedl et al., 2013), (v) implicit rating mechanisms, such as idea markets (e.g. Soukhoroukova, Spann, and Skiera, 2012), and (vi) adaptive idea screening and outsourcing evaluations to users or employees (Velamuri et al., 2015; Magnusson, Wästlund, and Netz, 2016; Onarheim and Christensen, 2012).

As a general theoretical contribution towards research on the proficient evaluation of early stage new product ideas, this study successfully expands this research beyond the process design aspect to include characteristics at the individual evaluator level. This research thus contributes to a field of research that has received little attention to date (Magnusson, Wästlund, and Netz, 2016). Consequently, this focus on the human side of new product idea evaluation has a number of theoretical implications for innovation management literature.

First, by acknowledging that characteristics at the individual evaluator's level play an important role with regard to the proficient evaluation of early-stage new product ideas, the study encourages the development of theories and the empirically testing of other characteristics at the individual level. This is especially relevant in respect of aspects that may influence idea evaluation proficiency, such as individuals' professional experience (Behrens, Ernst, and Shepherd, 2014), roles, and positions within the firm (Behrens, Ernst, and Shepherd, 2014; Behrens and Ernst, 2014; Melone, 1994) "thought worlds" (Dougherty, 1992), cognitive styles (Kozhevnikov, 2007), personality traits (Goldberg, 1990), and risk aversion (Tversky and Kahnemann, 1974).

Second, the study empirically supports voices in the literature reasoning that domain knowledge – comprising a user perspective (need knowledge) and a producer perspective (solution knowledge) – is a crucial factor to effectively evaluate new product ideas (von Hippel, 1988, 1994, 1998). This understanding encourages the development of new theories to improve the composition of new product idea evaluation teams and screening gate committees that go beyond the focus on functional backgrounds and firm tenure (Galbraith et al., 2010).

Third, this is the first study in the field of idea evaluation that explicitly investigates the interplay between an individual evaluator's domain knowledge and an idea's degree of innovativeness, as well as the influence of this interplay on evaluation proficiency. In this context, the study's results show that an evaluator's characteristics might be especially important for increasing the proficiency of radical new product idea evaluation. This is therefore a first attempt to answer the important question: "Should the gatekeepers vary depending on whether the innovation is incremental or radical?" (Barczak, 2014). This study does so by indicating that the type of ideas to be evaluated should be taken into cognizance when selecting appropriate evaluators. This finding also expands the current view in the literature that ideas in different domains may require more, or less, domain knowledge to be proficiently evaluated to also take the influence of the innovativeness of the subject under evaluation into account. Future research should thus always take the innovativeness of the ideas to be evaluated into consideration, because as antecedents of proficient idea evaluation, individual characteristics may differ markedly between the evaluations of more incremental rather than more radical new product ideas.

Fourth, in line with prior research, revealing the mediating effect of comprehension allows the conclusion that uncertainty is a significant driver of evaluation behavior (Blair and Mumford, 2007; Licuanan, Dailey, and Mumford, 2007; Mugge and Dahl, 2013; Veryzer, 1998b). The study's findings substantiates that domain knowledge helps an evaluator engage in internal knowledge transfer to discern appropriate meaning even when provided with limited and ambiguous information (Gregan-Paxton and Roedder John, 1997). Future research should thus further investigate the influence of uncertainty and comprehension on new product idea evaluation. A promising avenue for future research may be to explore whether or not elaborate idea descriptions, design sketches (Mugge and Dahl, 2013), and analogies from other domains (Gregan-Paxton et al., 2002) could enable individuals with lower domain knowledge to overcome comprehension problems and, thus, increase the efficiency of their new product idea evaluations.

Fifth, the study's results support the argument that consumer generally especially have difficulties with evaluating radical new product ideas accurately (e.g., Hoeffler, 2003; Veryzer, 1998). However, this has been verified as only being the case in respect of consumers with lower domain knowledge (in this study's sample classified as "laymen"), because the highest domain knowledge in the sample was found among members of 3D printing communities. Consequently, this study's findings support the premise that specific consumers (i.e., with high domain knowledge) are well equipped to proficiently evaluate early-stage radical new product ideas (Ozer, 2009; Pitta and Fowler, 2005). Additional analysis of the study's data also corroborates a strong correlation between the respondents' domain knowledge and their lead userness[81] (Faullant et al., 2012). The study's findings thus further promote utilizing the abilities of lead users beyond the

---

[81] A definition of lead users is stated by, for example, von Hippel (1986), Franke, von Hippel, and Schreier (2006) or von Hippel, Franke, and Prügl (2009). Seven items, adapted to the context of 3D printing, were included in the study to capture the individual evaluator's degree of lead userness (Faullant et al. (2012). Correlation analysis between the two constructs of lead userness and domain knowledge revealed a high correlation ($r = .879$; $p < .001$).

generation of new product ideas to also include the evaluation of new product ideas (Ozer, 2009). Future research could explore this possibility further.

Finally, the results of this study deliver a possible new explanation for prior ambiguous findings regarding the role of "experts" and "non-experts" in idea evaluation. Whereas management research studies have advocated involving users (Magnusson, Wästlund, and Netz, 2016; Kornish and Ulrich, 2014) or employees outside the R&D department (Onarheim and Christensen, 2012) to complement, or even substitute, firm-internal expert evaluators, creativity research has argued that experts cannot be easily replaced (Kaufman et al., 2008). Unfortunately, the definitions of "experts" and "non-experts" have varied substantially in these studies and, in most cases, these definitions were not explicitly associated with evaluators' domain knowledge. The current study's sample statistics have shown that individuals with high domain knowledge can be found among industry professionals – traditionally defined as "experts" in prior research – as well as among community members previously defined as "users." Consequently, this study encourages future researchers to identify further underlying characteristics at the individual evaluator level that might inform different idea evaluation outcomes between the groups previously defined as "experts," "quasi-experts," "users," or "novices."

6.3 Managerial implications

The question of how to increase the proficiency of new product idea evaluation at the front-end of innovation is of crucial importance. Firms have to evaluate a multitude of possibilities during their quest to identify promising new product ideas that can be developed into successful new products. In this context, a basic question for management practice is: "Who can be considered a suitable evaluator for the assessment of early-stage new product ideas?"

The study's findings suggest that management practice needs to employ evaluators with a comprehensive knowledge of the users' needs and wants, and of the chances, as well as limitations, of the available technology in the new product ideas' domain. Individual evaluators without such domain knowledge struggle to accurately evaluate early-stage new product ideas in their most relevant dimensions, i.e., originality, user value, and feasibility. This impedes decision makers' abilities to proficiently select high potential new product ideas based on these evaluations. Allowing individuals with insufficient domain knowledge to evaluate new product ideas is thus likely to increase false negatives in respect of radical new product ideas and false positives relating to incremental new product ideas. In this context, it is worth acknowledging that this effect applies equally to criteria-based and holistic evaluation tasks.

Consequently, these findings have implications with regard to the selection of appropriate individual evaluators and in respect of the composition of idea evaluation teams, internally, as well as externally. In selecting evaluators internally, managers should expand their selection criteria beyond the established criteria, such as general experience in research and development, marketing, and sales, to include domain knowledge as a major selection criterion. In an open evaluation process, managers should reconsider the common practice of inviting all registered participants to contribute to the idea evaluation task (Poetz and Schreier, 2012; Haller, 2013), irrespective of their domain knowledge (Velamuri et al., 2015) and the evaluation task by selecting evaluators more carefully.

Managers should identify individuals with high domain knowledge to enable the study's findings to be utilized in practice. They should therefore be aware of, especially, the value of lead users - who are agued to possess superior domain knowledge - in evaluating new product ideas (Ozer, 2009). To successfully identify these lead users, managers can revert to established methods of lead user identification, such as pyramiding and screening (von Hippel, Franke, and Prügl, 2009). Managers should also recognize that lead users can be sourced from within the firm (Schweisfurth and Herstatt, 2015), as well as from active members of relevant online communities (Marchi, Giachetti, and Genarro, 2011).

Given the fact that evaluators with high domain knowledge may likely remain a very limited resource for firms, the study's findings imply that idea evaluation efficiency may be increased by relating the choice of evaluator to the specific evaluation purpose (Runco, McCarthy, and Svenson, 1994). Even evaluators with low to moderate domain knowledge seem to generally recognize the most incremental ideas, especially in terms of them having a low user value. In practice, this could be leveraged by a two-step evaluation process, combining the strength in numbers of non-expert-evaluations and the evaluation proficiency of individuals with high domain knowledge (see Figure 6). In a first step, employees (Onarheim and Christensen, 2012) or consumers (Magnusson, Wästlund, and Netz, 2016) with low to moderate domain knowledge could be leveraged to identify those ideas with the lowest user value. This helps the firm significantly reduce the number of ideas by eliminating those that do not provide the customer with superior user value and cannot be considered a suitable starting point for high potential innovations. After discarding all ideas with very low user value scores, evaluators with high domain knowledge could evaluate the remaining ideas along all three dimensions in order to discern promising incremental ideas from high potential radical ones. This approach may be especially helpful for firms that generate large numbers of new product ideas with a very high variance in the idea quality when using crowdsourcing (Bayus, 2013) or innovation tournaments (Terwiesch and Ulrich, 2009). Such firms thus might be willing to trade some level of effectiveness for higher efficiency.[82]

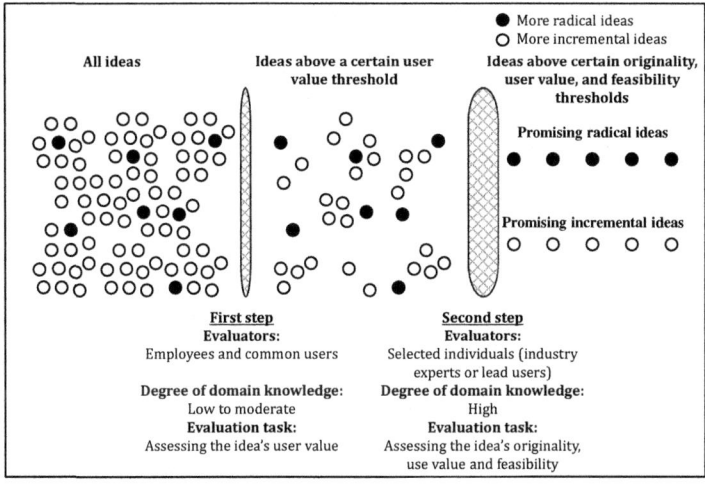

Figure 37: Two-step evaluation process combining "expert" and "non-expert" evaluations

6.4 Limitations and future research

A number of this study's imitations are noteworthy and offer several opportunities for future research.

---

[82] Although such a step-wise approach has been suggested before, e.g. by Terwiesch and Ulrich (2009) and Magnusson, Wästlund, and Netz (2016), the study's data do not allow for ignoring the possibility that valuable ideas may be rejected in the first step of such a process due to inaccurate evaluations. Managers should thus be aware that such a process is always a trade-off between efficiency and effectiveness Terwiesch and Ulrich (2009).

The first limitation is the study's focus on domain knowledge only. Additional types of knowledge, such as functional knowledge in R&D, manufacturing, marketing or sales (Dougherty, 1992), and knowledge of analog domains (Dahl and Moreau, 2002; Gregan-Paxton et al., 2002), may also play a role in evaluating new product ideas; future research should thus take this into account.

Second, this study is concerned with the evaluation of early-stage new product ideas in respect of which the evaluators have to specifically rely on their pre-existing knowledge. However, once the idea is developed into a more detailed concept in the later stages of the NPD process, considerably more quantitative, formal, and precise information becomes available to guide evaluators' judgments (Kim and Wilemon, 2002). Thus, researchers should further investigate the role of domain knowledge in the evaluation decisions on projects in the later NPD stages.

Third, this study focuses at the individual level, although many idea selection decisions in the front-end of innovation are taken at the team level. Future research should explore the possibility of combining different types of knowledge in idea evaluation teams, i.e., how to effectively combine individuals who may only have access to the need knowledge that is available to users of the product (i.e., users) with those who may only possess solution knowledge (i.e., new product developers).

Fourth, some limitations arise from the study's choice of domain. I selected the domain of 3D printing, because it requires particular knowledge to understand and evaluate new product ideas. I specifically chose this domain to isolate the influence of domain knowledge. By acknowledging that some domains may require more, or less, knowledge than others to accurately evaluate new product ideas (Amabile, 1996; Kaufman, Baer, and Cole, 2009), future research should analyze different domains, industries, and product categories.

Finally, the majority of the variables in the research framework are measured using self-ratings collected from a single source, consequently exposing the study's data to common method bias. However, several established precautions were taken in the study's design to control for this possible bias and the data were checked by means of Harman's single-factor test to confirm that no common method variance is observable (Malhotra, Kim, and Patil, 2006; Podsakoff, 1986; Podsakoff et al., 2003).

7 References

Agent3D. 2015. Available at: http://www.agent3d.de.

Agor W.H. 1984. *Intuitive management*. Englewood Cliffs, New Jersey: Prentice-Hall.

Aiken, L. S. and West, S. G. 1991. *Multiple regression: testing and interpreting interactions*. Newbury Park, CA: Sage Publications.

Akinci, C. and Sadler-Smith, E. 2012. "Intuition in Management Research: A Historical Review." *International Journal of Management Reviews* 14 (1): 104–122.

Alba, J. W. and Hutchinson, J. W. 1987. "Dimensions of consumer expertise." *Journal of Consumer Research* 13 (4): 411–454.

Alexy, O., George, G., Salter, A. 2013. "Cui bono? The selective revealing of knowledge and its implications for innovative activity." *Academy of Management Review* 13 (2): 270–291.

Amabile, T. M. 1982. "Children's artistic creativity: Detrimental effects of competition in a field setting." *Personality and Social Psychology Bulletin* 8 (3): 573–578.

Amabile, T. M. 1983. "The social psychology of creativity: A componential conceptualization." *Journal of Personality and Social Psychology* 45 (2): 357–376.

Amabile, T. M. 1996. *Creativity in context: Update to "The Social Psychology of Creativity"*. Boulder, CO, US: Westview Press.

Amabile, T. M., Barsade, S. G., Mueller, J. S., Staw, B. M. 2005. "Affect and creativity at work." *Administrative Science Quarterly* 50: 367–403.

Anastasi, A. and Urbina, S. 1998. *Psychological testing*. 7th ed. Upper Saddle River, NJ: Prentice Hall.

Anderson, J. R. 2015. *Cognitive psychology and its implications*. 8th ed. New York: Worth Publishers.

Andrew, J. and Sirkin, H. 2003. "Innovating for cash." *Harvard Business Review* 81 (9): 76–83.

Backhaus, K., Erichson, B., Plinke, W., Weiber, R. 2011. *Multivariate Analysemethoden: Eine anwendungsorientierte Einführung*. 13th ed. Berlin: Springer.

Baer, J. 1993. *Creativity and divergent thinking: A task-specific approach*. Hillsdale, NJ: Lawrence Erlbaum Associates.

Baer, J., Kaufman, J. C., Gentile, C. A. 2004. "Extension of the consensual assessment technique to nonparallel creative products." *Creativity Research Journal* 16 (1): 113–117.

Baker, Kenneth, G. and Albaum, G. S. 1986. "Modeling New Product Screening Decisions." *Journal of Product Innovation Management* 1: 32–39.

Balachandra, R. and Friar, J. H. 1997. "Factors for success in R&D projects and new product innovation. A contextual framework." *IEEE Transactions on Engineering Management* 44 (3): 276–287.

Barczak, G. 2014. "JPIM research priorities." *Journal of Product Innovation Management* 31 (4): 640–641.

Barczak, G., Griffin, A., Kahn, K. B. 2009. "PERSPECTIVE: Trends and drivers of success in NPD practices: Results of the 2003 PDMA best practices study." *Journal of Product Innovation Management* 26: 3–23.

Baron, R. M. and Kenny, D. A. 1986. "The moderator-mediator variable distinction in social psychological research: Conceptual, strategic, and statistical considerations." *Journal of Personality and Social Psychology* 51: 1173–1182.

Bayus, B. L. 2013. "Crowdsourcing new product ideas over time: An analysis of the Dell IdeaStorm community." *Management Science* 59 (1): 226–244.

Bédard, J. and Chi, M. T. H. 1992. "Expertise." *Current Directions in Psychological Science* 1 (4): 135–139.

Behrens, J. and Ernst, H. 2014. "What Keeps Managers Away from a Losing Course of Action? Go/Stop Decisions in New Product Development." *Journal of Product Innovation Management* 31 (2): 361–374.

Behrens, J., Ernst, H., Shepherd, D. A. 2014. "The decision to exploit an R&D project: Divergent thinking across middle and senior managers." *Journal of Product Innovation Management* 31 (1): 144–158.

Berekhoven, L., Eckert W., Ellenrieder P. 2004. *Marktforschung. Methodische Grundlagen und praktische Anwendungen.* Wiesbaden: Gabler.

Berg, J. M. 2016. "Balancing on the creative highwire: Forecasting the success of novel ideas in organizations." *Administrative Science Quarterly* (forthcoming).

Besemer S. P. and O'Quinn, K. 1987. "Creative Product Analysis: Testing a Model by Developing Judging Instruments." In: *Frontiers of creativity research*, edited by S. G. Isaksen, 341–357. Buffalo, NY: Bearly Limited.

Bettman, J. R. and Sujan, M. 1987. "Effects of framing on evaluation of omparable and noncomparable alternatives by expert and novice consumers." *Journal of Consumer Research* 14 (2): 141–154.

Blair, C. S. and Mumford, M. D. 2007. "Errors in idea evaluation: Preference for the unoriginal." *Journal of Creative Behavior* 41 (3): 197–222.

Blohm, I., Leimeister, J. M., Krcmar, H. 2013. "Crowdsourcing: How to benefit from (too) many great ideas." *MIS Quarterly Executive* 12 (4).

Blohm, I., Riedl, C., Leimeister, J. M., Krcmar, H. (Eds.). 2011. Idea Evaluation Mechanisms for Collective Intelligence in Open Innovation Communities: Do Traders outperform Raters? 32. International Conference on Information, Shanghai, China.

Boeddrich, H.-J. 2004. "Ideas in the Workplace: A New Approach Towards Organizing the Fuzzy Front End of the Innovation Process." *Creativity and Innovation Management* 13 (4).

Bogers, M. and West, J. 2012. "Managing distributed innovation. Strategic utilization of open and user innovation." *Creativity and Innovation Management* 21 (1): 61–75.

Bortz, J. and Schuster, C. 2010. *Statistik für Human- und Sozialwissenschaftler.* 7th ed. Berlin, Heidelberg: Springer.

BoXZY. 2015. Can your 3D printer shape metal? Avalaible at: http://www.boxzy.com/.

Breusch, T. S. and Pagan, A. R. 1979. "A simple test for heteroscedasticity and random coefficient variation." *Econometrica* 47 (5): 1287.

Broniarczyk, S. M. and Alba, J. W. 1994. "The role of consumers' intuitions in inference making." *Journal of Consumer Research* 21 (December): 393–407.

Bryman, A. 2008. *Social research methods.* 3rd ed. Oxford, UK: Oxford University Press.

Buhrmester, M., Kwang, T., Gosling, S. D. 2011. "Amazon's mechanical turk: A new source of on expensive, yet high-quality, data?" *Perspectives on psychological science: a journal of the Association for Psychological Science* 6 (1): 3–5.

Calantone, R. J., Chan, K., Cui, A. S. 2006. "Decomposing Product innovativeness and its effects on new product success." *Journal of Product Innovation Management* 23 (5): 408–421.

Calantone, R. J., DiBenedetto, A. C., Schmidt, J. B. 1999. "Using the analytic hierarchy process in new product development." *Journal of Product Innovation Management* 16: 65–76.

Campbell, D. T. and Fiske, D. W. 1959. "Convergent and discriminant validation by the multitrait-multimethod matrix." *Psychlogical Bulletin* 56 (2): 81.

Carbonell-Foulquié, P., Munuera-Alemán, J. L., Rodriguez-Escudero, A. I. 2004. "Criteria employed for go/no-go decisions when developing successful highly innovative products." *Industrial Marketing Management* 33 (4): 307–316.

Carson, S. 2006. *Creativity and mental illness.* Invitational Panel Discussion Hosted by Yale's Mind (April 19th). New Haven, CT.

Chandy, R. K. and Tellis, G. J. 1998. "Organizing for radical product innovation: The overlooked role of willingness to cannibalize." *Journal of Marketing Research* 35 (4): 474–487.

Chao, R. O. and Kavadias, S. 2008. "A theoretical framework for managing the new product development portfolio. When and how to use strategic buckets." *Management Science* 54 (5): 907–921.

Chesbrough, H. 2006a. "Open innovation: A new paradigm for understanding industrial innovation." In: *Open innovation: Researching a new paradigm*, edited by Henry Chesbrough, Wim Vanhaverbeke, and Joel West, 1–12. Oxford, UK: Oxford University Press.

Chesbrough, H., Vanhaverbeke, W., West, J. (Eds.). 2006. Open innovation: Researching a new paradigm. Oxford, UK: Oxford University Press.

Chesbrough, H. W. 2006b. *Open innovation: The new imperative for creating and profiting from technology.* Boston, Mass.: Harvard Business School Press.

Chi, M., Glaser, R., Rees, E. 1982. "Expertise in Problem Solving." In: *Advances in the Psychology of Human Intelligence*, edited by Robert J. Sternberg, 7–76. Hillsdale, NJ: Erlbaum.

Chi, M. T. H. and Glaser, R. 1988. *The nature of expertise.* Hillsdale, N.J.: Lawrence Erlbaum Associates.

Chin, W. W. 1998a. "Issues and opinion on structural equation modeling." *MIS Quarterly* 22 (1): vii–xvi.

Chin, W. W. 1998b. "The partial least squares approach to structural equation modeling." In: *Modern Methods for Business Research*, edited by George A. Marcoulides, 295–336. Mahwah, N.J: Lawrence Erlbaum.

Christiaans, H. 2002. "Creativity as a design criterion." *Creativity Research Journal* 14 (1): 41–54.

Cohen, J., Cohen P., West, S. G., Aiken, L. S. 2003. *Applied multiple regression/correlation analysis for the behavioral sciences.* Mahwah, N.J: Erlbaum.

Cohen, W. M. and Levinthal, D. A. 1990. "Absorptive Capacity: A New Perspective on Learning and Innovation." *Administrative Science Quarterly* 35: 128–152.

Colin Cameron, A. and Miller, D. L. 2015. "A practitioner's guide to cluster-robust inference." *Journal of Human Resources* 50 (2): 317–372.

Conchar, M. P. 2004. "An Integrated Framework for the Conceptualization of Consumers' Perceived-Risk Processing." *Journal of the Academy of Marketing Science* 32 (4): 418–436.

Conway, J. M. and Huffcutt, A. I. 1997. "Psychometric properties of multisource performance ratings. A meta-analysis of subordinate, supervisor, peer, and self-Ratings." *Human Performance* 10 (4): 331–360.

Cooper, R. G. 1979. "The dimensions of industrial new product success and failure." *Journal of Marketing* 43: 93–103.

Cooper, R. G. 1983. "A process model for industrial new product development." *IEEE Transactions on Engineering Management* EM-30 (1): 2–11.

Cooper, R. G. 1988. "Predevelopment activities determine new product success." *Industrial Marketing Management* 17 (3): 237–247.

Cooper, R. G. 1999. "From Experience: The invisible success factors in product innovation." *Journal of Product Innovation Management* 16: 115–133.

Cooper, R. G. 2008. "Perspective: The Stage-Gate ® idea-to-launch process. Update, what's New, and NexGen systems." *Journal of Product Innovation Management* 25 (3): 213–232.

Cooper, R. G. 2011. *Winning at new products: Creating value through innovation.* 4th ed. New York: Basic Books.

Cooper, R. G., Edgett, S. J., Kleinschmidt, E. J. 2002. "Portfolio management: Fundamental for new product success." *The PDMA Toolbook 1 for New Product Development*: 331–364.

Cooper, R. G. and Kleinschmidt, E. J. 1986. "An investigation into the new product process: Steps, deficiencies, and impact." *Journal of Product Innovation Management* 3: 71–85.

Cooper, R. G. and Kleinschmidt, E. J. 1995. "Benchmarking the firm's critical success factors in new product development." *Journal of Product Innovation Management* 12 (5): 374–391.

Crawford, M. C. 1977. "Marketing research and the new product failure." *Journal of Marketing* April: 51–61.

Cronbach, L. J. 1951. "Coefficient alpha and the internal structure of tests." *Psychometrika* 16 (3): 297–334.

Crossan, M. M. and Apaydin, M. 2010. "A multi-dimensional framework of organizational innovation. A systematic review of the literature." *Journal of Management Studies* 47 (6): 1154–1191.

Csikszentmihalyi, M. 1996. *Creativity: Flow and the psychology of discovery and invention.* New York: HarperCollins.

Cui, G., Peng, L., Florès, L. P. 2015. "Selecting ideas for new product development." *European Journal of Innovation Management* 18 (3): 380–396.

Cureton, E. and D'Agostino, R. 1993. *Factor analysis: An applies approach.* New Jersey: Hillsdale.

Dahan, E. and Mendelson, H. 2001. "An Extreme-Value Model of Concept Testing." *Management Science* 47 (1): 102–116.

Dahan, E., Soukhoroukova, A., Spann, M. 2010. "New Product Development 2.0: Preference Markets. - How Scalable Securities Markets Identify Winning Product Concepts and Attributes." *Journal of Product Innovation Management* 27: 937–954.

Dahl, D. W. and Moreau, P. 2002. "The influence and value of analogical thinking during new product ideation." *Journal of Marketing Research* 39 (1): 47–60.

Dahlander, L. and Wallin, M. W. 2006. "A man on the inside. Unlocking communities as complementary assets." *Research Policy* 35 (8): 1243–1259.

Dane, E. 2010. "Reconsidering the trade-off between expertise and flexibility: a cognitive entrenchment perspective." *Academy of Management Review* 35 (4): 579–603.

Dane, E. and Pratt, M. G. 2007. "Exploring Intuition and its Role in Managerial Decision Making." *Academy of Management Review* 32 (1): 33–54.

Danneels, E. 2007. "The process of technological competence leveraging." *Strategic Management Journal* 28 (5): 511–534.

Davidson, R. 1976. "The Role of Metaphor and Analogy in Learning." In: *Cognitive Learning in Children: Theories and Strategies*, edited by Joel Levin and Vernon Allen. New York: Academic Press.

Dean, D. L., Hender, J. M., Rodgers, T. L., Santanen, E. L. 2006. "Identifying quality, novel, and creative ideas: Constructs and scales for idea evaluation." *Journal of the Association for Information Systems* 7 (10): 646–699.

Dougherty, D. 1992. "Interpretive barriers to successful product innovation in large firms." *Organization Science* 3 (2): 179–202.

Driscoll, M. 1994. *Psychology of learning for instruction.* Boston: Allyn and Bacon.

Duncker, K. 1945. "On problem-solving (Translated By Lees, L. S.)." *Psychological Monographs* 58 (5): i-113.

Durbin, J. and Watson, G. S. 1950. "Testing for serial correlation in least squares regression." *Biometrika* 37 (3/4): 409–428.

Dwyer, L. and Mellor, R. 1991. "Corporate environment and the proficiency of new product process activities." *Technovation* 11 (2): 63–78.

Ebner, W., Leimeister, J. M., Krcmar, H. 2009. "Community engineering for innovations: the ideas competition as a method to nurture a virtual community for innovations." *R&D Management* 39 (4).

Edwards, J. R. and Lambert, L. S. 2007. "Methods for integrating moderation and mediation: A general analytical framework using moderated path analysis." *Psychological Methods* 12 (1): 1–22.

Eling, K. 2014. "Investigating two unresolved issues in fuzzy front end execution." Doctorial Dissertation.   Eindhoven   University   of   Technology.   Available at: http://repository.tue.nl/766135.

Eling, K., Griffin, A., Langerak, F. 2014. "Using intuition in fuzzy front-end decision-making: A conceptual framework." *Journal of Product Innovation Management* 31 (5): 626–641.

Eling, K., Griffin, A., Langerak, F. 2016. "Consistency matters in formally selecting incremental and radical new product ideas for advancement." *Journal of Product Innovation Management*: (forthcoming).

Eling, K., Langerak, F., Griffin, A. 2013. "A stage-wise approach to exploring performance effects of cycle time reduction." *Journal of Product Innovation Management* 30 (4): 626–641.

Eling, K., Langerak, F., Griffin, A. 2015. "The performance effects of combining rationality and intuition in making early new product idea evaluation decisions." *Creativity and Innovation Management* 24 (3): 464–477.

Ericsson, K. A., Charness, N., Feltovich, P., Hoffmann, R. R. 2006. *The Cambridge handbook of expertise and expert performance.* Cambridge: Cambridge University Press.

Ericsson, K. A. and Lehmann, A. C. 1996. "Expert and exceptional performance. Evidence of maximal adaptation to task constraints." *Annual Review of Psychology* 47 (1): 273–305.

Evanschitzky, H., Eisend, M., Calantone, R. J., Jiang, Y. 2012. "Success factors of product innovation: An updated meta-analysis." *Journal of Product Innovation Management* 29: 21–37.

fastcodesign.com.   2015.   Wood,   limestone,   and   metal   printing.   Available at: http://www.fastcodesign.com/3040518/the-9-best-ideas-from-ces-2015.

Faullant, R., Schwarz, E. J., Krajger, I., Breitenecker, R. J. 2012. "Towards a comprehensive understanding of lead userness: The search for individual creativity." *Creativity and Innovation Management* 21 (1): 76–92.

Field, A. P. and Hole, G. 2003. *How to design and report experiments.* London, Thousand Oakes, CA: Sage Publications.

Fiske, S. and Taylor, S. 1991. "Conditions of Schema Use." In: *Social Cognition,* edited by Susan Fiske and Shelley Taylor, 142–179. New York: McGraw-Hill.

Fiske, S. T., Kinder, D. R., Larter, W. 1983. "The novice and the expert. Knowledge-based strategies in political cognition." *Journal of Experimental Social Psychology* 19 (4): 381–400.

Fleming, L. and Sorenson, O. 2004. "Science as a map in technological search." *Strategic Management Journal* 25: 909–928.

Fornell, C. and Larcker, D. F. 1981. "Evaluating structural equation models with unobservable variables and measurement error." *Journal of Marketing Research* 18 (1): 39–50.

Franke, N., Poetz, M. K., Schreier, M. 2014. "Integrating problem solvers from analogous markets in new product ideation." *Management Science* 60 (4): 1063–1081.

Franke, N., von Hippel, E., Schreier, M. 2006. "Finding commercially attractive user innovations: A test of lead-user theory." *Journal of Product Innovation Management* 23: 301–315.

Frazier, P. A., Tix, A. P., Barron, K. E. 2004. "Testing moderator and mediator effects in counseling psychology research." *Journal of Counseling Psychology* 51 (1): 115–134.

Galbraith, C. S., DeNoble, A. F., Ehrlich, S. B., Mesmer-Magnus, J. 2010. "Review panel consensus and post-decision commercial performance: a study of early stage technologies." *Journal of Technology Transfer* 35 (2): 253–281.

Galbraith, C. S., Ehrlich, S. B., DeNoble, A. F. 2006. "Predicting technology success: identifying key predictors and assessing expert evaluation for advanced technologies." *The Journal of Technology Transfer* 31 (6): 673–684.

Garcia, R. 2010. "Types of innovation." In: *Encyclopedia of technology and innovation management,* edited by V. K. Narayanan and Gina C. O'Connor, 89–95. Chichester: John Wiley & Sons, Inc.

Garcia, R. and Calantone, R. 2002. "A critical look at technological innovation typology and innovativeness terminology: a literature review." *Journal of Product Innovation Management* 19 (2): 110–132.

Garton, L., Haythornthwaite, C., Wellman, B. 2011. "Studying online social networks." In: *Doing internet research: Critical issues and methods for examining the net*, edited by S. Jones, 75–105. Thousand Oakes, CA: Sage.

Gatignon, H., Tushman, M. L., Smith, W., Anderson, P. 2002. "A structural approach to assessing innovation: Construct development of innovation locus, type, and characteristics." *Management Science* 48 (9): 1103–1122.

Gaubinger, K. and Rabl, M. 2014. "Structuring the front end of innovation." In: *Management of the fuzzy front end of innovations*, edited by O. Gassmann and F. Schweitzer, 15–30: Springer.

Gaubinger, K., Rabl, M., Swan, S., Werani, T. 2015. *Innovation and product management: A holistic and practical approach to uncertainty reduction.* Heidelberg: Springer.

Gemünden, H. G., Salomo, S., Hölzle, K. 2007. "Role models for radical innovations in times of open innovation." *Creativity and Innovation Management* 16 (4): 408–421.

George, D. and Mallery, P. 2012. *IBM SPSS statistics step by step: A simple guide and reference.* 12th ed.: Boston; Pearson Education.

Gerbing, D. W. and Anderson, J. C. 1988. "An updated paradigm for scale development incorporating unidimensionality and Its assessment." *Journal of Marketing Research* 25 (2): 186.

Girotra, K., Terwiesch, C., Ulrich, K. T. 2010. "Idea generation and the quality of the best idea." *Management Science* 56 (4): 591–605.

Goldberg, L. R. 1990. "An alternative "Description of Personality": The big-five factor structure." *Journal of Personality and Social Psychology* 59 (6): 1216–1229.

Good, P. I. 2001. *Resampling methods: a practical guide to data analysis.* Boston, MA: Birkhauser.

Graeff, T. R. and Olson, J. C. 1994. "Consumer inference as part of product comprehension." *Advances in Consumer Research* 21 (1): 201–207.

Green, S. G., Gavin M. B., Aiman-Smith, L. 1995. "Assessing a multidimensional measure of radical technological innovation." *IEEE Transactions on Engineering Management* 42: 203–214.

Gregan-Paxton, J., Hibbard, J., Brunel, F. F., Azar, P. 2002. ""So that's what that is" examining the impact of analogy on consumers' knowledge development for really new products." *Psychology and Marketing* 19 (6): 533–550.

Gregan-Paxton, J. and Roedder John, D. 1997. "Consumer learning by analogy: A model of internal knowledge transfer." *Journal of Consumer Research* 24 (3): 266–284.

Griffin, A. 1997. "PDMA research on new product development practices: Updating trends and benchmarking best practices." *Journal of Product Innovation Management* 14 (6): 429–458.

Hair, J. F., Black, W. C., Babin, B. J., Anderson, R. E. 2014a. *Multivariate data analysis.* 7th ed. Harlow: Pearson Education Limited.

Hair, J. F., Hult, G. Thomas M., Ringle, C. M., Sarstedt, M. 2014b. *A primer on partial least squares structural equations modeling (PLS-SEM).* Thousand Oakes, CA: Sage Publications.

Hair, J. F., Ringle, C. M., Sarstedt, M. 2011. "PLS-SEM: Indeed a silver bullet." *The Journal of Marketing Theory and Practice* 19 (2): 139–152.

Hair, J. F., Sarstedt, M., Ringle, C. M., Mena, J. A. 2012. "An assessment of the use of partial least squares structural equation modeling in marketing research." *Journal of the Academy of Marketing Science* 40 (3): 414–433.

Haller, J. 2013. *Open evaluation: Integrating users into the selection of new product ideas.* Wiesbaden, London: Gabler; Springer.

Hart, S., Hultink, E. J., Nikolaos, T., Commandeur, H. R. 2003. "Industrial companies' evaluation criteria in new product development gates." *Journal of Product Innovation Management* 20: 22–36.

Hartmann, P. 2014. *New business creation: Systems for institutionalized radical innovation management.* Wiesbaden: Springer Gabler.

Hauschildt, J. and Salomo, S. 2007. *Innovationsmanagement.* 4th ed. München: Vahlen.

Hayes, A. F. 2013. *Introduction to mediation, moderation, and conditional process analysis: A regression-based approach:* Guilford Press.

Hayes, A. F. and Cai, L. 2007. "Using heteroskedasticity-consistent standard error estimators in OLS regression: An introduction and software implementation." *Behavior Research Methods* 39 (4): 709–722.

Hedeker, D. and Gibbons, R. D. 1994. "A random-effects ordinal regression model for multilevel analysis." *Biometrics* 50 (4): 933–944.

Hekkert, P. and Wieringen, P. 1996. "Beauty in the eye of expert and nonexpert beholders. A Study in the Appraisal of Art." *The American Journal of Psychology* 109 (3): 389.

Herstatt, C. and Verworn, B. 2001. *The "fuzzy front end" of innovation.* Hamburg University of Technology.

Herstatt, C. and Verworn, B. (Eds.). 2007. Management der frühen Innovationsphasen: Grundlagen, Methoden, neue Ansätze. 2nd ed. Wiesbaden: Gabler.

Hoaglin, D. C. and Iglewicz, B. 1987. "Fine-tuning some resistant rules for outlier labeling." *Journal of the American Statistical Association* 82 (400): 1147–1149.

Hoaglin, D. C., Iglewicz, B., Tukey, J. W. 1986. "Performance of some resistant rules for outlier labeling." *Journal of the American Statistical Association* 81 (396): 991–999.

Hoeffler, S. 2003. "Measuring preferences for really new products." *Journal of Marketing Research* 40 (November): 406–420.

Hoffmann, R. R. 1992. *The psychology of expertise: Cognitive research and empirical AI.* New York: Springer-Verlag.

Hoffmann, R. R. 1998. "How can expertise be defined? Implications of research from cognitive psychology." In: *Exploring expertise*, edited by R. Williams, W. Faulkner, and J. Fleck, 81–100. New York: Macmillam.

Homburg, C. and Giering, A. 1996. "Konzeptualisierung und Operationalisierung komplexer Konstrukte: ein Leitfaden für die Marketingforschung." *Marketing ZFP* 18 (1): 5–24.

Homburg, C., Wieseke, J., Bornemann, T. 2009. "Implementing the marketing concept at the employee–customer interface: The role of customer need knowledge." *Journal of Marketing* 73 (July): 64–81.

Huang, S., Yeo, A. A., Li, S. D. 2007. "Modification of Kolmogorov-Smirnov test for DNA content data analysis through distribution alignment." *Assay and drug development technologies* 5 (5): 663–671.

Im, S., Montoya, M. M., Workman, J. P. 2013. "Antecedents and consequences of creativity in product innovation teams." *Journal of Product Innovation Management* 30 (1): 170–185.

Jaworski, B. J. and Kohli, A. K. 1993. "Market orientation: Antecedents and consequences." *Journal of Marketing* 57 (July): 53–70.

Jeppesen, L. B. and Lakani, K. R. 2010. "Marginality and problem-solving effectiveness in broadcast search." *Organization Science* 21 (5): 1016–1033.

Judd, C. M. and Kenny, D. A. 1981. "Estimating mediation in treatment evaluations." *Evaluation Review,* 5: 602–619.

Kaiser, H. F. 1970. "A second generation little jiffy." *Psychometrika* 35 (4): 401–415.

Kaiser, H. F. and Rice, J. 1974. "Little Jiffy, Mark IV." *Educational and Psychological Measurement* 34 (1): 111–117.

Kaufman, J. C., Baer, J., Cole, J. C. 2009. "Expertise, domains, and the consensual assessment technique." *The Journal of Creative Behavior* 43 (4): 223–233.

Kaufman, J. C., Baer, J., Cole, J. C., Sexton, J. D. 2008. "A comparison of expert and nonexpert raters using the consensual assessment technique." *Creativity Research Journal* 20 (2): 171–178.

Kaufman, J. C., Baer, J., Cropley, D. H., Reiter-Palmon, R., Sinnett, S. 2013. "Furious activity vs. understanding: How much expertise is needed to evaluate creative work?" Available at: http://digitalcommons.unomaha.edu/psychfacpub.

Kaufman, J. C., Lee, J., Baer, J., Lee, S. 2007. "Captions, consistency, creativity, and the consensual assessment technique. New evidence of reliability." *Thinking Skills and Creativity* 2 (2): 96–106.

Khurana, A. and Rosenthal, S. R. 1997. "Integrating the fuzzy front end of new product development." *Sloan Management Review* 38 (2): 103–120.

Kim, J. and Wilemon, D. 2002. "Focusing the fuzzy front-end in new product development." *R&D Management* 32 (4): 269–279.

Klein, G. 1998. *Sources of power: How people make decisions.* Cambridge, MA: MIT Press.

Klein, G. 2008. "Naturalistic decision making." *Human Factors* 50 (3): 456–460.

Klein, G. A., Orasanu J., Calderwood R., Zsambok, C. E. (Eds.). 1993. Decision making in action: Models and methods. Norwood, NJ: Ablex Publishing Corporation.

Kock, A., Heising, W., Gemünden, H. G. 2015. "How ideation portfolio management influences front-end success." *Journal of Product Innovation Management* 32 (4): 539–555.

Koen, P., Ajamian, G., Burkart, R., Clamen, A., Davidson, J., D'Amore, R., Elkins, C., Herald, K., Incorvia, M., Johnson, A., Karol, R., Seibert, R., Slavejkov, A., Wagner, K. 2001. "Providing clarity and a common language to the "fuzzy front end"." *Research-Technology Management* 44 (2): 46–55.

Kornish, L. J. and Ulrich, K. T. 2014. "The importance of the raw idea in innovation: testing the sow's ear hypothesis." *Journal of Marketing Research* 51 (1): 14–26.

Kozhevnikov, M. 2007. "Cognitive styles in the context of modern psychology: Toward an integrated framework of cognitive style." *Psychlogical Bulletin* 133 (3): 464–481.

Kristensson, P., Gustafsson, A., Archer, T. 2004. "Harnessing the creative potential among users." *Journal of Product Innovation Management* 21: 4–14.

Kristensson, P. and Magnusson, P. R. 2010. "Tuning users' innovativeness during ideation." *Creativity and Innovation Management* 19 (2): 147–159.

Kudrowitz, B. M. and Wallace, D. 2013. "Assessing the quality of ideas from prolific, early-stage product ideation." *Journal of Engineering Design* 24 (2): 120–139.

Landis, J. R. and Koch, G. G. 1977. "The measurement of observer agreement for categorical data." *Biometrics* 33 (1): 159.

Langerak, F., Hultink, E. J., Robben, H. S. 2004. "The role of predevelopment activities in the relationship between market orientation and performance." *R&D Management* 34 (3): 295–309.

Lerch, M. and Spieth, P. 2013. "Innovation project portfolio management. A Qualitative Analysis." *IEEE Transactions on Engineering Management* 60 (1): 18–29.

Licuanan, B. F., Dailey, L. A., Mumford, M. D. 2007. "Idea evaluation: Error in evaluating highly original ideas." *Journal of Creative Behavior* 41 (1): 1–27.

Lipshitz, R., Klein, G., Orasanu, J., Salas, E. 2001. "Focus Article: Taking Stock of Naturalistic Decision Making." *Journal of Behavioral Decision Making* 14: 331–352.

lithoz. 2015. LCM – Lithography-based ceramic manufacturing. Available at: http://www.lithoz.com/de/technologie/lcm-%E2%80%93-verfahren/.

Loch, C. H. and Kavadies, S. 2002. "Dynamic portfolio selection of NPD programs using marginal returns." *Management Science* 48 (10): 1227–1241.

Lüthje, C. 2000. *Kundenorientierung im Innovationsprozess.* Wiesbaden: Universitäts-Verlag.

Lüthje, C. 2004. "Characteristics of innovating users in a consumer goods field: An empirical study of sport-related product consumers." *Technovation* 24: 683–695.

MacKenzie, S. B., Podsakoff, P. M., Podsakoff, N. P. 2011. "Construct measurement and validation procedures in MIS and behavioral research: Integrating new and existing techniques." *MIS Quarterly* 35 (2): 293–334.

MacKinnon, D. P., Lockwood, C. M., Hoffman, J. M., West, S. G., Sheets, V. 2002. "A comparison of methods to test mediation and other intervening variable effects." *Psychological Methods* 7 (1): 83–104.

Magnusson, P. R. 2009. "Exploring the contributions of involving ordinary users in ideation of technology-based services." *Journal of Product Innovation Management* 26 (5): 578–593.

Magnusson, P. R., Netz, J., Wästlund, E. 2014. "Exploring holistic intuitive idea screening in the light of formal criteria." *Technovation* 34 (5-6): 315–326.

Magnusson, P. R., Wästlund, E., Netz, J. 2016. "Exploring users' appropriateness as a proxy for experts when screening new product/service ideas." *Journal of Product Innovation Management* 33 (1): 4–18.

Malhotra, N. K., Kim, S. S., Patil, A. 2006. "Common method variance in IS research: A comparison of alternative approaches and a reanalysis of past research." *Management Science* 52 (12): 1865–1883.

Mandler, G. 1982. "The structure of value: Accounting for taste." In: *Affect and Cognition: The 17th Annual Carnegie Symposium*, edited by M. S. Clark and S. T. Fiske, 3–36. Hillsdale, NJ: Lawrence Erlbaum Associates.

Marchi, G., Giachetti, C., Genarro, P. de. 2011. "Extending lead-user theory to online brand communities: The case of the community Ducati." *Technovation* 31: 350–361.

Markham, S. K. 2013. "The impact of front-end innovation activities on product performance." *Journal of Product Innovation Management* 30: 77–92.

Martinsuo, M. and Poskela, J. 2011. "Use of evaluation criteria and innovation performance in the front end of innovation." *Journal of Product Innovation Management* 28: 896–914.

Melone, N. P. 1994. "Reasoning in the executive suite: The influence of role/experience-based expertise on decision processes of corporate executives." *Organization Science* 5 (3): 438–455.

Meyers-Levy, J., Louie, T. A., Curren, M. T. 1994. "How does the congruity of brand names affect evaluations of brand name extensions?" *Journal of Applied Psychology* 79 (1): 46–53.

Meyers-Levy, J. and Tybout, A. 1989. "Schema congruity as a basis for product evaluation." *Journal of Consumer Research* 16 (June): 39–54.

Mitchell, A. W. and Dacin, P. A. 1996. "The assessment of alternative measures of consumer expertise." *Journal of Consumer Research* 23 (3): 219–239.

Mitchell, M. and Jolley, J. 2001. *Research design explained.* 4th ed. New York: Harcourt.

Moenart, R. K., Meyer, A. de, Souder, W. E., Deschoolmeester, D. 1995. "R&D/Marketing communication during the fuzzy front-end." *IEEE Transactions on Engineering Management* 42 (3): 243–258.

Moenart, R. K. and Souder, W. E. 1990. "An information transfer model for integrating marketing and R&D Personnel in new product development projects." *Journal of Product Innovation Management* 7 (2): 91–107.

Moreau, C. P., Lehmann, D. R., Markman, A. B. 2001. "Entrenched knowledge structures and consumer response to new products." *Journal of Marketing Research* 38 (1): 14–29.

Moreau, C. P., Markman, A. B., Lehmann, D. R. 2001. ""What is it?" Categorization flexibility and consumers' responses to really new products." *Journal of Marketing Research* 27 (March): 89–98.

Morrison, P. D., Roberts, J. H., Midgley, D. F. 2004. "The nature of lead users and measurement of leading edge status." *Research Policy* 33 (2): 351–362.

Mugge, R. and Dahl, D. W. 2013. "Seeking the ideal level of design newness: Consumer response to radical and incremental product design." *Journal of Product Innovation Management* 30 (S1): 34–47.

Mukherjee, A. and Hoyer, W. D. 2001. "The effect of novel attributes on product evaluation." *Journal of Consumer Research* 28 (December).

Mumford, M. D. and Gustafson, S. B. 1988. "Creativity syndrome: Integration, application, and innovation." *Psychological Bulletin* 103 (1): 27–43.

Murphy, S. A. and Kumar, V. 1996. "The role of predevelopment activities and firm attributes in new product success." *Technovation* 16 (8): 431–441.

Netz, J., Sukhov, A., Magnusson, P. R. 2015. "Exploring the merits of internal outsourcing to increase effectiveness and efficiency in idea screening."

Nunally, J. C. and Bernstein, I. H. 1994. *Psychometric Theory*. New York: McGraw.

Ocasio, W. 2011. "Attention to attention." *Organization Science* 22 (5): 1286–1296.

Onarheim, B. and Christensen, B. T. 2012. "Distributed idea screening in stage–gate development processes." *Journal of Engineering Design* 23 (9): 660–673.

O'Quin, K. and Besemer S. 1999. "Creative products." In: *Encyclopedia of creativity*, edited by Mark A. Runco and S. R. Pritzker, 267–278. San Diego, CA: Academic Press.

Osborne, J. W., Costello, A. B., Kellow, T. J. 2008. "Best practice in exploratory factor analysis." In: *Best practices in quantitative methods*, edited by Jason W. Osborne, 86–99. Thousand Oaks, Calif.: Sage Publications.

Osborne, J. W. and Overbay, A. 2008. "Best practices in data cleaning. How outliers and "fringeliers" can increase error rates and decrease the quality and precision of your results." In: *Best practices in quantitative methods*, edited by Jason W. Osborne, 205–213. Thousand Oaks, Calif.: Sage Publications.

Ozer, M. 1999. "A Survey of New Product Evaluation Models." *Journal of Product Innovation Management* 16: 77–94.

Ozer, M. 2005. "Factors which influence decision making in new product evaluation." *European Journal of Operational Research* 163: 784–801.

Ozer, M. 2009. "The roles of product lead-users and product experts in new product evaluation." *Research Policy* 38 (8): 1340–1349.

Paolacci, G. and Chandler, J. 2014. "Inside the turk: Understanding mechanical turk as a participant pool." *Current Directions in Psychological Science* 23 (3): 184–188.

Park, C. W. 1976. "The Effect of individual and situation-related factors on consumer selection of judgmental models." *Journal of Marketing Research* 13 (2): 144.

Parry, M. E. and Song, X. M. 1994. "Identifying new product successes in China." *Journal of Product Innovation Management* 11 (1): 15–30.

Pavlou, P. A., Liang, H., Xue, Y. 2007. "Understanding and mitigating uncertainty in online environments: A principal-agent perspective." *MIS Quarterly* 31 (1): 105–136.

Peracchio, L. A. and Tybout, A. M. 1996. "The moderating role of prior knowledge in schema-based product evaluation." *Journal of Consumer Research* 23 (3): 177–192.

Peterson, R. A. 1994. "A meta-analysis of Cronbach's coefficient alpha." *Journal of Consumer Research* 21 (2): 381–391.

Phillips, J. K., Klein, G., Sieck, W. R. 2004. "Expertise in judgment and decision making: A case for training intuitive decision skills." In: *Blackwell handbook of judgment and decision making*, edited by D. J. Koehler and N. Harvey, 297–315. Oxford, UK: Blackwell Publishing.

Piezunka, H. and Dahlander, L. 2015. "Distant search, narrow attention: How crowding alters organizations' filtering of suggestions in crowdsourcing." *Academy of Management Journal* 58 (3): 856–880.

Piller, F., Ihl, C., Vossen, A. 2011. "Customer co-creation: Open innovation with customers." In: *New forms of collaborative innovation and production on the internet*, edited by H. Hanekop and V. Wittke. Göttingen: Universitäts-Verlag Göttingen.

Piller, F. T. and Walcher, D. 2006. "Toolkits for idea competitions: a novel method to integrate users in new product development." *R&D Management* 36 (307-318).

Pisano, G. P. and Verganti, R. 2008. "Which kind of collaboration is right for you?" *Harvard Business Review* 86 (12): 78–86.

Pitta, D. A. and Fowler, D. 2005. "Online consumer communities and their value to new product developers." *Journal of Product & Brand Management* 14 (5): 283–291.

Podsakoff, P. M. 1986. "Self-Reports in organizational research: Problems and prospects." *Journal of Management* 12 (4): 531–544.

Podsakoff, P. M., MacKenzie, S. B., Lee, J.-Y., Podsakoff, N. P. 2003. "Common method biases in behavioral research: a critical review of the literature and recommended remedies." *The Journal of applied psychology* 88 (5): 879–903.

Poetz, M. K. and Schreier, M. 2012. "The value of crowdsourcing: Can users really compete with professionals in generating new product ideas?" *Journal of Product Innovation Management* 29 (2): 245–256.

Raasch, C., Herstatt, C., Lock, P. 2008. "The dynamics of user innovation: Drivers and impediments of innovation activities." *International Journal of Innovation Management* 12 (03): 377–398.

Reid, S. E. and Brentani, U. 2004. "The fuzzy front end of new product development for discontinuous innovations: A theoretical model." *Journal of Product Innovation Management* 21: 170–184.

Rhode, S. M. 1987. "An analysis of creativity." In: *Frontiers of creativity research*, edited by S. G. Isaksen, 216–222. Buffalo, NY: Bearly Limited.

Riedl, C., Blohm, I., Leimeister, J. M., Krcmar, H. 2013. "The effect of rating scales on decision quality and user attitudes in online innovation communities." *International Journal of Electronic Commerce* 17 (3): 7–36.

Rietzschel, E. F., Nijstad, B. A., Stroebe, W. 2010. "The selection of creative ideas after individual idea generation: Choosing between creativity and impact." *British Journal of Psychology* 101 (1): 47–68.

Robinson, J. P., Shaver, P. R., Wrightsman, L. S. 1991. "Criteria for scale selection and evaluation." In: *Measures of social psychological attitudes*, edited by J. P. Robinson, P. R. Shaver, and L. S. Wrightsman, 1–16: Academic Press.

Rochford, L. 1991. "Generating and screening new products ideas." *Industrial Marketing Management* 20 (4): 287–296.

Roedder John, D., Scott, C. A., Bettman, J. R. 1986. "Sampling data for covariation assessment: The effect of prior Beliefs on search patterns." *Journal of Consumer Research* 13 (1): 38–47.

Rousseau, D. M. 2001. "Schema, promise and mutuality: The building blocks of the psychological contract." *Journal of Occupational and Organizational Psychology* 74 (4): 511–541.

Runco, M. A., McCarthy, K. A., Svenson, E. 1994. "Judgments of the creativity of artwork from students and professional artists." *Journal of Psychology* 128 (1): 23–31.

Sadler-Smith, E. and Shefy, E. 2004. "The intuitive executive: Understanding and applying 'gut feel' in decision-making." *Academy of Management Executive* 18 (4): 76–91.

Salas, E., Rosen, M. A., DiazGranados, D. 2010. "Expertise-based intuition and decision making in organizations." *Journal of Management* 36 (4): 941–973.

Sanchez, A. M. and Elola, L. N. 1991. "Product innovation management in Spain." *Journal of Product Innovation Management* 8 (1): 49–56.

Schreier, M. and Prügl, R. 2008. "Extending lead-user theory: Antecedents and consequences of consumers' lead userness." *Journal of Product Innovation Management* 25 (4): 331–346.

Schultz, C., Salomo, S., Talke, K. 2013. "Measuring new product portfolio innovativeness: How differences in scale width and evaluator perspectives affect its relationship with performance." *Journal of Product Innovation Management* 30 (S1): 93–109.

Schweisfurth, T. 2012. *Embedded lead users inside the firm: How innovative user employees contribute to the corporate product innovation process.* Wiesbaden: Springer Gabler.

Schweisfurth, T. G. and Herstatt, C. 2015. "Embedded (lead) users as catalysts to product diffusion." *Creativity and Innovation Management* 24 (1): 151–168.

Shah, J. J., Smith, S. M., Vargas-Hernandez, N. 2003. "Metrics for measuring ideation effectiveness." *Design Studies* 24 (2): 111–134.

Shanteau and James. 1992. "Competence in experts: The role of task characteristics." *Organizational Behavior and Human Decision Processes* 53 (2): 252–266.

Simon, M., Houghton, S. M., Aquino, K. 1999. "Cognitive biases, risk perception, and venture formation: How individuals decide to start companies." *Journal of Business Venturing* 15: 113–134.

Smith, M. and Taffler, R. 1992. "Readability and understandability. Different measures of the textual complexity of accounting narrative." *Accounting, Auditing & Accountability Journal* 5 (4).

Song, X. M. and Montoya-Weiss, M. M. 1998. "Critical development activities for really new versus incremental products." *Journal of Product Innovation Management* 15 (2): 124–135.

Soukhoroukova, A., Spann, M., Skiera, B. 2012. "Sourcing, filtering, and evaluating new product ideas: An empirical exploration of the performance of idea markets." *Journal of Product Innovation Management* 29 (1): 100–112.

Spiller, S. A., Fitzsimons, G. J., Lynch J. G., McClelland, G. H. 2013. "Spotlights, floodlights, and the magic number zero: Simple effects tests in moderated regression." *Journal of Marketing Research* 31 (3): 277–288.

Stone-Romero, E. F., Alliger, G. M., Aguinis, H. 1994. "Type II error problems in the use of moderated multiple regression for the detection of moderating effects of dichotomous variables." *Journal of Management* 20 (1): 167–178.

stratasys. 2015. Objet500 and Objet350 Connex3: Color and multi-material 3D printing. Available at: http://www.stratasys.com/3d-printers/production-series/connex3-systems.

SunP Biotech. 2015. 3D print chocolate from your own 3D printer! Available at: https://www.kickstarter.com/projects/361249064/chocolate-printhead-for-open-source-3d-printer?ref=category_newest.

Szymanski, D. M., Kroff, M. W., Troy, L. C. 2007. "Innovativeness and new product success: insights from the cumulative evidence." *Journal of the Academy of Marketing Science* 35 (1): 35–52.

Terwiesch, C. and Ulrich, K. T. 2009. *Innovation tournaments: Creating and selecting exceptional opportunities.* Boston: Harvard Business Press.

Terwiesch, C. and Xu, Y. 2008. "Innovation contests, open innovation, and multiagent problem solving." *Management Science* 54 (9): 1529–1543.

Toubia, O. and Florès, L. 2007. "Adaptive idea screening using consumers." *Marketing Science* 26 (3): 342–360.

Tversky, A. and Kahnemann, D. 1974. "Judgment under uncertainty: Heuristics and biases." *Science* 185 (4157): 1124–1131.

Tzokas, N., Hultink, E. J., Hart, S. 2004. "Navigating the new product development process." *Industrial Marketing Management* 33 (7): 619–626.

UCLA: Statistical Consulting Group. 2016. Stata web books: Regression with stata: Chapter 2 - Regression diagnostics. Available at: http://statistics.ats.ucla.edu/stat/stata/webbooks/reg/chapter2/statareg2.htm.

van Selst, M. and Jolicoeur, P. 1994. "A solution to the effect of sample size on outlier elimination." *The Quarterly Journal of Experimental Psychology Section A* 47 (3): 531–650.

Velamuri, V. K., Schneckenberg, D., Haller, Jörg B. A., Moeslein, K. M. 2015. "Open evaluation of new product concepts at the front end of innovation: objectives and contingency factors." *R&D Management* in press.

Verworn, B. and Herstatt, C. 2007. "Bedeutung und Charakteristika der frühen Phasen des Innovationsprozesses." In: *Management der frühen Innovationsphasen: Grundlagen, Methoden, neue Ansätze*, edited by C. Herstatt and B. Verworn, 4–19. Wiesbaden: Gabler.

Veryzer, R. W. 1998a. "Discontinuous innovation and the new product development process." *Journal of Product Innovation Management* 15: 304–321.

Veryzer, R. W. 1998b. "Key factors affecting customer evaluation of discontinuous new products." *Journal of Product Innovation Management* 15 (March): 136–150.

von Hippel, E. 1986. "Lead users: a source of novel product concepts." *Management Science* 32 (7): 791–805.

von Hippel, E. 1988. *The sources of innovation.* New York: Oxford University Press.

von Hippel, E. 1994. ""Sticky Information" and the locus of problem solving: Implications for innovation." *Management Science* 40 (4): 429–439.

von Hippel, E. 1998. "Economics of product development by users: The impact of "Sticky" local information." *Management Science* 44 (5): 629–644.

von Hippel, E., Franke, N., Prügl, R. 2009. "Pyramiding: Efficient search for rare subjects." *Research Policy* 38 (9): 1397–1406.

Voxel8. 2015. The world's first 3D electronics printer. Available at: http://www.voxel8.co/.

Walliman, N. S. R. 2006. *Social science research methods.* London: Sage Publications.

Weiber, R. and Mühlhaus, D. 2010. *Strukturgleichungsmodellierung: Eine anwendungsorientierte Einführung in die Kausalanalyse mit Hilfe von AMOS, SmartPLS und SPSS.* Heidelberg: Springer.

Wellner, K. 2014. *User innovators in the silver market: An empirical study among camping tourists.* Hamburg: Springer Gabler.

West, J. and Bogers, M. 2014. "Leveraging external sources of innovation: A review of research on open innovation." *Journal of Product Innovation Management* 31 (4): 814–831.

West, J., Salter, A., Vanhaverbeke, W., Chesbrough, H. 2014. "Open innovation: The next decade." *Research Policy* 43 (5): 805–811.

Wheeler, A. 2015a. Breakthrough! Layerless 3D printing! 25-100x faster prints! Available at: http://3dprintingindustry.com/2015/03/17/breakthrough-layerless-3d-printing-25-100x-faster-prints/.

Wheeler, A. 2015b. Conductive graphene filament for 3D printing. Available at: http://www.engineering.com/3DPrinting/3DPrintingArticles/ArticleID/9797/Conductive-Graphene-Filament-for-3D-Printing.aspx.

Wheelwright, S. C. and Clark, K. B. 1995. *Leading product development.* New York: The Free Press.

White, H. 1980. "A heteroskedasticity-consistent covariance matrix estimator and a direct test for heteroskedasticity." *Econometrica* 48 (4): 817.

Wood, M. 2005. "Bootstrapped confidence intervals as an approach to statistical inference." *Organizational Research Methods* 8 (4): 454–470.

Wyer, R. S. and Srull, T. K. 1994. *Handbook of social cognition.* 2nd ed. Hillsdale, N.J.: L. Erlbaum Associates.

Zaichkowsky, J. L. 1985. "Measuring the involvement construct." *Journal of Consumer Research* 12 (3): 341–352.

Zhang, Q. and Doll, W. J. 2001. "The fuzzy front end and success of new product development: a causal model." *European Journal of Innovation Management* 4 (2): 95–112.

8 Appendix

8.1 Appendix A – Core literature

Table 56: Core literature for thesis I – (Innovation-) Management research studies (part I)

Authors, year	Title	Journal
Alexy et al., 2013	Cui bono? The selective revealing of knowledge and its implications for innovative activity	Academy of Management Review
Barczak et al., 2009	PERSPECTIVE: Trends and drivers of success in NPD practices: Results of the 2003 PDMA best practices study	Journal of Product Innovation Management
Berg, 2016	Balancing on the creative highwire: Forecasting the success of novel ideas in organizations	Administrative Science Quarterly
Carbonell-Foulquié et al., 2004	Criteria employed for go/no-go decisions when developing successful highly innovative products	Industrial Marketing Management
Dane, 2010	Reconsidering the trade-off between expertise and flexibility: a cognitive entrenchment perspective	Academy of Management Review
Dean et al., 2006	Identifying quality, novel, and creative ideas: Constructs and scales for idea evaluation	Journal of the Association for Information Systems
Evanschitzky et al., 2012	Success factors of product innovation: An updated meta-analysis	Journal of Product Innovation Management
Franke et al., 2014	Integrating problem solvers from analogous markets in new product ideation	Management Science
Garcia and Calantone, 2002	A critical look at technological innovation typology and innovativeness terminology: a literature review	Journal of Product Innovation Management
Girotra et al., 2010	Idea generation and the quality of the best idea	Management Science
Hart et al., 2003	Industrial companies' evaluation criteria in new product development gates	Journal of Product Innovation Management
Kim and Wilemon, 2002	Focusing the fuzzy front-end in new product development	R&D Management
Kristensson et al., 2004	Harnessing the creative potential among users	Journal of Product Innovation Management
Kudrowitz and Wallace, 2013	Assessing the quality of ideas from prolific, early-stage product ideation	Journal of Engineering Design
Langerak et al., 2004	The role of predevelopment activities in the relationship between market orientation and performance	R&D Management

Table 57: Core literature for thesis II – (Innovation-) Management research studies (part II)

Authors, year	Title	Journal
Magnusson et al., 2014	Exploring holistic intuitive idea screening in the light of formal criteria	Technovation
Magnusson et al., 2016	Exploring users' appropriateness as a proxy for experts when screening new product/service ideas	Journal of Product Innovation Management
Magnusson, 2009	Exploring the contributions of involving ordinary users in ideation of technology-based services	Journal of Product Innovation Management
Martinsuo and Poskela, 2011	Use of evaluation criteria and innovation performance in the front end of innovation	Journal of Product Innovation Management
Mugge and Dahl, 2013	Seeking the ideal level of design newness: Consumer response to radical and incremental product design	Journal of Product Innovation Management
Piezunka and Dahlander, 2015	Distant search, narrow attention: How crowding alters organizations' filtering of suggestions in crowdsourcing	Academy of Management Journal
Poetz and Schreier, 2012	The value of crowdsourcing: Can users really compete with professionals in generating new product ideas?	Journal of Product Innovation Management
Salas et al., 2010	Expertise-based intuition and decision making in organizations	Journal of Management
Shanteau and James, 1992	Competence in experts: The role of task characteristics	Organizational Behavior and Human Decision Processes
Terwiesch et al., 2008	Innovation contests, open innovation, and multiagent problem solving	Management Science
Velamuri et al., 2015	Open evaluation of new product concepts at the front end of innovation: objectives and contingency factors	R&D Management
Veryzer, 1998	Discontinuous innovation and the new product development process	Journal of Product Innovation Management
Veryzer, 1998	Key factors affecting customer evaluation of discontinuous new products	Journal of Product Innovation Management
von Hippel, 1986	Lead users: a source of novel product concepts	Management Science
von Hippel, 1994	Sticky Information and the Locus of Problem Solving: Implications for Innovation	Management Science

Table 58: Core literature for thesis III – Marketing and consumer behavior research studies

Authors, year	Title	Journal
Alba and Hutchinson, 1987	Dimensions of consumer expertise	Journal of Consumer Research
Bettman and Sujan, 1987	Effects of framing on evaluation of omparable and noncomparable alternatives by expert and novice consumers	Journal of Consumer Research
Graeff and Olson, 1994	onsumer inference as part of product comprehension	Advances in Consumer Research
Gregan-Paxton and Roedder John, 1997	Consumer learning by analogy: A model of internal knowledge transfer	Journal of Consumer Research
Gregan-Paxton et al., 2002	"So that's what that is" examining the impact of analogy on consumers' knowledge development for really new products	Psychology and Marketing
Kornish and Ulrich, 2014	The importance of the raw idea in innovation: testing the sow's ear hypothesis	Journal of Marketing Research
Moreau et al., 2001	Entrenched knowledge structures and consumer response to new products	Journal of Marketing Research
Mukherjee and Hoyer, 2001	The effect of novel attributes on product evaluation	Journal of Consumer Research
Peracchio and Tybout, 1996	he moderating role of prior knowledge in schema-based product evaluation	Journal of Consumer Research
Toubia and Florès, 2007	Adaptive idea screening using consumers	Marketing Science

Table 59: Core literature for thesis IV – Psychology and creativity research studies

Authors, year	Title	Journal
Amabile, 1983	The social psychology of creativity: A componential conceptualization	Journal of Personality and Social Psychology
Baer et al., 2004	Extension of the consensual assessment technique to nonparallel creative products	Creativity Research Journal
Blair and Mumford, 2007	Errors in idea evaluation: Preference for the unoriginal	Journal of Creative Behavior
Eling et al., 2015	The performance effects of combining rationality and intuition in making early new product idea evaluation decisions	Creativity and Innovation Management
Kaufman and Baer, 2012	Beyond New and Appropriate: Who Decides What Is Creative?	Creativity Research Journal
Kaufman et al., 2008	A comparison of expert and nonexpert raters using the consensual assessment technique	Journal of Creative Behavior
Kaufman et al., 2009	Expertise, domains, and the consensual assessment technique	Creativity Research Journal
Licuanan et al., 2007	Idea evaluation: Error in evaluating highly original ideas	Journal of Creative Behavior
Meyers-Levy and Tybout, 1989	How does the congruity of brand names affect evaluations of brand name extensions?	Journal of Applied Psychology
Rietzschel et al., 2010	The selection of creative ideas after individual idea generation: Choosing between creativity and impact	British Journal of Psychology

8.2 Appendix B – Online survey

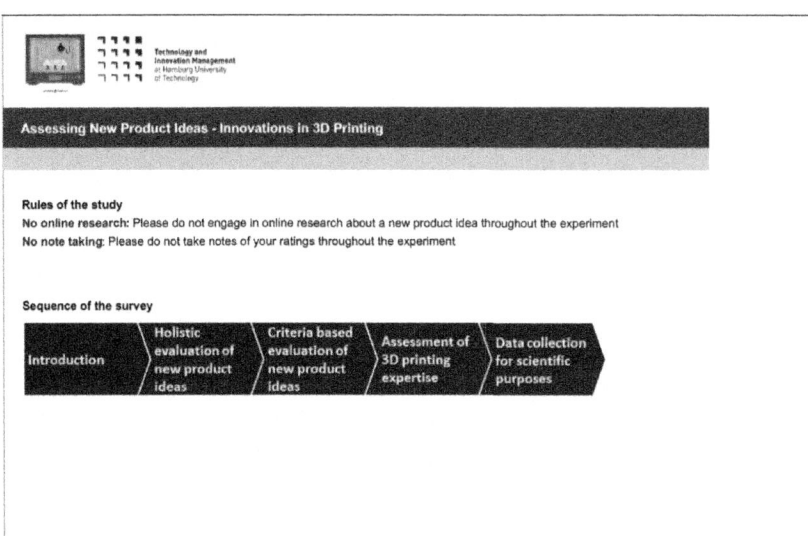

Rules of the study
No online research: Please do not engage in online research about a new product idea throughout the experiment
No note taking: Please do not take notes of your ratings throughout the experiment

Sequence of the survey

Imagine you just started in a **new job as a senior manager** in a multinational company. Among other things, it is **your responsibility to evaluate various new product ideas** from different business units. Your evaluation will be taken into account in deciding which ideas should be taken further in future development processes and eventually be brought to market. Therefore **your decisions can have a significant impact on the firm's future success.**

Today you are requested to evaluate ideas in the domain of **3D printing.** Although you are new to the job and might not posses deep expertise in 3D printing, you are requested to **evaluate the ideas to the best of your knowledge.**

Technology and
Innovation Management
at Hamburg University
of Technology

Assessing New Product Ideas - Innovations in 3D Printing

Part 1: introduction

On the next pages, you will be asked to evaluate 8 new product ideas in the domain of 3D printing.

First you will be asked to state your overall impression of the ideas, followed by a more detailed assessment of the ideas along several criteria.

In your assessments, please ensure to use the full range of the evaluation scale.

It might very well be that you will encounter difficulties understanding some of the 3D printing innovations. If that should be the case, we kindly ask you to follow your intuition and gut feeling in the ideas' evaluation.

Technology and
Innovation Management
at Hamburg University
of Technology

Assessing New Product Ideas - Innovations in 3D Printing

Part 2: holistic evaluation of new product ideas

Stating your overall impression

Please indicate your overall impression of the following 8 new product ideas. For your evaluation, you are free to consider all potential benefits and shortcomings of the product ideas as you feel is best.

Technology and Innovation Management at Hamburg University of Technology

Assessing New Product Ideas - Innovations in 3D Printing

Part 2: holistic evaluation of new product ideas

Tripple-jetting 3D printer

The triple-jetting 3D printer will combine up to three base resins to print a range of material properties from rubber to rigid, transparent to opaque, neutral to vibrantly colored and standard to biocompatible in pre-set configurations to produce more than 50 materials in a single build.

	very negative	negative	somewhat negative	moderate	somewhat positive	positive	very positive
Overall impression	O	O	O	O	O	O	O

Wood, stone and metal filament

The idea is to create a filament that contains tiny particles of wood, limestone or metal resulting in 3D printed products that can mimic the finish of the contained particles.

	very negative	negative	somewhat negative	moderate	somewhat positive	positive	very positive
Overall impression	O	O	O	O	O	O	O

Lithography-based ceramic 3D-Printer

This printer will allow the production of functioning ceramic parts as green bodies that can be further processed to obtain a completely dense ceramic part. The technology is based on the selective curing of a photosensitive resin which contains homogeneously dispersed ceramic particles. The centerpiece of the process is a specifically designed imaging system which enables the transfer of the layer information by means of the latest LED-technology.

	very negative	negative	somewhat negative	moderate	somewhat positive	positive	very positive
Overall impression	O	O	O	O	O	O	O

Chocolate printhead for 3D printer

The chocolate printhead will be a nozzle that is customized to print low viscous material, i.e. chocolate. This nozzle will not require proprietary materials so that chocolate found in the local supermarkets can be used.

	very negative	negative	somewhat negative	moderate	somewhat positive	positive	very positive
Overall impression	O	O	O	O	O	O	O

Conductive graphene filament

This filament will incorporate highly conductive nano-carbon platelets to enhance the properties of standard filament, allowing a variety of new applications, including the 3D printing of conductive traces, capacitive touch sensors, electromagnetic and radiofrequency shielding and production of high-strength mechanical and functional parts.

	very negative	negative	somewhat negative	moderate	somewhat positive	positive	very positive
Overall impression	O	O	O	O	O	O	O

3D electronics printer

The idea is to create the first 3D desktop printer that can co-print matrix materials such as thermoplastics and highly conductive silver inks enabling to print customized electronic devices like quadcopters, electromagnets and fully functional 3D electromechanical assemblies.

	very negative	negative	somewhat negative	moderate	somewhat positive	positive	very positive
Overall impression	◯	◯	◯	◯	◯	◯	◯

All-In-One 3D Printer, CNC Machine, & Laser Engraver

The all-in-one 3d printer will combine a 3D Printer, CNC Mill, and Laser Engraver in one compact cube. By utilizing quick-change heads, the user will be able to shape a block of aluminum, hardwood, or plastic into intricate designs, 3D print complex plastic shapes, or laser engrave into objects made of wood, leather or plastic with a single machine.

	very negative	negative	somewhat negative	moderate	somewhat positive	positive	very positive
Overall impression	◯	◯	◯	◯	◯	◯	◯

Continuous liquid interface production printer

This printer will use light and oxygen to continuously grow objects from a pool of resin instead of printing them layer by layer. The idea is to use a photochemical process by carefully controlling the interaction of UV light, which creates the photopolymerization, and oxygen, which inhibits the reaction to create 3D printed products.

	very negative	negative	somewhat negative	moderate	somewhat positive	positive	very positive
Overall impression	◯	◯	◯	◯	◯	◯	◯

Technology and
Innovation Management
at Hamburg University
of Technology

Assessing New Product Ideas - Innovations in 3D Printing

Part 3: criteria based evaluation of new product ideas

Please evaluate **the same ideas** in more detail along the following 4 criteria:

Originality: Determines how novel, unusual and unique you consider the idea to be. You are not to think about whether the idea is realizable or not or about the user value, this will be evaluated in the other dimensions (user value & feasibility).

User value: Can be offering new forms of usage, new and/or more features, being less expensive than similar product, or in a broader sense offering an experience or something else that provides the user with added value.

Feasibility: Concerns questions such as whether it is feasible to develop, produce and successfully commercialize the product within 'reasonable time' and under 'reasonable investments'

Understandability: Indicates how well you understood the idea, e.g. did the relationship between an addressed user need and the recommended solution became clear to you?

Technology and
Innovation Management
at Hamburg University
of Technology

Assessing New Product Ideas - Innovations in 3D Printing

Part 3: criteria based evaluation of new product ideas

Tripple-jetting 3D printer
The triple-jetting 3D printer will combine up to three base resins to print a range of material properties from rubber to rigid, transparent to opaque, neutral to vibrantly colored and standard to biocompatible in pre-set configurations to produce more than 50 materials in a single build.

	very low	low	somewhat low	moderate	somewhat high	high	very high
Originality	○	○	○	○	○	○	○
User Value	○	○	○	○	○	○	○
Feasibility	○	○	○	○	○	○	○
Understandability	○	○	○	○	○	○	○

Technology and
Innovation Management
at Hamburg University
of Technology

Assessing New Product Ideas - Innovations in 3D Printing

Part 3: criteria based evaluation of new product ideas

Wood, stone and metal filament
The idea is to create a filament that contains tiny particles of wood, limestone or metal resulting in 3D printed products that can mimic the finish of the contained materials.

	very low	low	somewhat low	moderate	somewhat high	high	very high
Originality	○	○	○	○	○	○	○
User Value	○	○	○	○	○	○	○
Feasibility	○	○	○	○	○	○	○
Understandability	○	○	○	○	○	○	○

Technology and
Innovation Management
of Hamburg University
of Technology

Assessing New Product Ideas - Innovations in 3D Printing

Part 3: criteria based evaluation of new product ideas

Conductive graphene filament
This filament will incorporate highly conductive nano-carbon platelets to enhance the properties of standard filament, allowing a variety of new applications, including the 3D printing of conductive traces, capacitive touch sensors, electromagnetic and radiofrequency shielding and production of high-strength mechanical and functional parts.

	very low	low	somewhat low	moderate	somewhat high	high	very high
Originality	○	○	○	○	○	○	○
User Value	○	○	○	○	○	○	○
Feasibility	○	○	○	○	○	○	○
Understandability	○	○	○	○	○	○	○

Technology and
Innovation Management
of Hamburg University
of Technology

Assessing New Product Ideas - Innovations in 3D Printing

Part 3: criteria based evaluation of new product ideas

3D electronics printer
The idea is to create the first 3D desktop printer that can co-print matrix materials such as thermoplastics and highly conductive silver inks enabling to print customized electronic devices like quadcopters, electromagnets and fully functional 3D electromechanical assemblies.

	very low	low	somewhat low	moderate	somewhat high	high	very high
Originality	○	○	○	○	○	○	○
User Value	○	○	○	○	○	○	○
Feasibility	○	○	○	○	○	○	○
Understandability	○	○	○	○	○	○	○

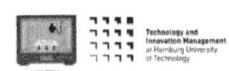

Assessing New Product Ideas - Innovations in 3D Printing

Part 3: criteria based evaluation of new product ideas

Chocolate printhead for 3D printer
The chocolate printhead will be a nozzle that is customized to print low viscous material, i.e. chocolate. This nozzle will not require proprietary materials, so that chocolate found in the local supermarkets can be used.

	very low	low	somewhat low	moderate	somewhat high	high	very high
Originality	○	○	○	○	○	○	○
User Value	○	○	○	○	○	○	○
Feasibility	○	○	○	○	○	○	○
Understandability	○	○	○	○	○	○	○

Assessing New Product Ideas - Innovations in 3D Printing

Part 3: criteria based evaluation of new product ideas

Continuous liquid interface production printer
This printer will use light and oxygen to continuously grow objects from a pool of resin instead of printing them layer by layer. The idea is to use a photochemical process by carefully controlling the interaction of UV light, which creates the photopolymerization, and oxygen, which inhibits the reaction to create 3D printed products.

	very low	low	somewhat low	moderate	somewhat high	high	very high
Originality	○	○	○	○	○	○	○
User Value	○	○	○	○	○	○	○
Feasibility	○	○	○	○	○	○	○
Understandability	○	○	○	○	○	○	○

Technology and Innovation Management at Hamburg University of Technology

Assessing New Product Ideas - Innovations in 3D Printing

Part 3: criteria based evaluation of new product ideas

All-In-One 3D Printer, CNC Machine, & Laser Engraver
The all-in-one 3d printer will combine a 3D Printer, CNC Mill, and Laser Engraver in one compact cube. By utilizing quick-change heads, the user will be able to shape a block of aluminum, hardwood, or plastic into intricate designs, 3D print complex plastic shapes, or laser engrave into objects made of wood, leather or plastic with a single machine.

	very low	low	somewhat low	moderate	somewhat high	high	very high
Originality	○	○	○	○	○	○	○
User Value	○	○	○	○	○	○	○
Feasibility	○	○	○	○	○	○	○
Understandability	○	○	○	○	○	○	○

Technology and Innovation Management at Hamburg University of Technology

Assessing New Product Ideas - Innovations in 3D Printing

Part 3: criteria based evaluation of new product ideas

Lithography-based Ceramic 3D-Printer
This printer will allow the production of functioning ceramic parts as green bodies that can be further processed to obtain a completely dense ceramic part. The technology is based on the selective curing of a photosensitive resin which contains homogeneously dispersed ceramic particles. The centerpiece of the process is a specifically designed imaging system which enables the transfer of the layer information by means of the latest LED-technology.

	very low	low	somewhat low	moderate	somewhat high	high	very high
Originality	○	○	○	○	○	○	○
User Value	○	○	○	○	○	○	○
Feasibility	○	○	○	○	○	○	○
Understandability	○	○	○	○	○	○	○

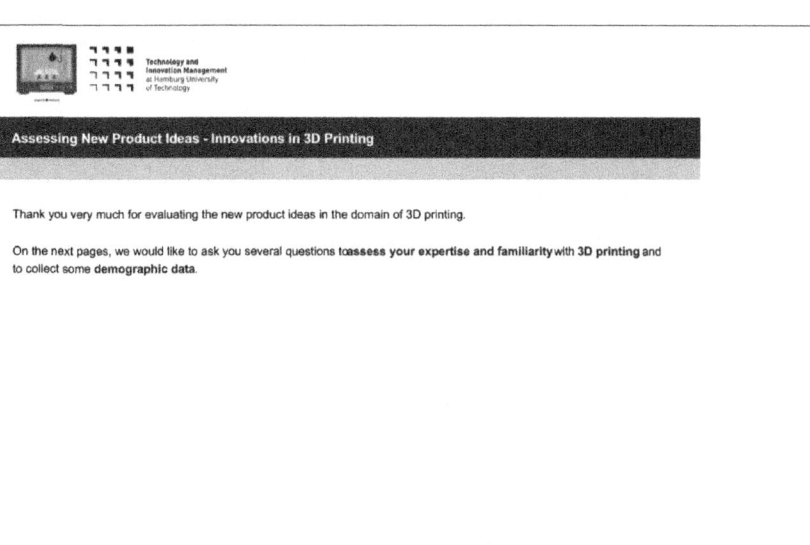

Thank you very much for evaluating the new product ideas in the domain of 3D printing.

On the next pages, we would like to ask you several questions to assess your expertise and familiarity with 3D printing and to collect some demographic data.

Assessing New Product Ideas - Innovations in 3D Printing

Part 4: assessment of 3D printing expertise

For how many years have you been using 3D printing equipment?

Do you own a 3D printer?

○ Yes

○ No

In your work environment or in your leisure time, how frequently do use 3D printing?

		3 =	4 =	5 =		7 = most of
	1 = never	2 = rarely	occasionally	sometimes	frequently	6 = usually	the time
Frequency of use	○	○	○	○	○	○	○

Do you agree or disagree with the following statements about 3D printing?

	1 = strongly disagree	2 = disagree	3 = somewhat disagree	4 = neither agree nor disagree	5 = somewhat agree	6 = agree	7 = strongly agree
I can repair 3D printing equipment	○	○	○	○	○	○	○
I always try to keep up to date with regard to the materials, innovations, and possibilities with regard to 3D printing	○	○	○	○	○	○	○
I can help other users solve problems with 3D printers	○	○	○	○	○	○	○
I can make technical changes to 3D printers on my own	○	○	○	○	○	○	○
I am a huge fan of the technical aspects of 3D printing	○	○	○	○	○	○	○
I am handy and enjoy tinkering	○	○	○	○	○	○	○
I come from a technical background in my profession or education (e.g. engineering)	○	○	○	○	○	○	○

	1 = strongly disagree	2 = disagree	3 = somewhat disagree	4 = neither agree nor disagree	5 = somewhat agree	6 = agree	7 = strongly agree
Compared to the average person, I do not know much about 3D Printing	○	○	○	○	○	○	○
I am very familiar with 3D printing	○	○	○	○	○	○	○
I am not skilled at utilizing 3D printing technology	○	○	○	○	○	○	○
I am very interested in 3D printing	○	○	○	○	○	○	○
I use 3D printing products and services a lot	○	○	○	○	○	○	○
My friends use 3D printing products and services a lot	○	○	○	○	○	○	○
I read articles related to 3D printing all the time	○	○	○	○	○	○	○

	1 = strongly disagree	2 = disagree	3 = somewhat disagree	4 = neither agree or disagree	5 = somewhat agree	6 = agree	7 = strongly agree
I usually find out about new 3D printing products and solutions earlier than others	○	○	○	○	○	○	○
I have benefited significantly from the early adoption and use of 3D printing	○	○	○	○	○	○	○
I am regarded as being on the 'cutting edge' in the field of 3D printing	○	○	○	○	○	○	○
I have a comprehensive knowledge of the 3D printing equipment available on the market	○	○	○	○	○	○	○
I have often noticed technical problems with 3D printers	○	○	○	○	○	○	○
I have needs which are not satisfied by existing 3D printing equipment	○	○	○	○	○	○	○
I am dissatisfied with the existing 3D printing equipment offered on the market	○	○	○	○	○	○	○

	1 = strongly disagree	2 = disagree	3 = somewhat disagree	4 = neither agree nor disagree	5 = somewhat agree	6 = agree	7 = strongly agree
In general, I am among the last in my circle of friends to adopt new 3D printing products	○	○	○	○	○	○	○
If I heard that a new 3D printing product was available, I would be interested to try it out	○	○	○	○	○	○	○
Compared to my friends, I do not adopt a lot of 3D printing products	○	○	○	○	○	○	○
In general, I am the first in my circle of friends to know about a new 3D products	○	○	○	○	○	○	○
I will adopt a new 3D printing product, even if I haven't heard of it before	○	○	○	○	○	○	○
I get to know many 3D printing products before other people do	○	○	○	○	○	○	○

Technology and Innovation Management at Hamburg University of Technology

Assessing New Product Ideas - Innovations in 3D Printing

Part 5: data collection for scientific purposes

Do you agree or disagree with the following statements?

	1 = strongly disagree	2 = disagree	3 = somewhat disagree	4 = neither agree nor disagree	5 = somewhat agree	6 = agree	7 = strongly agree
I believe that higher financial risks are worth taking for higher rewards	○	○	○	○	○	○	○
I accept occasional new product failures as being normal	○	○	○	○	○	○	○
I only implement plans if I am certain that they will work	○	○	○	○	○	○	○
I like to take big financial risks	○	○	○	○	○	○	○
I would encourage the development of innovative new product ideas, knowing well that some will fail	○	○	○	○	○	○	○
I like to "play it safe" in regard to product development projects	○	○	○	○	○	○	○

	1 = strongly disagree	2 = disagree	3 = somewhat disagree	4 = neither agree nor disagree	5 = somewhat agree	6 = agree	7 = strongly agree
I enjoy spending time looking beyond the initial view of the problems	○	○	○	○	○	○	○
I enjoy working on ill-defined, novel problems	○	○	○	○	○	○	○
I enjoy stretching my imagination to produce many ideas	○	○	○	○	○	○	○
I like to work with unique ideas	○	○	○	○	○	○	○

Technology and Innovation Management at Hamburg University of Technology

Assessing New Product Ideas - Innovations in 3D Printing

Part 5: data collection for scientific purposes

In conducting new product development activities my level of ...

	1 = very low	2 = low	3 = somewhat low	4 = moderate	5 = somewhat high	6 = high	7 = very high
Experience is ...	○	○	○	○	○	○	○
Knowledge is ...	○	○	○	○	○	○	○

How many years of professional experience do you have in the following areas?

	< 1	1-2	2-3	3-4	4-5	5-10	10-15	> 15
R&D	○	○	○	○	○	○	○	○
Manufacturing	○	○	○	○	○	○	○	○
Engineering	○	○	○	○	○	○	○	○
Design	○	○	○	○	○	○	○	○
Marketing	○	○	○	○	○	○	○	○
Sales	○	○	○	○	○	○	○	○
Strategy	○	○	○	○	○	○	○	○
Finance/Controlling	○	○	○	○	○	○	○	○
IT	○	○	○	○	○	○	○	○

I have had experience with the evaluation of ideas and/or creative products...

	1 = strongly disagree	2 = disagree	3 = somewhat disagree	4 = neither agree or disagree	5 = somewhat agree	6 = agree	7 = strongly agree
... in general	○	○	○	○	○	○	○
... at work	○	○	○	○	○	○	○
... in my leisure time	○	○	○	○	○	○	○

For which industry do you currently work for?

- ○ Basic materials (incl. chemicals & oil & gas)
- ○ Aerospace & defense
- ○ Automobiles and parts
- ○ Food & beverages
- ○ Personal & household goods
- ○ Health care
- ○ Consumer services (incl. retail, media, travel & leisure)
- ○ Telecommunications
- ○ Financials (incl. banks, insurance & real estate)
- ○ IT technology
- ○ Utilities
- ○ Research & education
- ○ Other (please specify)

[   ]

How old are you?

[▲▼]

What is your gender?

- ○ Male
- ○ Female

What is your highest educational degree?

- ○ Middle School (Realschulabschluss)
- ○ High School (Abitur)
- ○ Bachelor's Degree
- ○ Master's Degree (or Diplom)
- ○ PhD or Doctorate
- ○ Professor

What is your country of origin?

- ○ Germany
- ○ Netherlands
- ○ Austria
- ○ Switzerland
- ○ United Kingdom
- ○ United States
- ○ Other (please specify)

[   ]

Technology and Innovation Management at Hamburg University of Technology

Assessing New Product Ideas - Innovations in 3D Printing

Thank you!!!

Thank you very much for participating in this survey! Your help in this important research is highly appreciated!!!

Please do not talk to other participants about the content of this study. Any pre-knowledge could bias the results and make them useless for our study.

Please provide your email below, if you would like to be informed about the research outcome

We appreciate any further comments or feedback you might have

Code: X5I0#7

8.3 Appendix C – Additional mediation effects

Domain knowledge, as well as the interaction effect between domain knowledge and idea innovativeness, have been hypothesized to influence the perception and evaluation of new product ideas' originality, user value, feasibility, and perceived overall impression (see chapter 3.6). With regard to the holistic judgment of overall impression, research scholars have argued that evaluators inadvertently take different evaluation criteria into consideration, which then influence their judgments (Sadler-Smith and Shefy, 2004; Salas, Rosen, and DiazGranados, 2010). Empirical research studies have supported this expectation by showing that the evaluation criteria originality, user value, and feasibility account for about 50 per cent of the deviation in holistic new service idea evaluations (Magnusson, Netz, and Wästlund, 2014). This is in line with Anderson's information integration theory, that suggests that attribute ratings provide the building blocks for overall product evaluations (Wyer and Srull, 1994). Consequently, I propose that:

H19: Perceived originality has a positive influence on the overall impression of early-stage new product ideas.

H20: Perceived user value has a positive influence on the overall impression of early-stage new product ideas.

H21: Perceived feasibility has a positive influence on the overall impression of early-stage new product ideas.

I tested these hypotheses with multiple regression analyses. The results of model D-5, D-6 and D-7 reveal that perceived originality (b = .292; p < .001), perceived user value (b = .541; p < .001), and perceived feasibility (b = .201; p < .001) have a significant positive influence on perceived overall impression (see Table 61). Acknowledging that domain knowledge and the interaction effect between domain knowledge and idea innovativeness have been shown to have a significant influence on perceived originality, user value, and feasibility, it can be assumed that domain knowledge indirectly affects overall impression through its influence on perceived originality, user value, and feasibility. I thus propose that originality, user value, and feasibility act as mediators in the perception of overall impression. Furthermore, acknowledging that the influence of domain knowledge on perceived originality, user value, and feasibility has been found to be moderated by idea innovativeness, it is logical that the mediated relationships between domain knowledge and overall impression are moderated by ideas innovativeness (see Figure 38).

H22: Perceived originality mediates the effects of domain knowledge on overall impression originality of early-stage new product ideas.

H23: Perceived user value mediates the effects of domain knowledge on overall impression originality of early-stage new product ideas.

H24: Perceived feasibility mediates the effects of domain knowledge on overall impression originality of early-stage new product ideas.

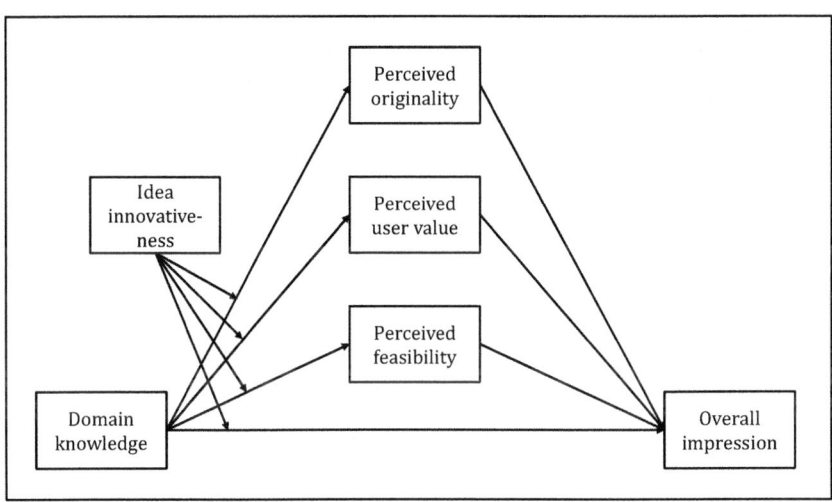

Figure 38: Moderated mediation model for overall impression[83]

I tested these hypotheses following the procedure outlined in chapter 5.2.3.4. I applied conditional process analysis, which enabled me to show that perceived originality, perceived user value, and perceived feasibility mediate the effect of domain knowledge on

---

[83] Author's illustration.

overall impression (see Table 60). Thus, H15, H16 and H17 are supported. Furthermore, the results show that the new product ideas' degree of innovativeness moderates these indirect effects. Thus H18, H19 and H20 are supported.

Table 60: Results of additional conditional process analyses

Conditional effects of domain knowledge on overall impression (OI)	Effect	Sig.	LLCI	ULCI
Conditional direct effects				
Idea innovativess (-1SD)	.017	.431	-.025	.058
Idea innovativess (mean)	.026	.091	-.004	.056
Idea innovativess (+1 SD)	.035	.089	-.005	.075
Conditional indirect effects through perceived originality				
Idea innovativess (-1SD)	-.050		-.066	-.036
Idea innovativess (mean)	-.026		-.036	-.018
Idea innovativess (+1 SD)	-.003		-.011	.004
Conditional indirect effects through perceived user value				
Idea innovativess (-1SD)	-.026		-.052	-.001
Idea innovativess (mean)	.012		-.006	.029
Idea innovativess (+1 SD)	.050		.026	.073
Conditional indirect effects through perceived feasibility				
Idea innovativess (-1SD)	.035		.025	.049
Idea innovativess (mean)	.025		.018	.035
Idea innovativess (+1 SD)	.015		.007	.026
Indirect effect of highest order product (moderated mediation index)				
Originality	.041		.029	.057
User value	.067		.037	.099
Feasibility	-.018		-.031	-.008

Note: Number of bootstrap samples for bias-corrected bootstrap confidence intervals: 10.000; analysis carried out with Hayes' PROCESS macro model 8.

In summary, the results of the conditional process analyses reveal that the total effect of domain knowledge on perceived overall impression is mediated through the idea's perceived originality, user value, and feasibility (see Table 60). The moderated mediation analysis shows that, in respect of ideas with low innovativeness, domain knowledge exerts a negative indirect effects through perceived originality (effect size: -.050) and perceived user value (effect size: -.026), and a positive effect through perceived feasibility (effect size: .035). With regard to ideas with moderate innovativeness, domain knowledge exerts a negative indirect effect through perceived originality (effect size: -.026) and a positive effect through perceived feasibility (effect size: .025). Finally, for ideas with high innovativeness, domain knowledge exerts a positive indirect effect through perceived user value (effect size: .050) perceived feasibility (effect size: .015).

Acknowledging the effects of domain knowledge that have been proposed in chapter 3.6, domain knowledge thus leads to a more positive perception of highly innovative new product ideas through a more positive perception of their user value and feasibility.

Table 61: Regression results for overall impression with perceived originality, user value and feasibility as mediators

	Model D (overall impression)									
	Model D-3		Model D-5		Model D-6		Model D-7		Model D-8	
	B	Sig.	B	Sig.	B	Sig.	B	Sig.	B	Sig.
Constant	3.740	.000 ***	.885	.001 **	1.643	.000 ***	1.467	.000 ***	.723	.002 **
Age	-.003	.365	-.001	.818	-.002	.510	-.002	.576	-.002	.518
Native English speaker	-.033	.623	-.016	.800	-.042	.447	-.052	.417	-.028	.602
University degree	-.121	.114	-.078	.267	-.138	.028 *	-.121	.096	-.094	.124
R&D tenure > 5 years	-.231	.013 **	-.180	.034 *	-.128	.091	-.198	.025 *	-.055	.457
Marketing tenure > 5 years	-.057	.682	-.036	.779	-.032	.779	-.046	.727	-.040	.719
Sales tenure > 5 years	.014	.918	.063	.601	-.024	.823	-.044	.724	-.005	.959
Top-level management	-.366	.003 **	-.396	.001 **	-.192	.061	-.312	.008 **	-.218	.030 *
Risk aversion	-.006	.809	.022	.322	.000	.993	-.004	.865	.021	.283
Idea innovativeness	.568	.000 ***	.504	.000 ***	.237	.000 ***	.792	.000 ***	.229	.000 ***
Domain knowledge	.037	.048 *	.028	.112	.006	.718	-.036	.048 *	.022	.153
Interaction (Inno. x DK)	.107	.001 **	.002	.940	.023	.366	.114	.000 ***	.014	.591
Comprehension			.284	.000 ***	.079	.000 ***	.190	.000 ***	.025	.227
H15: Perceived originality									.147	.000 ***
H16: Perceived user value			.292	.000 ***	.541	.000 ***			.463	.000 ***
H17: Perceived feasibility							.201	.000 ***	.153	.000 ***
R^2	.063		.222		.377		.167		.407	
Adjusted R^2	.059		.218		.373		.162		.404	
Adj. R^2 change	.004		.159		.314		.103		.345	
F-statistic	14.269	.000 ***	51.003	.000 ***	107.650	.000 ***	35.633	.000 ***	106.099	.000 ***
F change	11.747	.001 **	254.542	.000 ***	889.984	.000 ***	82.105	.000 ***	351.988	.000 ***

Note: Unstandardized regression coefficients reported; * p < .05; ** p < .01; *** p < .001; n = 2.331 (333 respondents with each 7 idea evaluations)

Adj. R^2 change and F change of Models D-5, D-6, D-7 and D-8 are in reference to Model D-3 (moderated effects model)

8.4 Appendix D – Robustness checks

In order to ensure the robustness of the OLS regression results, I conducted five additional regression models that are able to (i) compensate for deviations from the homoscedasticity assumption, and (ii) take into account statistical inference for regression when data are grouped into clusters.

I ran the models with heteroscedasticity-consistent standard error (HCSE) estimators to compensate for deviations from the homoscedasticity assumption (see chapter 5.2.2.2). Following the suggestion of Hayes and Cai (2007), I applied HC3 and HC4 estimators to all four models to double-check the results obtained from the OLS regression models. The models based on the HCSE estimators show that the significance levels for the proposed effects do not change recognizably (see columns HC3estimimators, HC4 estimators and Robust regr. in Table 62, Table 63, Table 64 and Table 65).

I checked the robustness of the OLS regression models by comparing them to cluster-robust regression models (Colin Cameron and Miller, 2015) and to random effect regression models (Hedeker and Gibbons, 1994) to take into account statistical inferences that might result from the structure of the data (see chapter 5.2.1). Although there are some changes in the significance levels, these changes are mostly connected to the control variables in the models. The significance levels of the hypothesized, direct, interaction and mediation effects do not change substantially.[84] Thus, these models confirm the findings of the OLS regression models (see columns Clustered and Random regr. in Table 62, Table 63, Table 64, and Table 65).

To summarize, by applying state-of-the-art regression analysis methods, I was able to confirm the reported results of the OLS regression models. I was therefore also able to suspend the possibility that violations of the OLS regression's assumption, or the structure of the data, distorts my findings in any significant way.

---

[84] One exception is observed in model C (feasibility). Whereas the OLS regression shows that domain knowledge has a positive direct effect on perceived feasibility (b = .043; p = .011), the regression model with cluster-robust estimators (b = .043; p = .074) and the random effect regression model (b = .040; p = .081) show that the effect is only significant at a level of p < .10 when accounting for cluster effects in the data. However, considering that the moderation effect remains highly significant (p < .000), it can still be concluded that domain knowledge has a significant influence on perceived feasibility.

Table 62: Robustness checks – Model A (originality)

	Model A (originality)										
	OLS		HC3 estimators		HC4 estimators		Robust regr.		Clustered		Random regr.	
	B	Sig.	B	Sig.	B	Sig.	B	Sig.	B	Sig.	B	Sig.
Constant	3.830	.000 ***	3.830	.000 ***	3.830	.000 ***	3.830	.000 ***	3.830	.000 ***	4.261	.000 ***
Age	-.002	.519	-.002	.535	-.002	.536	-.002	.534	-.002	.744	-.002	.667
Native English speaker	-.115	.100	-.115	.115	-.115	.116	-.115	.114	-.115	.395	-.111	.372
University degree	-.207	.009 **	-.207	.012 *	-.207	.012 *	-.207	.012 *	-.207	.170	-.203	.151
R&D tenure > 5 years	-.287	.003 **	-.287	.004 **	-.287	.004 **	-.287	.004 **	-.287	.101	-.279	.103
Marketing tenure > 5 years	-.001	.993	-.001	.994	-.001	.994	-.001	.994	-.001	.997	-.006	.980
Sales tenure > 5 years	-.267	.050 *	-.267	.086	-.267	.086	-.267	.083	-.267	.372	-.260	.283
Top-level management	.184	.156	.184	.169	.184	.169	.184	.165	.184	.452 *	.178	.440
Risk aversion	-.114	.000 ***	-.114	.000 ***	-.114	.000 ***	-.114	.000 ***	-.114	.009 **	-.112	.011 *
Idea innovativeness	.815	.000 ***	.815	.000 ***	.815	.000 ***	.815	.000 ***	.815	.000 ***	.772	.000 ***
H1: Domain knowledge	-.189	.000 ***	-.189	.000 ***	-.189	.000 ***	-.189	.000 ***	-.189	.000 ***	-.173	.000 ***
H5: Interaction (Inno. x DK)	.280	.000 ***	.280	.000 ***	.280	.000 ***	.280	.000 ***	.280	.000 ***	.286	.000 ***
H11: Comprehension	.037	.102	.037	.127	.037	.127	.037	.125	.037	.278	.036	.093
R^2	.168		.168		.168		.168		.168		.164	
Adjusted R^2	.164		n.a.		n.a.		n.a.		n.a.		n.a.	
F-statistic	38.956	.000 ***	38.811	.000 ***	38.953	.000 ***	39.120	.000 ***	37.130	.000 ***	n.a.	
Wald chi²	n.a.		n.a.		n.a.		n.a.		n.a.		484.590	.000 ***

Note: unstandardized regression coefficients reported; * p < .05; ** p < .01; *** p < .001; n = 2.331 (333 respondents with each 7 idea evaluations); OLS = reference model A-4

Table 63: Robustness checks – Model B (user value)

	Model B (user value)											
	OLS		HC3 estimators		HC4 estimators		Robust regr.		Clustered		Random regr.	
	B	Sig.	B	Sig.	B	Sig.	B	Sig.	B	Sig.	B	Sig.
Constant	.667	.008 ***	.667	.006 ***	.667	.006 ***	.667	.006 ***	.667	.015 *	.642	.020 *
Age	.001	.792	.001	.794	.001	.794	.001	.793	.001	.830	.001	.825
Native English speaker	-.013	.833	-.013	.836	-.013	.835	-.013	.835	-.013	.871	-.013	.861
University degree	-.001	.994	-.001	.994 *	-.001	.994 *	-.001	.994 *	-.001	.995	-.001	.993
R&D tenure > 5 years	-.250	.004 **	-.250	.004 **	-.250	.004 **	-.250	.004 **	-.250	.015 *	-.251	.019 *
Marketing tenure > 5 years	-.008	.954	-.008	.954	-.008	.954	-.008	.954	-.008	.960	-.007	.964
Sales tenure > 5 years	.017	.893	.017	.897	.017	.897	.017	.896	.017	.906	.016	.915
Top-level management	-.279	.017 *	-.279	.023 *	-.279	.023 *	-.279	.022 *	-.279	.075	-.278	.052
Risk aversion	-.021	.356	-.021	.378	-.021	.377	-.021	.376	-.021	.451	-.021	.450
Idea innovativeness	.932	.000 ***	.932	.000 ***	.932	.000 ***	.932	.000 ***	.932	.000 ***	.935	.000 ***
H2: Domain knowledge	-.060	.001 **	-.060	.001 **	-.060	.001 **	-.060	.001 **	-.060	.005 **	-.061	.005 **
H6: Interaction (Inno. x DK)	.113	.000 ***	.113	.000 ***	.113	.000 ***	.113	.000 ***	.113	.000 ***	.112	.000 ***
H12: Comprehension	.398	.000 ***	.398	.000 ***	.398	.000 ***	.398	.000 ***	.398	.000 ***	.402	.000 ***
R^2	.208		.208		.208		.208		.208		.208	
Adjusted R^2	.204		n.a.		n.a.		n.a.		n.a.		n.a.	
F-statistic	50.876	.000 ***	57.607	.000 ***	57.902	.000 ***	58.110	.000 ***	53.080	.000 ***	n.a.	
Wald chi²	n.a.		n.a.		n.a.		n.a.		n.a.		602.200	.000 ***

Note: unstandardized regression coefficients reported; * p < .05; ** p < .01; *** p < .001; n = 2.331 (333 respondents with each 7 idea evaluations); OLS = reference model B-4

Table 64: Robustness checks – Model C (feasibility)

	OLS		HC3 estimators		HC4 estimators		Robust regr.		Clustered		Random regr.	
	B	Sig.	B	Sig.	B	Sig.	B	Sig.	B	Sig.	B	Sig.
Constant	2.673	.000 ***	2.673	.000 ***	2.673	.000 ***	2.673	.000 ***	2.673	.000 ***	2.597	.000 ***
Age	.002	.487	.002	.495	.002	.494	.002	.493	.002	.600	.002	.602
Native English speaker	.013	.829	.013	.828	.013	.828	.013	.827	.013	.873	.012	.882
University degree	-.087	.199	-.087	.209	-.087	.208	-.087	.207	-.087	.341	-.088	.348
R&D tenure > 5 years	-.330	.000 ***	-.330	.000 ***	-.330	.000 ***	-.330	.000 ***	-.330	.007 **	-.332	.004 **
Marketing tenure > 5 years	.049	.691	.049	.695	.049	.695	.049	.693	.049	.784	.050	.769
Sales tenure > 5 years	.144	.217	.144	.211	.144	.211	.144	.207	.144	.343	.143	.376
Top-level management	-.152	.170	-.152	.160	-.152	.160	-.152	.156	-.152	.339	-.151	.324
Risk aversion	-.038	.078	-.038	.104	-.038	.103	-.038	.102	-.038	.239	-.038	.199
Idea innovativeness	-.251	.000 ***	-.251	.000 ***	-.251	.000 ***	-.251	.000 ***	-.251	.000 ***	-.244	.000 ***
H3: Domain knowledge	.043	.011 *	.043	.014 *	.043	.013 *	.043	.013 *	.043	.074	.040	.081
H7: Interaction (Inno. x DK)	-.150	.000 ***	-.150	.000 ***	-.150	.000 ***	-.150	.000 ***	-.150	.000 ***	-.151	.000 ***
H13: Comprehension	.523	.000 ***	.523	.000 ***	.523	.000 ***	.523	.000 ***	.523	.000 ***	.535	.000 ***
R^2	.301		.301		.301		.301		.301		.301	
Adjusted R^2	.297		n.a.		n.a.		n.a.		n.a.		n.a.	
F-statistic	83.026	.000 ***	92.152	.000 ***	92.496	.000 ***	92.830	.000 ***	78.810	.000 ***	n.a.	
Wald chi²	n.a.		n.a.		n.a.		n.a.		n.a.		949.740	.000 ***

Note: unstandardized regression coefficients reported; * $p < .05$; ** $p < .01$; *** $p < .001$; n = 2.331 (333 respondents with each 7 idea evaluations); OLS = reference model C-4

Table 65: Robustness checks – Model D (overall impression)

	Model D (overall impression)																	
	OLS			HC3 estimators			HC4 estimators			Robust regr.			Clustered			Random regr.		
	B	Sig.		B	Sig.		B	Sig.		B	Sig.		B	Sig.		B	Sig.	
Constant	2.003	.000	***	2.004	.000	***	2.004	.000	***	2.004	.000	***	2.004	.000	***	1.991	.000	***
Age	-.001	.673		-.001	.690		-.001	.690		-.001	.689		-.001	.787		-.001	.776	
Native English speaker	-.049	.449		-.049	.458		-.049	.457		-.049	.457		-.049	.611		-.049	.605	
University degree	-.138	.061		-.138	.064		-.138	.063		-.138	.063		-.138	.212		-.138	.202	
R&D tenure > 5 years	-.264	.003	**	-.264	.005	**	-.264	.004	**	-.264	.004	**	-.264	.041	*	-.264	.044	*
Marketing tenure > 5 years	-.036	.787		-.036	.813		-.036	.813		-.036	.811		-.036	.881		-.036	.855	
Sales tenure > 5 years	-.015	.905		-.015	.916		-.015	.916		-.015	.915		-.015	.946		-.015	.934	
Top-level management	-.343	.004	**	-.343	.007	**	-.343	.007	**	-.343	.006	**	-.343	.070		-.343	.053	
Risk aversion	-.011	.622		-.011	.654		-.011	.653		-.011	.652		-.011	.779		-.011	.736	
Idea innovativeness	.742	.000	***	.742	.000	***	.742	.000	***	.742	.000	***	.742	.000	***	.743	.000	***
H4: Domain knowledge	-.027	.141		-.027	.147		-.027	.147		-.027	.145		-.027	.315		-.027	.300	
H8: Interaction (Inno. x DK)	.084	.005	**	.084	.007	**	.084	.007	**	.084	.007	**	.084	.004	**	.084	.002	**
H14: Comprehension	.295	.000	***	.295	.000	***	.295	.000	***	.295	.000	***	.295	.000	***	.297	.000	***
R^2	.137			.137			.137			.137			.137			.137		
Adjusted R^2	.133			n.a.			n.a.			n.a.			n.a.			n.a.		
F-statistic	30.687	.000	***	31.890	.000	***	31.923	.000	***	32.080	.000	***	25.180	.000	***	n.a.		
Wald chi²	n.a.			n.a.			n.a.			n.a.			n.a.			366.040	.000	***

Note: unstandardized regression coefficients reported; * p < .05; ** p < .01; *** p < .001; n = 2.331 (333 respondents with each 7 idea evaluations); OLS = reference model D-4

8.5 Appendix E – Idea rankings

Prior studies have compared the ability between different groups' evaluators to effectively evaluate new products/services based on the ranking of ideas that resulted from the criteria-based or holistic evaluation of the ideas (Magnusson, Wästlund, and Netz, 2016).

Thus, I derived a ranking of the ideas based on the average ratings of the participants' groups (i.e., 3D printing professionals, community members, NPD professionals, and laymen). These comparisons reveal that the ranking based on the 3D printing online community members' idea evaluations are indeed a good proxy for the ranking based on the 3D printing industry professionals' idea evaluations. Conversely, the ranking based on the laymen's idea evaluations are not. The rankings based on the overall impression evaluations (holistic evaluation), originality, and user value of the ideas are actually almost identical between 3D printing professionals' and 3D printing online community members (see Table 66, Table 67, and Table 68). The only substantial difference between these two groups is that the most innovative idea ranks higher based on the evaluations of the 3D printing industry professionals (see Table 69). Not surprisingly, the rating based on the laymen's idea evaluations is very different from the rating of the 3D printing industry professionals. For example, the laymen considered the "All-In-One 3D printer" to be the best idea (ranking 1st in overall impression, 5th in originality, 1st in user value, and 1st in feasibility). In comparison, 3D printing industry professionals considered the idea to be rather bad (ranking 5th in overall impression, 5th in originality, 4th in user value, and 2nd in feasibility).

However, it should be acknowledged that, in my sample, the community members stated that they have very high domain knowledge. Their stated domain knowledge was, on average, even higher than those of 3D printing industry professionals (see chapter 5.1.2). Thus, I also derived a ranking of the ideas based on the average ratings of the different domain knowledge groups that I used for the descriptive analysis of the evaluation outcomes (see chapter 5.1.3). These rankings confirm the major findings of this study. First, a ranking based on the idea evaluations would be very different between the higher domain knowledge groups (groups 3 and 4) and the lower domain knowledge groups (groups 1 and 2). Second, the higher domain knowledge groups ranked the more innovative ideas higher in terms of overall impression, originality, and user value. Three out of the four most innovative ideas were ranked among the top three ideas in terms of the overall impression, originality, and user value rankings of groups 3 and 4.

To conclude, the ranking analysis shows that, following the suggested approach of Magnusson, Wästlund, and Netz (2016) to leverage the evaluations of users to select the best ideas for further elaboration, would have proven to be successful in this case. The rankings based on the evaluations of 3D printing industry professionals and the rankings based on the user evaluations were very similar. However, the results also indicate that this is the case only because both groups reported to have very high knowledge in the domain of 3D printing. The ranking analysis, comparing groups with different degrees of domain knowledge, clearly suggests that, basing the selection of early-stage new product ideas on the ranking of a "crowd" of evaluators with low domain knowledge, is likely to lead to the rejection of valuable ideas (false negatives) and the selection of less valuable ideas (false positives).

Table 66: Idea rankings by participant group (overall impression)

		Ranking - overall impression			
Idea	Innova- tiveness	3D printing professionals [DK mean = 4.81, SD = 1.06; N = 27]	Community members [DK mean = 5.87, SD = 1.01; N = 156]	NPD professionals [DK mean = 3.72, SD = 1.29; N = 35]	Laymen [DK mean = 2.73, SD = 1.05; N = 115]
3D electronics printer	3.59	1	1	3	3
CLIP	3.37	4	4	4,5	6
Tripple-jetting 3D	3.07	3	2	1	2
Conductive graphene filament	2.93	2	3	2	4
All-In-One 3D Printer	2.80	5	6	6	1
Wood, stone and metal filament	2.09	6	5	4,5	5
Chocolate printhead	1.98	7	7	7	7

Table 67: Idea rankings by participant group (originality)

		Ranking - originality			
Idea	Innova- tiveness	3D printing professionals [DK mean = 4.81, SD = 1.06; N = 27]	Community members [DK mean = 5.87, SD = 1.01; N = 156]	NPD professionals [DK mean = 3.72, SD = 1.29; N = 35]	Laymen [DK mean = 2.73, SD = 1.05; N = 115]
3D electronics printer	3.59	1	3	2	2,5
CLIP	3.37	3	2	5	1
Tripple-jetting 3D	3.07	4	1	3	6
Conductive graphene filament	2.93	5	4	1	4
All-In-One 3D Printer	2.80	5	5	6	5
Wood, stone and metal filament	2.09	6	6	4	2,5
Chocolate printhead	1.98	7	7	7	7

Table 68: Idea rankings by participant group (user value)

		Ranking - user value			
Idea	Innova-tiveness	3D printing professionals [DK mean = 4.81, SD = 1.06; N = 27]	Community members [DK mean = 5.87, SD = 1.01; N = 156]	NPD professionals [DK mean = 3.72, SD = 1.29; N = 35]	Laymen [DK mean = 2.73, SD = 1.05; N = 115]
3D electronics printer	3.59	1	2	3	3
CLIP	3.37	6	5	6	6
Tripple-jetting 3D	3.07	2	1	2	2
Conductive graphene filament	2.93	3	3	1	4
All-In-One 3D Printer	2.80	4	4	4	1
Wood, stone and metal filament	2.09	5	6	5	5
Chocolate printhead	1.98	7	7	7	7

Table 69: Idea rankings by participant group (feasibility)

		Ranking - feasibility			
Idea	Innova-tiveness	3D printing professionals [DK mean = 4.81, SD = 1.06; N = 27]	Community members [DK mean = 5.87, SD = 1.01; N = 156]	NPD professionals [DK mean = 3.72, SD = 1.29; N = 35]	Laymen [DK mean = 2.73, SD = 1.05; N = 115]
3D electronics printer	3.59	3,5	6	3	5
CLIP	3.37	6	5	6	7
Tripple-jetting 3D	3.07	5	7	2	2
Conductive graphene filament	2.93	7	3	4	6
All-In-One 3D Printer	2.80	2	4	7	1
Wood, stone and metal filament	2.09	3,5	2	5	3
Chocolate printhead	1.98	1	1	1	4

Table 70: Idea rankings by domain knowledge group (overall impression)

Ranking - overall impression

Idea	Innova-tiveness	Group 1: "none to low DK" [DK >1 SD; N = 68]	Group 2: "low to moderate" [DK <-1 SD; N = 91]	Group 3: "moderate to high DK" [DK <+1 SD; N = 102]	Group 4: "very high DK" [DK >+1 SD; N = 72]
3D electronics printer	3.59	3	4	1	2
CLIP	3.37	7	6	4	4
Tripple-jetting 3D	3.07	1	1	3	1
Conductive graphene filament	2.93	5	3	2	3
All-In-One 3D Printer	2.80	2	2	6	7
Wood, stone and metal filament	2.09	4	5	5	5
Chocolate printhead	1.98	6	7	7	6

Table 71: Idea rankings by domain knowledge group (originality)

Ranking - originality

Idea	Innova-tiveness	Group 1: "none to low DK" [DK >1 SD; N = 68]	Group 2: "low to moderate" [DK <-1 SD; N = 91]	Group 3: "moderate to high DK" [DK <+1 SD; N = 102]	Group 4: "very high DK" [DK >+1 SD; N = 72]
3D electronics printer	3.59	2	3	1	2,5
CLIP	3.37	1	2	3	1
Tripple-jetting 3D	3.07	7	5	2	2,5
Conductive graphene filament	2.93	4	1	4	4
All-In-One 3D Printer	2.80	6	6	5	5
Wood, stone and metal filament	2.09	3	4	6	6
Chocolate printhead	1.98	5	7	7	7

Table 72: Idea rankings by domain knowledge group (user value)

Idea	Innovativeness	Ranking - user value			
		Group 1: "none to low DK" [DK >1 SD; N = 68]	Group 2: "low to moderate" [DK <-1 SD; N = 91]	Group 3: "moderate to high DK" [DK <+1 SD; N = 102]	Group 4: "very high DK" [DK >+1 SD; N = 72]
3D electronics printer	3.59	2	3	1	2
CLIP	3.37	7	6	5	5
Tripple-jetting 3D	3.07	3	2	2	1
Conductive graphene filament	2.93	5	4	3	3
All-In-One 3D Printer	2.80	1	1	4	4
Wood, stone and metal filament	2.09	4	5	6	6
Chocolate printhead	1.98	6	7	7	7

Table 73: Idea rankings by domain knowledge group (feasibility)

Idea	Innovativeness	Ranking - feasibility			
		Group 1: "none to low DK" [DK >1 SD; N = 68]	Group 2: "low to moderate" [DK <-1 SD; N = 91]	Group 3: "moderate to high DK" [DK <+1 SD; N = 102]	Group 4: "very high DK" [DK >+1 SD; N = 72]
3D electronics printer	3.59	5	5	6	6
CLIP	3.37	7	7	3	5
Tripple-jetting 3D	3.07	2	1	7	4
Conductive graphene filament	2.93	6	6	5	3
All-In-One 3D Printer	2.80	1	3	4	7
Wood, stone and metal filament	2.09	3,5	4	2	1
Chocolate printhead	1.98	3,5	2	1	2

Printed by Printforce, the Netherlands